ANCIENT MAGICKS AND FEELINGS AND STUFF

The Aversion Bureau: Volume Two

S.R. Ringuette

ANCIENT MAGICKS AND FEELINGS AND STUFF
© 2014 Sebastien Ringuette

This book consists of material originally posted on aversionbureau.com,
no portion of this book may be used or reproduced in any form
or in any way without written consent of the author.
Scanning, uploading or reproduction of this book by any means is illegal
without written consent of the author.

The Aversion Bureau is © Sebastien Ringuette. All rights reserved.

ISBN: 978-0-9879414-3-5

SRR Comics

- DEDICATED DEFACEMENT AREA -

Foreword by Trenton Q. Broens

In this book there's a strip called "Denial" which contains the Averson Bureau's boss, Director Thomas Bilge, tumbling through space wearing nothing at all. His pasty butt cheeks are overlaid onto a cosmic background and as his characteristic rectangular glasses turn toward the reader, words that may either be drunken ramblings or deep insight into our metaphysical awareness provide commentary on gods. The strip is hilarious (as usual) but it got me thinking about broader notions of gods and creation. I came to one conclusion:

Being a god must be kinda crazy.

You see, gods create worlds (in theory or reality- I'm not here to tell you what to believe). Gods create, manipulate and seek reverence. They conceive things in their metaphysical minds and put them out into the world to be seen, tested, and give rise to other things. Their aims may be selfish or altruistic, kind or condemnatory, calculated or impulsive. Like I said, being a god would be pretty nuts. So is being a webcomic creator.

The task of creating worlds is not, of course, limited to gods. Like gods, storytellers create worlds, build narratives, and seek reverence. Their aims are varied but their desire to put something novel into the world is uniform. Now Sebastien's humble demeanour and plethora of anxieties would probably make him want to stifle the comparison of himself to gods but it is impossible to understate his ability to create a world in which flying whales, fluffy mammoths, warp goats, Tesla raptors and a plethora of other wildly imaginative creations exist within the building of a fake insurance company. The time, dedication, and sacrifice it takes to be a webcomic creator is admirable in so many ways but it is the exciting ideas, funny jokes, and ability to translate thoughts into comics that are truly worthy of any reverence he gets and equally worthy of any questions raised about his sanity. And, unlike 'capital-g' God, Seb doesn't take Sundays off. In fact, the 'Sunday strip' is one of the new and exciting additions to the second collection of his comic. Seb may not in fact be a god, but his storytelling ability and inclination to build worlds makes him worthy of all the divine reverence and cosmic confusion that I was contemplating after seeing Bilge's butt cheeks floating amongst the stars.

In this second volume (Ancient Magicks And Feelings And Stuff), Seb has a clear conception of the Aversion Bureau and its cast. While the heavy lifting of the world building is largely complete, the world of the Aversion Bureau continues to expand in new and exciting ways. I truly feel like the humour of the book begins to hit its stride in the storyline that opens this volume and a clear conception of the comic's overall vision provides the opportunity for Seb to more freely experiment with his own creative capabilities. In this volume you will see larger, more expansive storylines as well as shorter but equally satisfying Sunday strips. The addition of Sunday strips in this volume are visual treats and hit you with punchy lines and visual gags that you'll want to revisit frequently. The longer stories, meanwhile, help to raise the stakes and show that underneath the veneer of silliness, the Aversion Bureau exists in a world with alarming (but still hilarious) dangers. Stories like the action-packed 'Iron Tide' arc at the ending of the first volume are exhilarating, fun, and tremendously well executed. The momentum continues into the second volume, where, contrasting with the large-scale action are moments of profound pathos found in the quieter moments of growing up, reflecting on relationships, and living your day-to-day life. Wade and Max in particular are featured in moments of reflection and realization while a wordless story featuring Agent Stone shows a day in the life of an Aversion Bureau agent. Taken together, these operate as perfect examples of how a more fully developed world can lend itself to more a reflective tone and a more nuanced form of storytelling.

There are also rhymes galore with rap battles, slam poetry, and a Christmas tale all showing a tremendous amount of wordplay and what I can only assume is Seb's latent desire to become a famous rapper. There's romance, crazy creatures, and more wacky science. There's explosions, robots, and gangster dogs. There's everything you could want and more. Did I mention the butt cheeks?

Over the course of creating and building the world of the Aversion Bureau I've been lucky enough to also see the growth and change of a friend. By pushing the boundaries of his creativity and art I think Seb started to gain clearer understanding of what he wanted to build for his own life. This volume contains the end of Seb's regular additions of TAB strips yet, like many gods, he wasn't quite ready to leave his creation in stasis. After he stopped updating the comic regularly he may have spent more time away from his computer but his mind was still firmly entrenched in the world of the Aversion Bureau. While this second volume marks the end of an era, it also marks the beginning of a new one where the Aversion Bureau expands into other realms. Already he has new prose content and is expanding his talents into many other areas. This creator isn't content and never will be. By exploring the world of the Aversion Bureau, he was earnestly exploring his own talents and capabilities. Where those talents take him is uncertain but, like most gods and storytellers, whether the impacts he make may be big or small the act of creation is always worth revering.

In your hands you have the last of the Aversion Bureau's regular comics (for now). While I already miss regular looks at the lives of Max, Stone, Davison, Bilge, Wade, and the various other inhabitants of the Aversion Bureau, I look forward to the adventure that they can take both the creator and the reader on next. Now dear god, stop reading my words and start reading his. Trust me, they'll make you laugh a whole lot more.

—Trenton Q. Broens
June 2014
Edmonton, AB

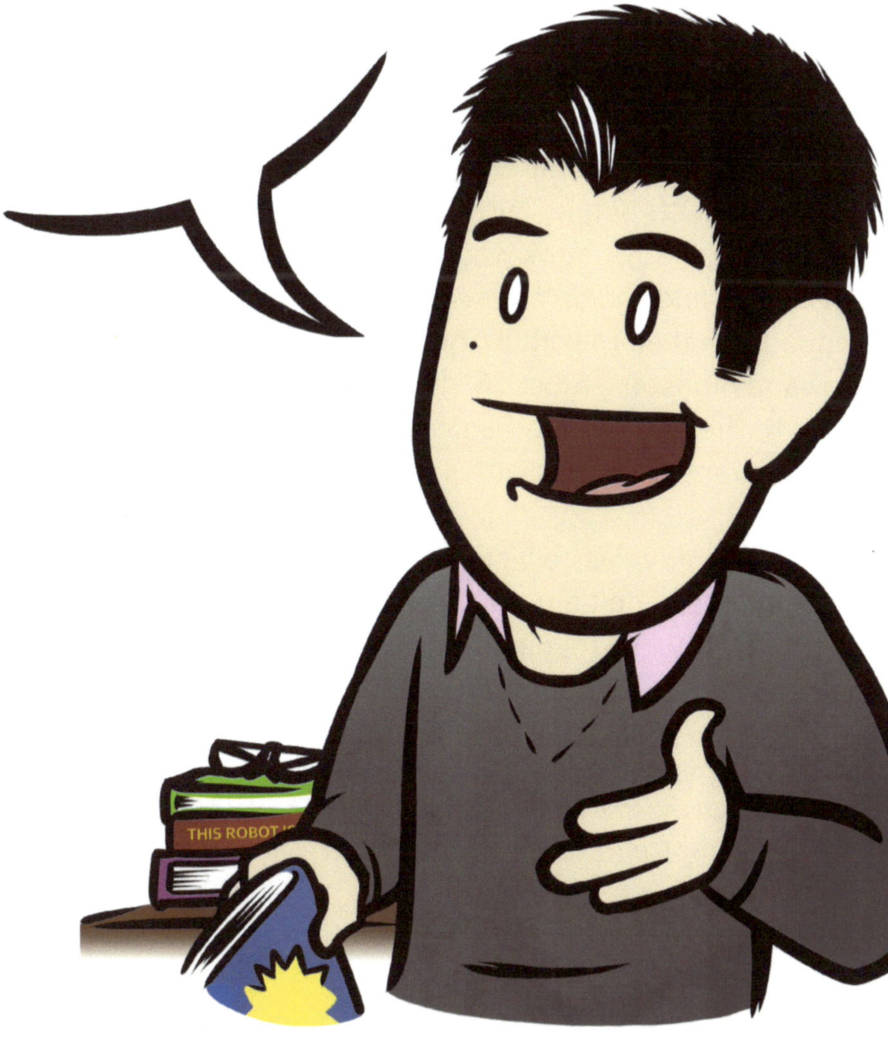
THIS ROBOT

After a foreword that good, there's almost never anything left to say...
But perhaps the one, *true* superpower I've experienced in this brief existence
is making words, *often too many words*, appear out of thin air. *Like so:*

Get ready for a whole bunch of great stories that tie directly into the previous year's with the ultimate goal of conclusion, but sometimes just drag them out to an even **more** remote cliff from which to hang. The longest adventure in this collection, "*Calculo Dominum*" has got to be the ***most*** fun I had with any story in the whole run. Between the chance to finally use Aversion Bureau *specific* self-referential humour and re-visit one of the dumbest (read: greatest) ideas I had in the series, there was no way it couldn't be a blast.

Yet, the fun really starts where the regular weekly strips finally peter out and the Sunday strips and One-Offs begin. This book has comics that predate the weekly adventures it contains because the last book was in black and white. The Sunday strips were big full-page colourful comics and couldn't be wasted on something so greyscale, so now they get to be here, rendered in their maximum glory. Those strips delivered a ton of the series' greatest villains and monsters, most of which I've crammed onto the back cover of this book.
Thanks to their non-chronological nature they could ***go*** anywhere and ***do*** anything.
I took great advantage of this with some of them. Seagull soldiers, fish militia, you name it.

So I hope you enjoy this collection of every scrap of *The Aversion Bureau* left that made to the internet and hadn't already been put into a book. I've done my best to ensure it's big, colourful and quality. Re-reading these strips brought a real smile to my face, and I expect it will do the same to you. Whether you've read the others ones or not, it's just *plain old fun*.

*This book is dedicated to anyone who ever visited aversionbureau.com
to read the strip while it was still going. The only gift I know I can bring the world
consistently, is entertainment. But I didn't know that until you showed up.*

TABLE OF CONTENTS

Character Re-Introduction ---------------------------------- *Page 8*
Makes an appearance in the event you're an animal who starts with the second book in a series.

The Story Thus Far Colon ---------------------------------- *Page 10*
Can't remember what happened in The Aversion Bureau before now? You could have just asked...

All Of The Comics ---------------------------------- *Page 11*
Most of the comics.

Sunday Strips ---------------------------------- *Page 64*
But wait, there's more! More comics, that is. There are more comics.

One-Offs ---------------------------------- *Page 102*
The rest of the comics, under a different titling.

The Lost Sunday Strip ---------------------------------- *Page 126*
Not anymore!

Running The Bureau Is Hard, You Know ------------------ *Page 128*
Even MORE silly, rhyming poetry. Because I love to write it, and you love to read it(?)

Outtrofarewelladuction® ---------------------------------- *Page 130*
I say goodbye (to you) with an additional page that may or may not be necessary at all

Character Re-Introductions

(This section returns just incase you started with book 2, but why would you do a silly thing like that?)

1. Max Martin
Taken under the wing of the Aversion Bureau after a fateful day at the beach, Max is a loyal and gullible person with a heart of gold. He's also a bit of a wuss, but beneath his unimposing demeanor beats the heart of a true hero. And on top of that one beats the heart of desperate and paranoid young man that will take a pass at anything even *resembling* a woman.

2. Director Thomas Bilge
Thomas Bilge is the founder of the Aversion Bureau, a secret organization that endeavors to thwart any and all apocalyptic threats to the world. Bilge's history is shrouded in mystery (whose isn't?) and very little is known about this eccentric older gentleman... that is until you get a drink into his hand. **Bilge has a problem with booze.**

3. Agent Stone
A calculating and articulate woman who ranks highly within the bureau, a personal favourite of the director. Agent Stone is a natural leader and ass-kicker, she excels in hand to hand combat and having to take care of literally everything for everyone all the time. Stone finds it exhausting dealing with the buffoonery of others and the more eccentric aspects of Bilge's personality, but she holds it all together nonetheless and is a rallying point of reason for the entire team.

4. Dick Davison
Dick Davison is a total bro. He is competitive, pugnacious and a violently sore loser. But having said that, it must also be clear that agent Davison is an incredibly loyal, although headstrong, companion who is un-deniably combat-effective. Deep-down, everybody loves Dick.

5. Wade Andersen
Wade Andersen is a man of few words. He is head of the science, research and technology departments within the bureau and boasts a sizeable lab with which to work. People try to talk to Wade sometimes, though it is questionable whether he recognizes that they exist in the same space at the same time. He has this problem with most people.

Additional Rubes In This Never Ending Farce...

Jim the intern:
Jim is a timid, yet competent worker with a bright future in accounting. Or at least he used to be. Jim is the kind of guy who's always getting swept up in grandiose schemes and ultimately being corrupted by the residual evil in the power-vacuum created when his dark master falls. You know the type. Jim likes football and playing the castanets.
His favourite colour is orange.

Jackie the roommate:
Jackie is the girl who shares her apartment with Max on the condition that he pay rent on time and never hit on her. Jackie exists solely so that Max has someone to talk to when the story dictates that he should go home for a bit. There, I said it. She owns a cat but the cat seems to think that it's clothes or something because it's always attached to her in some way.

Reception Lady:
The ever vigilant keeper-of-appointments and confirmer-of-identification. Reception Lady keeps watch at the reception desk by the entrance to the building that houses both RGI and the Aversion Bureau, though she is none the wiser to the latter. Everyone seems to think she's pretty good looking but we've never seen her face so who knows.

Agent Whiskers:
Agent Whiskers is a semi-psychotic investigator type who runs long-term undercover investigations away from the bureau and prefers to work alone as his methods for interrogation and apprehension often fall into a grey area with the Geneva Convention. I've mentioned before that there are "barely a dozen agents" working for the bureau and as the main cast only consists of five, that leaves me some space to have fun. Meow.

THE STORY THUS FAR COLON

After nearly being killed on the beach by a robotic super-plague, everyman Max Martin is hired, to the shock of all, by the Aversion Bureau. He receives training in the martial and culinary arts before experiencing another near-death situation during the containment breach of two large, lightning-firing bird monsters.

The trauma of this latest fantastical ordeal sends his mind hurdling towards the dark calls of accounting. Attempting to hide behind the RGI Insurance alter-ego he was given upon joining the Bureau, Max transforms the department into a mad kingdom with sheer force of willful ignorance. Dragging a certain intern, poor timid Jim, along in the process.

Max attempts to learn the nature of the robotic Scoria nano-bots present in his body as the Bureau looks for a cure. He undergoes further training in the arts of espionage and the opposite sex (courtesy of the infamous agent Dick Davison). Max meets a beautiful woman out at 'Tha Club' but is interrupted before they get a chance to totally make out. He gets her number, but has not the testicular fortitude to call.

Many wacky adventures and side-quests later find the Scoria army on the doorstep of the Aversion Bureau. The brave agents manage to defend their home base and Max is cured of his robo-affliction in the process. Eventually, he sacs up and calls the nice girl from the club. That's where we are now. Out for dinner at a fancy Omelette repository.

OMELETTE DU FROMAGE

"PAWS"

It is a starry night in the city.
Perhaps *too* starry...

Some time has passed since the Scoria hordes broke themselves against the bureau's vigilant defenses. Life is begining to return to normal for the young agent Max Martin, or, about as normal as it gets, now-a-days...

Omelette du Fromage
So you're saying that a **dog**.
Yes.
That you didn't know.
I did not know the dog.
-**Ate** your phone?
Whole.
Whole.
Like a shark.
Like a *land*-**shark**.
SNAP
SNAP

"Never Forget"

Well, *honestly* I was **convinced** after a while that you just weren't interested.
I had made it *pretty* easy for you.
You had! I thought you were *incredible*... But it was ***so*** out of the ordinary, I could *barely* believe it happened...
And then *every* time I tried to, or even ***thought*** about calling you, I had so much **anxiety**.
And *geez*, there was that time at **three am** when I ***called*** *but couldn't even make words come out!*
MENU
Oh my ***God..***
You *were the three-am creepy breathing guy!* ***I knew it***
Hey, YOU went home with dinosaur Sean Connery!!

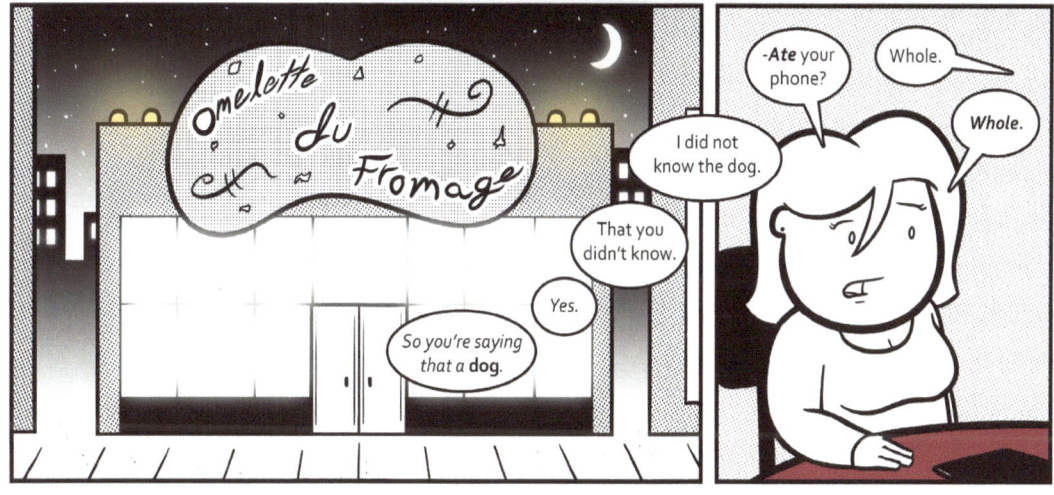

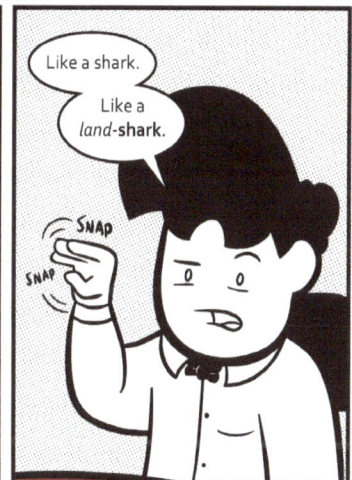

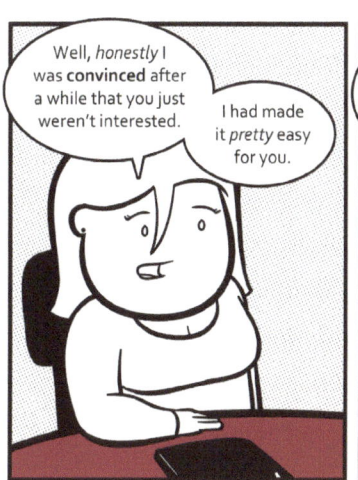

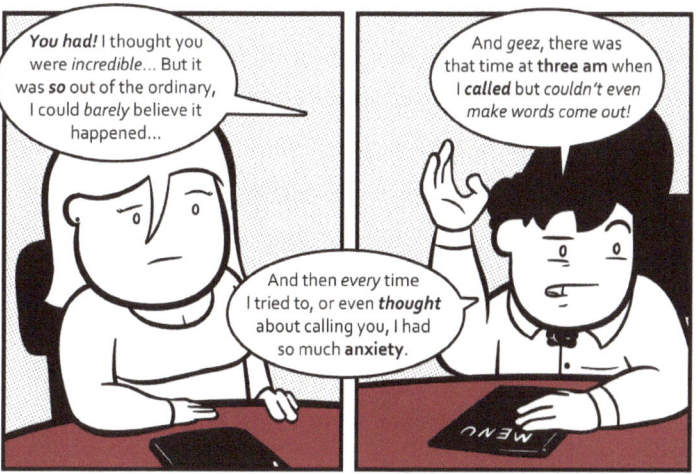

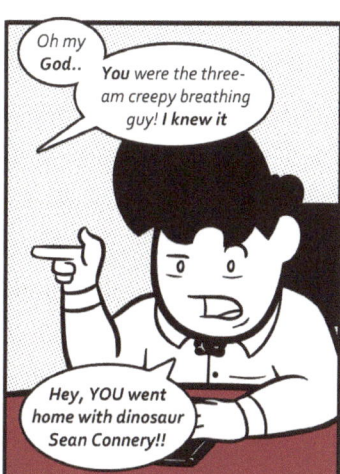

"Le Haute Dog"

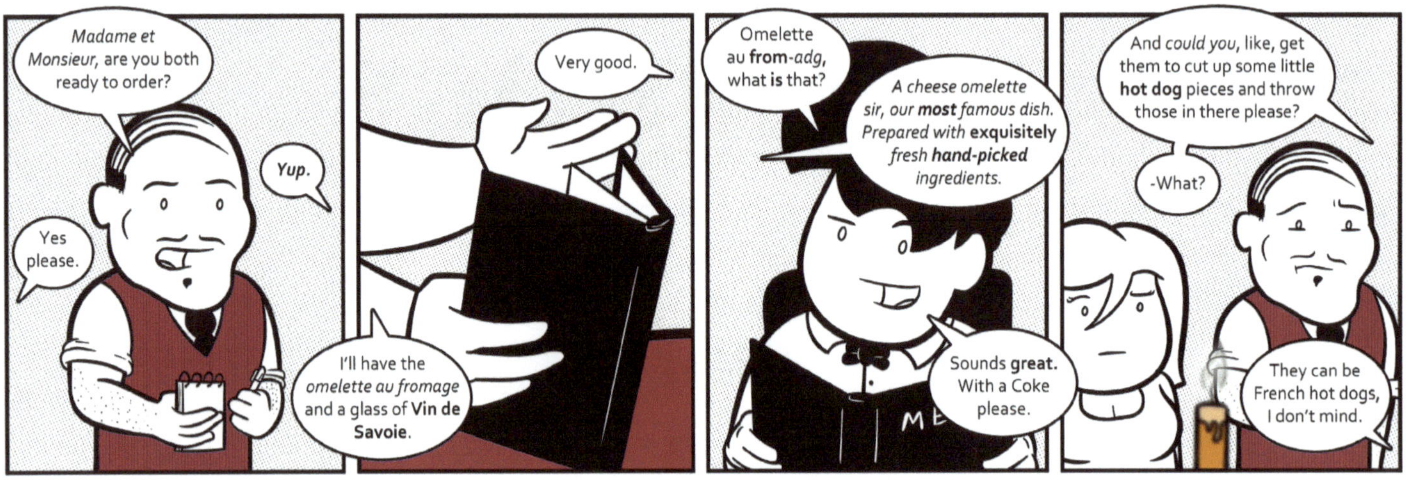
Madame et Monsieur, are you both ready to order?
Yup.
Yes please.
Very good.
I'll have the *omelette au fromage* and a glass of **Vin de Savoie.**
Omelette au **from**-*adg*, what **is** that?
A cheese omelette sir, our ***most*** *famous dish. Prepared with* ***exquisitely*** *fresh* ***hand-picked*** *ingredients.*
Sounds **great.** With a Coke please.
And *could you*, like, get them to cut up some little **hot dog** pieces and throw those in there please?
-What?
They can be French hot dogs, I don't mind.

"Making Progress"

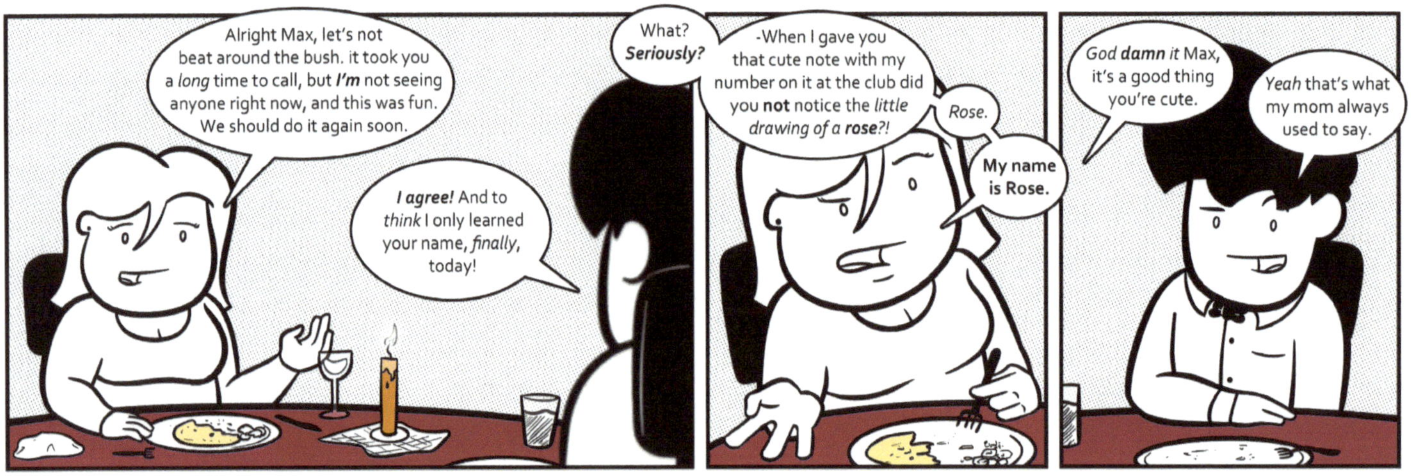
Alright Max, let's not beat around the bush. it took you a *long* time to call, but ***I'm*** not seeing anyone right now, and this was fun. We should do it again soon.
I agree! And to *think* I only learned your name, *finally*, today!
What? ***Seriously?***
-When I gave you that cute note with my number on it at the club did you **not** notice the *little drawing of a* ***rose****?!*
Rose.
My name is Rose.
God ***damn*** *it* Max, it's a good thing you're cute.
Yeah that's what my mom always used to say.

"Yes That Is A Foreshadow"

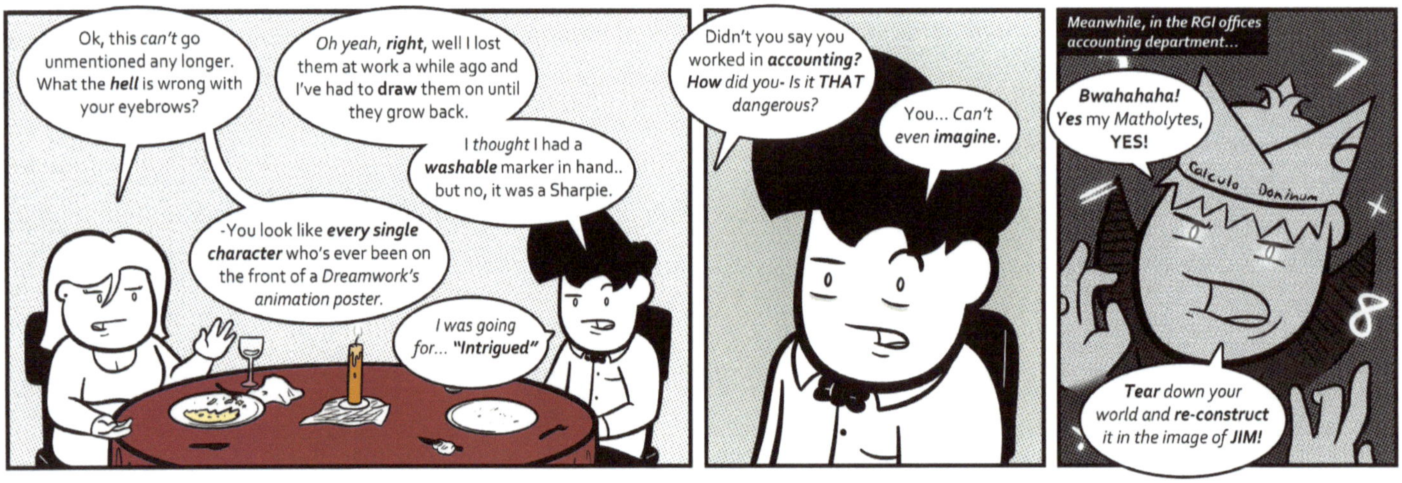
Ok, this *can't* go unmentioned any longer. What the ***hell*** is wrong with your eyebrows?
Oh yeah, ***right****,* well I lost them at work a while ago and I've had to **draw** them on until they grow back.
I thought I had a ***washable*** marker in hand.. but no, it was a Sharpie.
-You look like ***every single character*** who's ever been on the front of a *Dreamwork's animation poster.*
I was going for... ***"Intrigued"***
Didn't you say you worked in ***accounting?*** ***How*** *did you- Is it* ***THAT*** *dangerous?*
You... *Can't even* ***imagine.***
Meanwhile, in the RGI offices accounting department...
Bwahahaha!
Yes *my Matholytes,* **YES!**
Calculo Dominum
Tear *down your world and* ***re-construct*** *it in the image of* ***JIM!***

"Shattering Expectations"

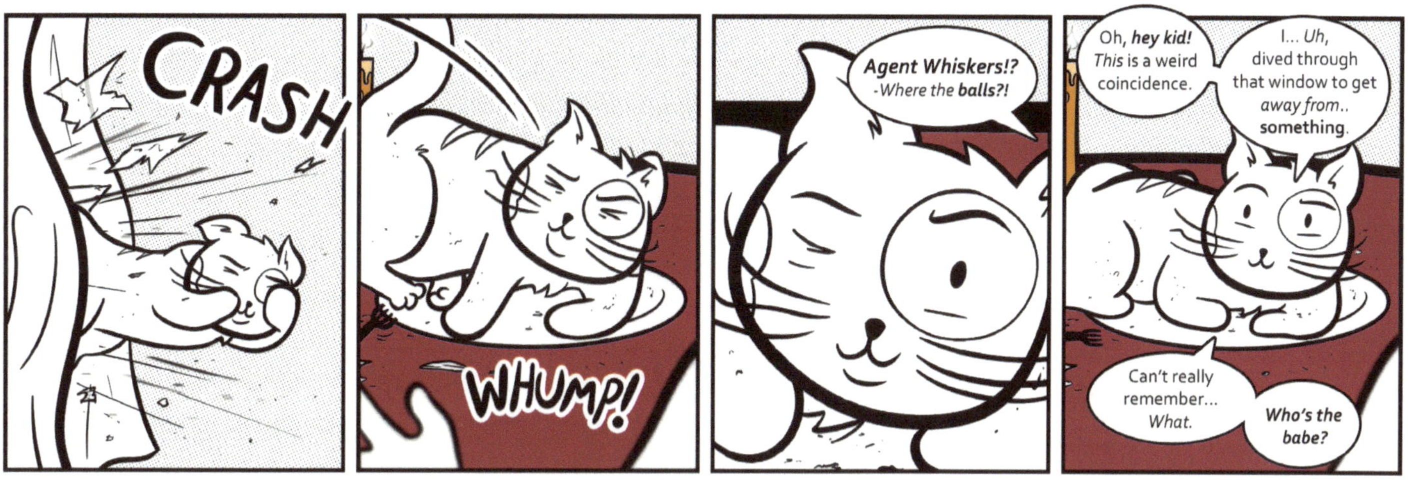

CRASH
WHUMP!
Agent Whiskers!? -Where the balls?!
Oh, hey kid! This is a weird coincidence.
I... Uh, dived through that window to get away from.. something.
Can't really remember... What.
Who's the babe?

"Upon Closer Inspection"

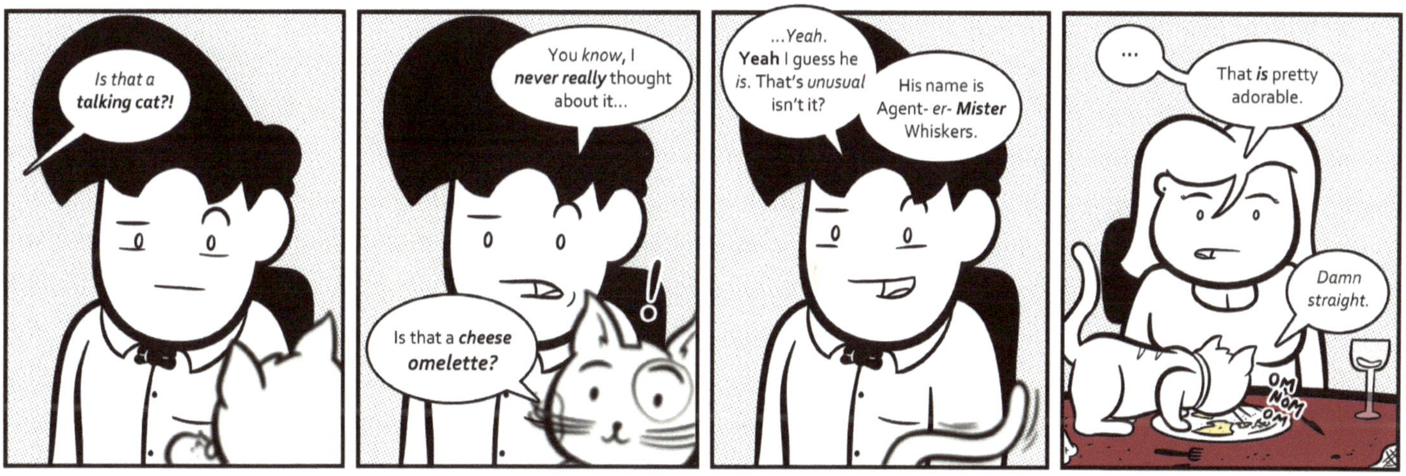

Is that a talking cat?!
You know, I never really thought about it...
Is that a cheese omelette?
...Yeah. Yeah I guess he is. That's unusual isn't it?
His name is Agent- er- Mister Whiskers.
...
That is pretty adorable.
Damn straight.

"Hope That Missed The Waiter"

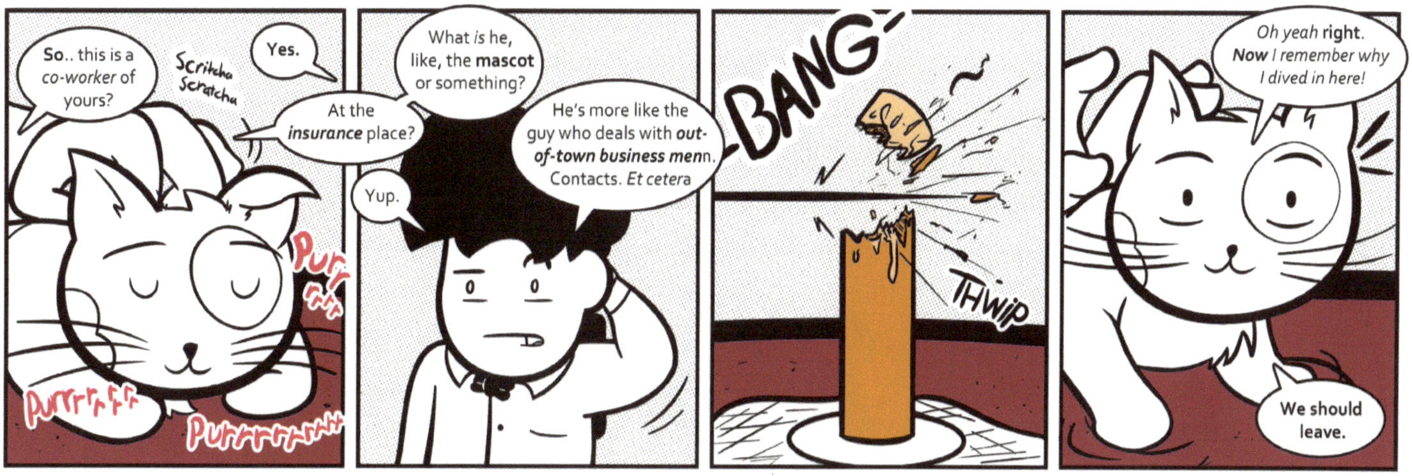

So.. this is a co-worker of yours?
Scritcha Scratcha
Yes.
At the insurance place?
What is he, like, the mascot or something?
Yup.
He's more like the guy who deals with out-of-town business menn. Contacts. Et cetera
BANG
THWIP
Oh yeah right. Now I remember why I dived in here!
We should leave.

"Surprisingly Leader-Like"

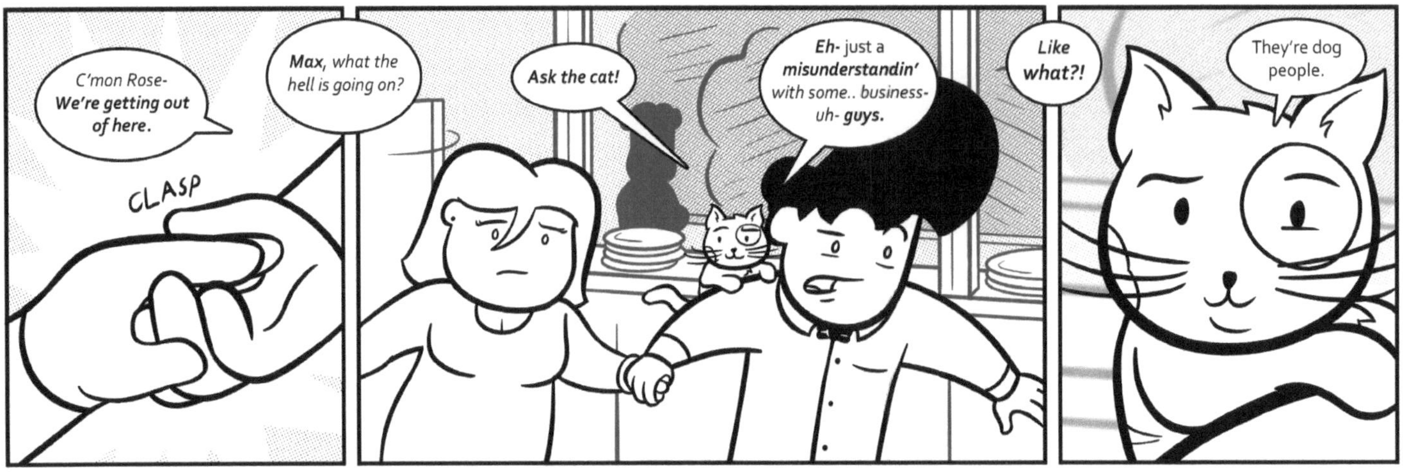
C'mon Rose- **We're getting out of here.**
CLASP
Max, what the hell is going on?
Ask the cat!
Eh- just a **misunderstandin'** with some.. business- uh- **guys.**
Like what?!
They're dog people.

"Just Like In The Movies"

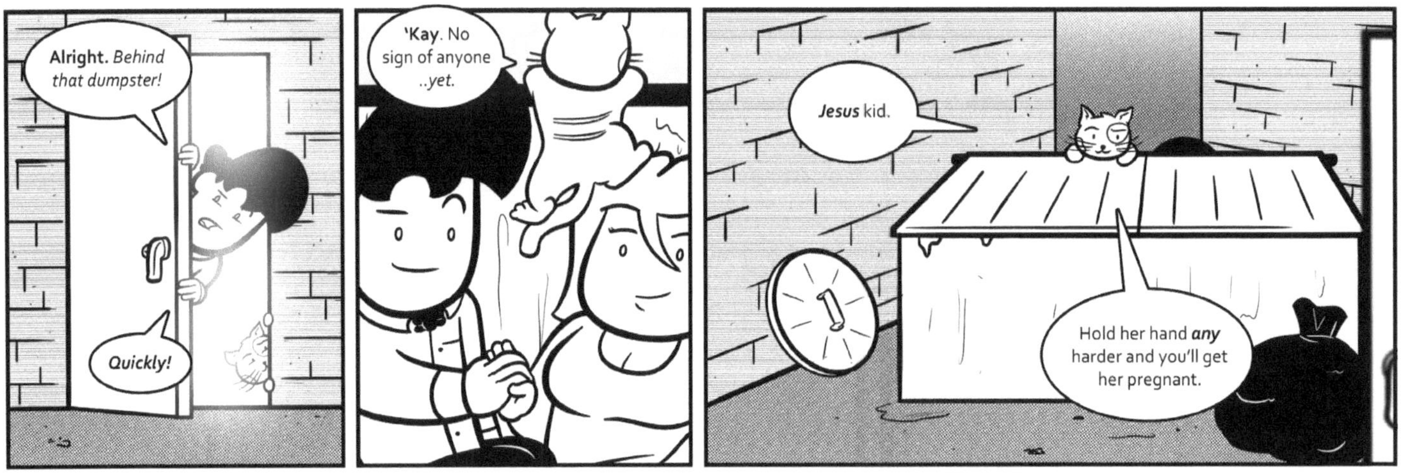
Alright. *Behind that dumpster!*
Quickly!
'Kay. No sign of anyone *..yet.*
Jesus kid.
Hold her hand ***any*** harder and you'll get her pregnant.

"Cats Are Always On Top Of Things"

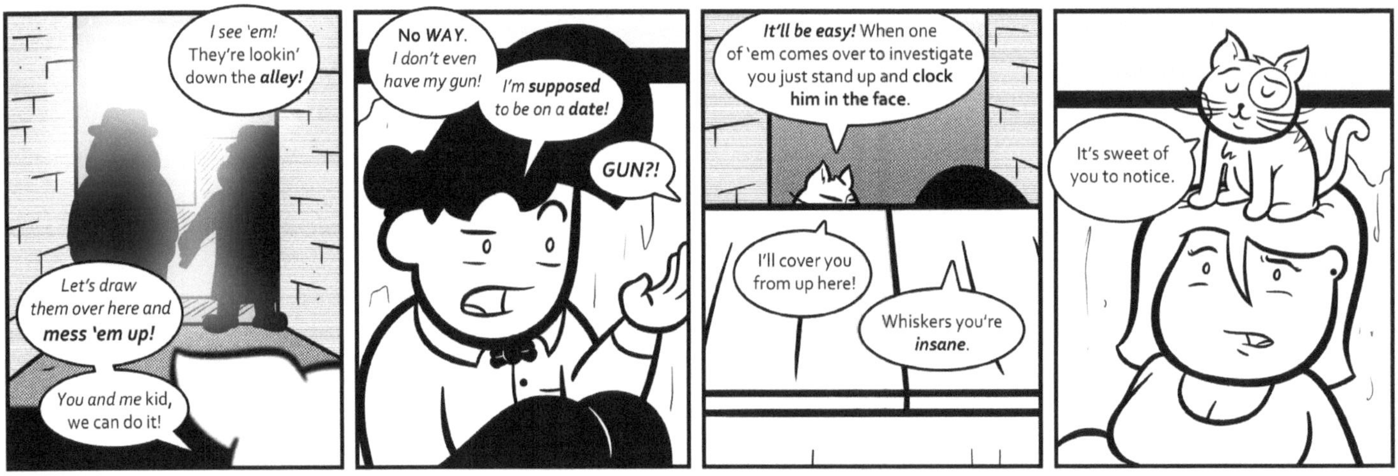
I see 'em! They're lookin' down the ***alley!***
Let's draw them over here and ***mess 'em up!***
You and me kid, we can do it!
No *WAY. I don't even have my gun!*
I'm ***supposed*** *to be on a* ***date!***
GUN?!
It'll be easy! When one of 'em comes over to investigate you just stand up and **clock him in the face.**
I'll cover you from up here!
Whiskers you're ***insane.***
It's sweet of you to notice.

"Max In The Box"

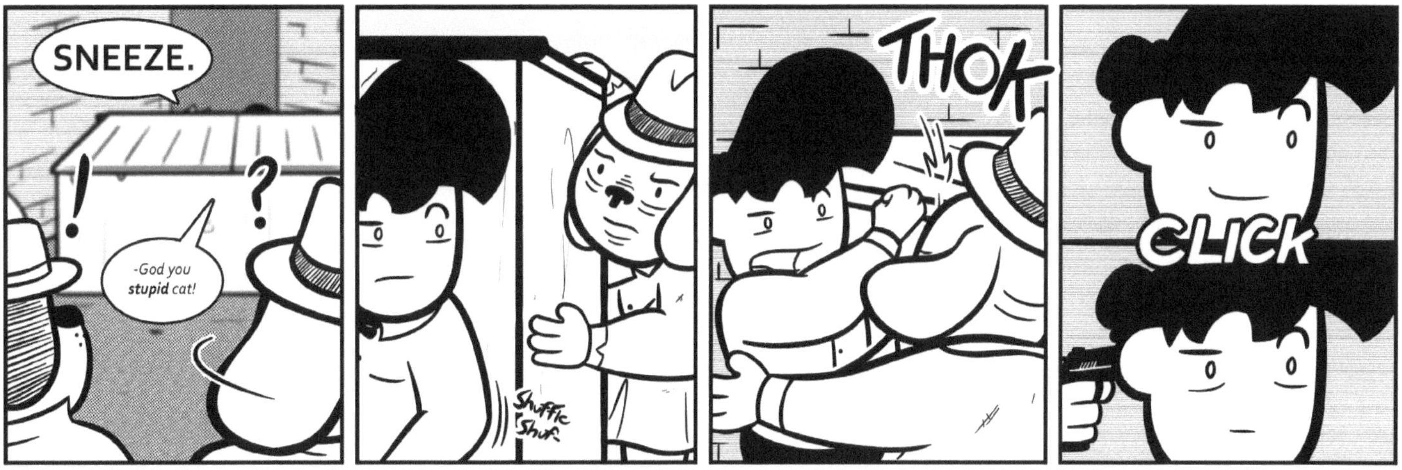
SNEEZE.
!
?
-God you **stupid** cat!
Shuffle Shuf
THOK
CLICK

"Valkyrie"

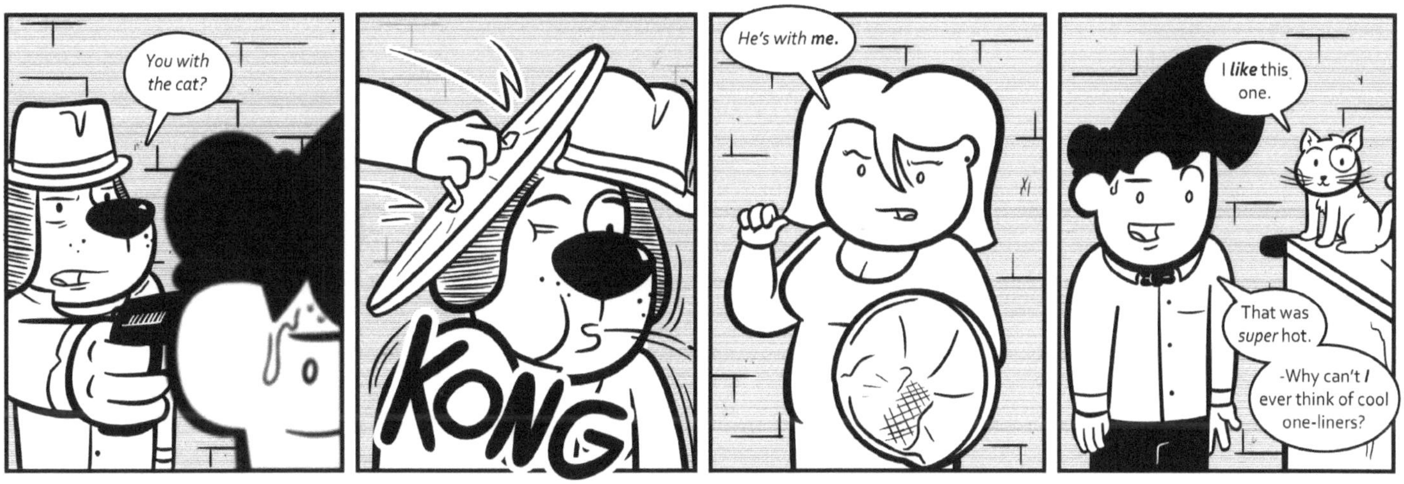
You with the cat?
KONG
*He's with **me.***
I ***like*** this one.
That was *super* hot.
-Why can't ***I*** ever think of cool one-liners?

"Need To Practice This Part"

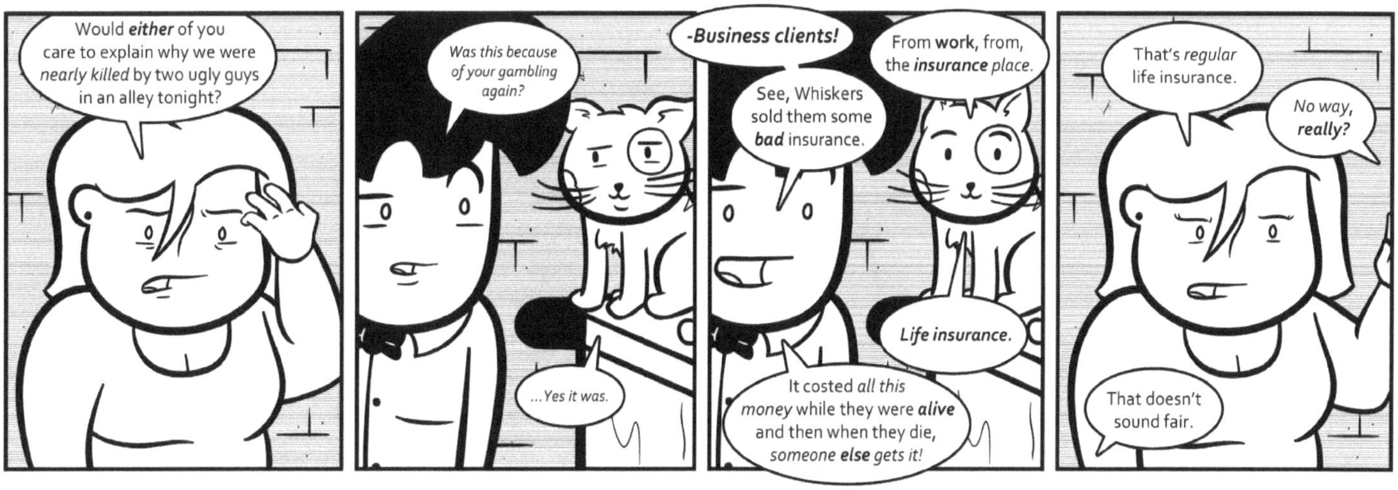
Would ***either*** of you care to explain why we were *nearly killed* by two ugly guys in an alley tonight?
Was this because of your gambling again?
...Yes it was.
-Business clients!
From **work**, from, the ***insurance** place.*
See, Whiskers sold them some ***bad*** insurance.
Life insurance.
It costed *all this money* while they were ***alive*** and then when they die, *someone **else** gets it!*
That's *regular* life insurance.
*No way, **really?***
That doesn't sound fair.

"Miami Nights"

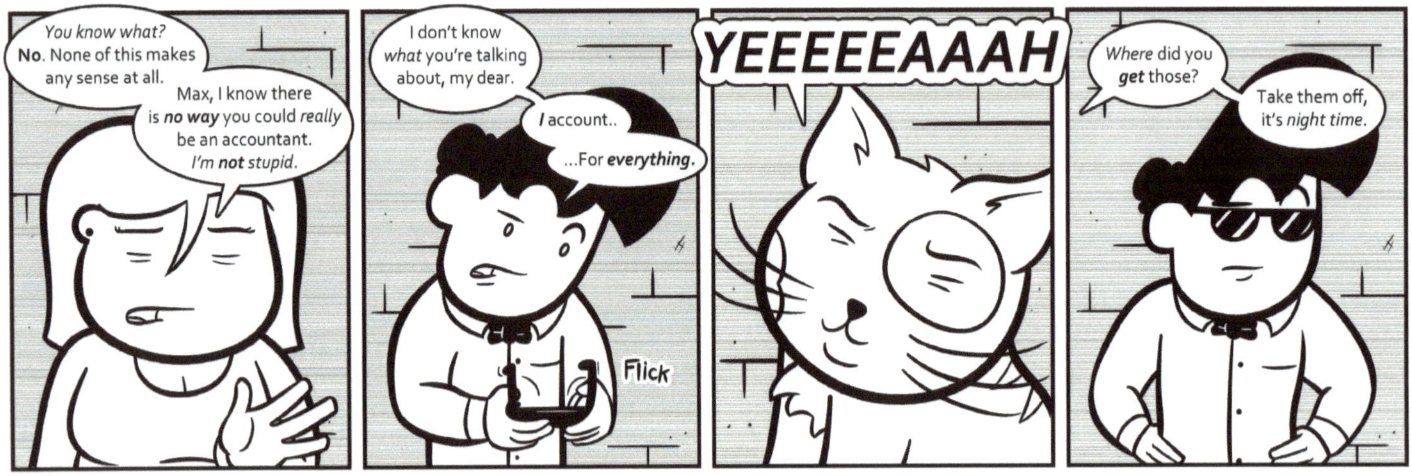
You know what? No. None of this makes any sense at all.
Max, I know there is no way you could really be an accountant. I'm not stupid.
I don't know what you're talking about, my dear.
I account..
...For everything.
Flick
YEEEEEAAAH
Where did you get those?
Take them off, it's night time.

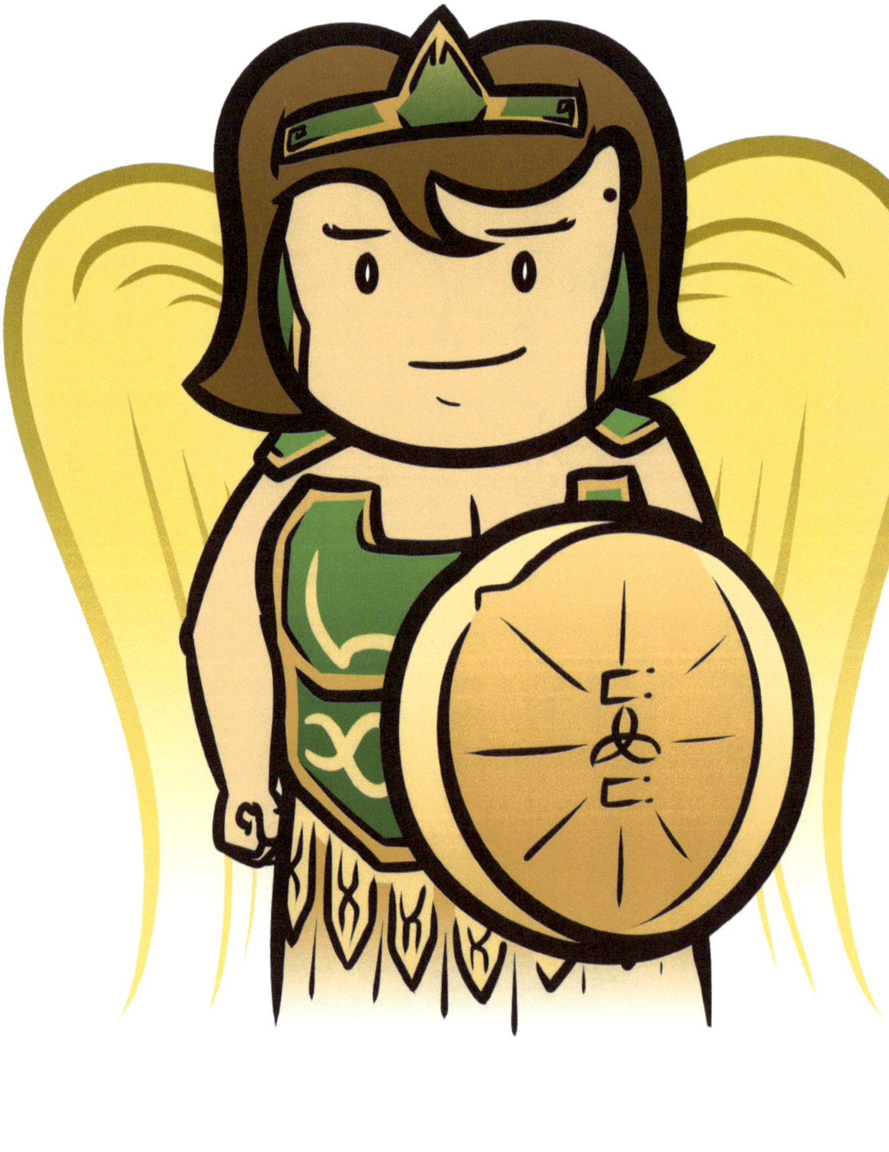

THE BIGGEST DEAL EVER

"Denial"

Sir.
Sir?
Gods are but a masquerade on the true face of the universe.
I swirl in the cold heart of infinity.
Now seeing beyond this veil,
Blimey.

"Anger"

Normalcy and reason get together and *bunk off* while reality itself re-arranges simply to confound me.
Suddenly a million men are swallowing knives.
Though none of them are performers.
The chorus of their agony begets the creation of an entirely new world.
This one favours me no more than the last.

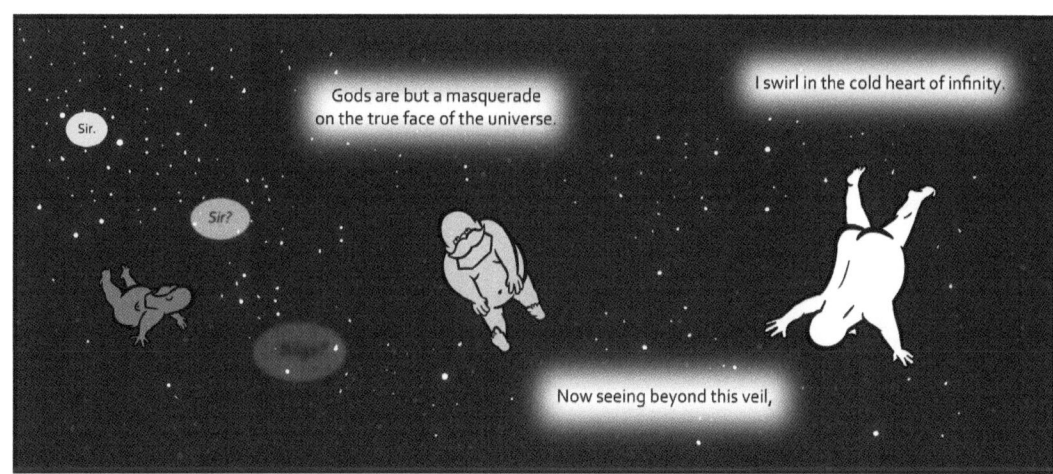

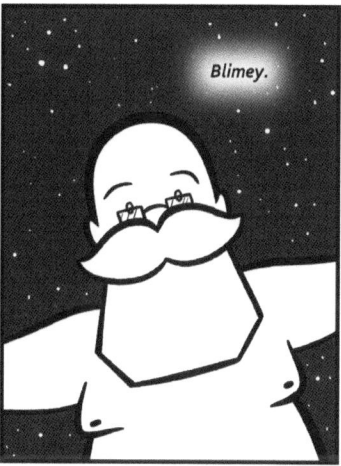

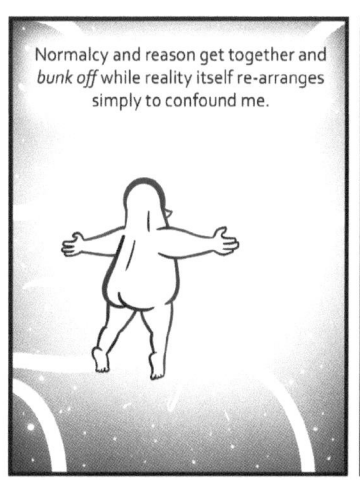

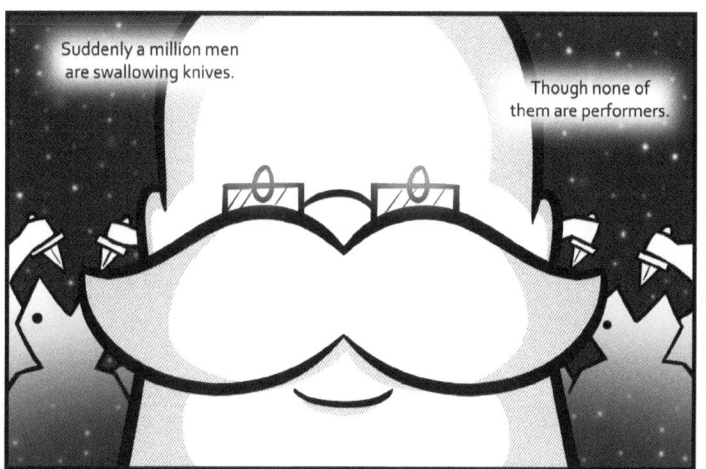

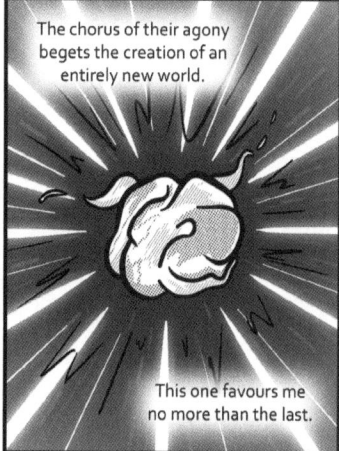

"Bargaining"

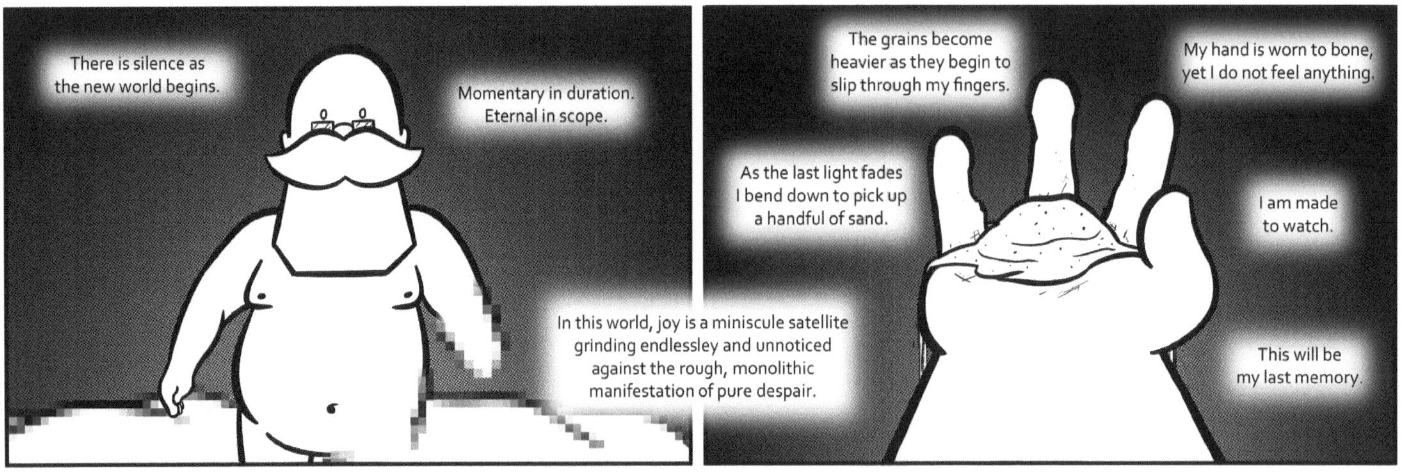
There is silence as the new world begins.
Momentary in duration. Eternal in scope.
In this world, joy is a miniscule satellite grinding endlessley and unnoticed against the rough, monolithic manifestation of pure despair.
The grains become heavier as they begin to slip through my fingers.
As the last light fades I bend down to pick up a handful of sand.
My hand is worn to bone, yet I do not feel anything.
I am made to watch.
This will be my last memory.

"Depression"

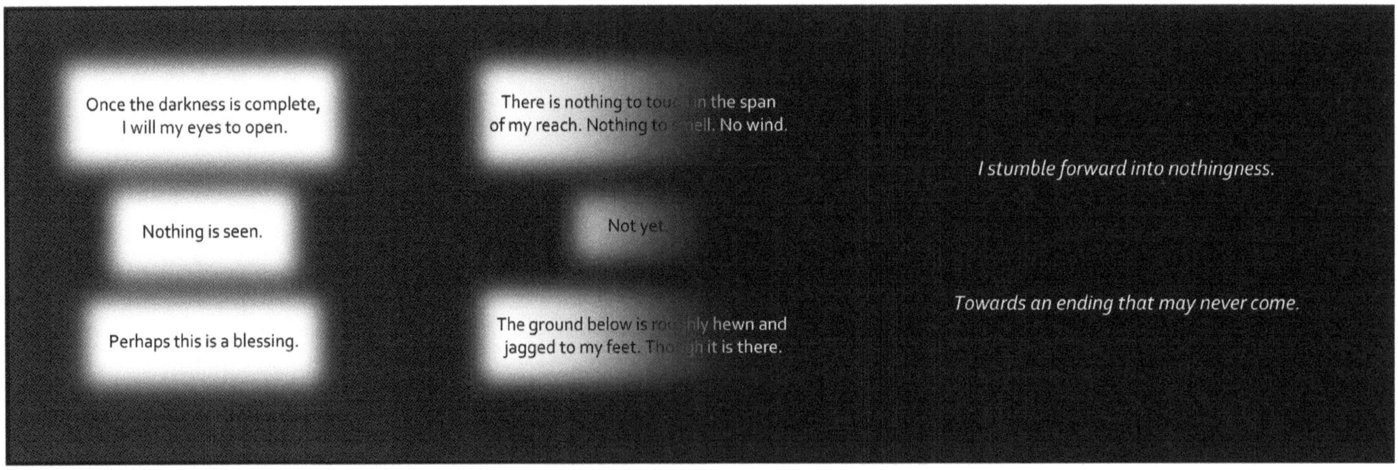
Once the darkness is complete, I will my eyes to open.
Nothing is seen.
Perhaps this is a blessing.
There is nothing to tou the span of my reach. Nothing to ell. No wind.
Not yet.
The ground below is ro hly hewn and jagged to my feet. Th h it is there.
I stumble forward into nothingness.
Towards an ending that may never come.

"Acceptance"

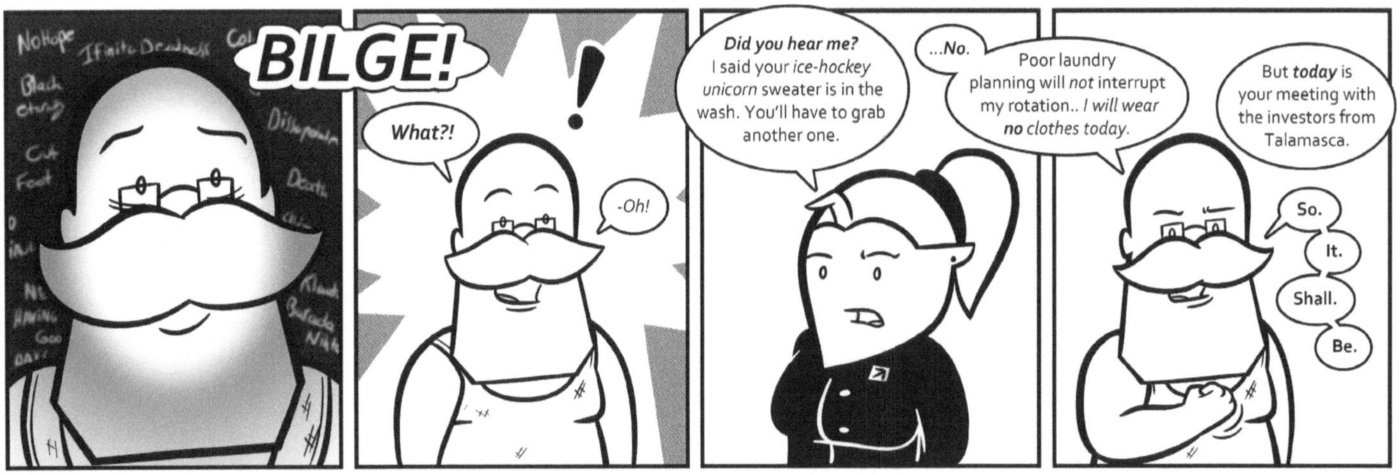
BILGE!
What?!
!
-Oh!
Did you hear me? I said your *ice-hockey unicorn* sweater is in the wash. You'll have to grab another one.
...**No.**
Poor laundry planning will *not* interrupt my rotation.. *I will wear* ***no*** *clothes today.*
But ***today*** is your meeting with the investors from Talamasca.
So.
It.
Shall.
Be.

A DAY IN THE LIFE

"Preemptive Strike"

"Fuel"

"Duties"

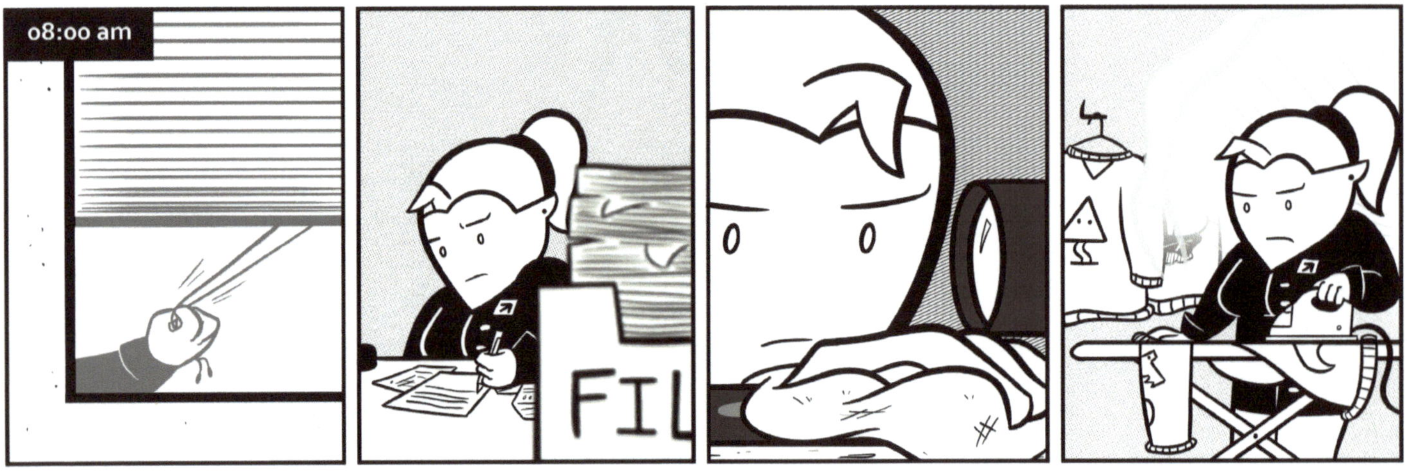
08:00 am
FIL

"Can You Make The Burger Taste Like A Gun"

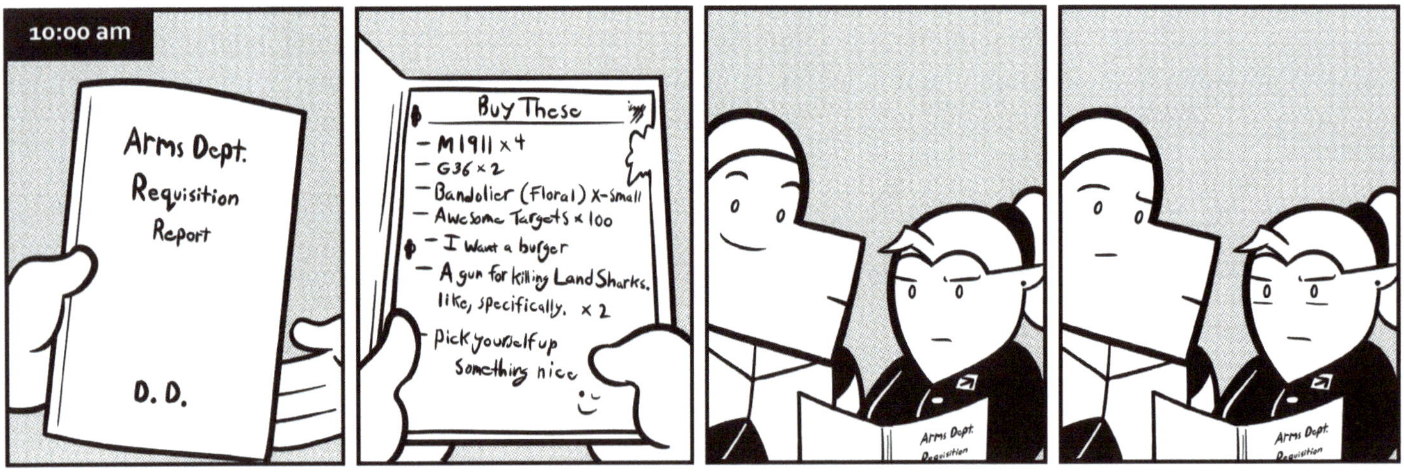
10:00 am
Arms Dept.
Requisition
Report
D. D.
Buy These
- M1911 x 4
- G36 x 2
- Bandolier (Floral) X-Small
- Awesome Targets x 100
- I Want a burger
- A gun for killing Land Sharks. like, specifically. x 2
- Pick yourself up Something nice
Arms Dept.
Requisition
Arms Dept.
Requisition

"Now That's A Throwback"

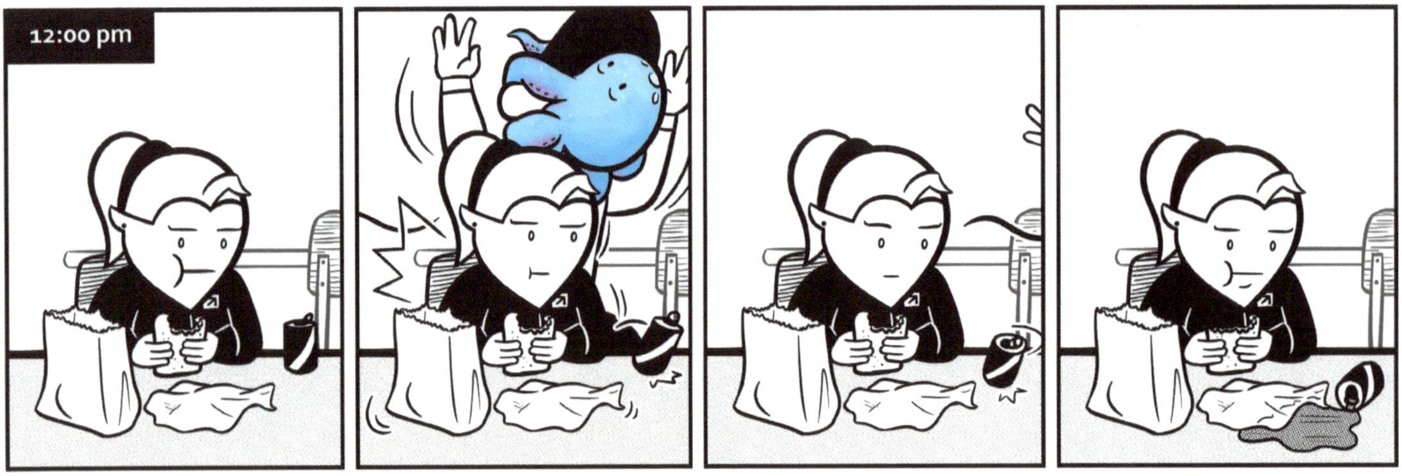
12:00 pm

"Getting Somewhere Now"

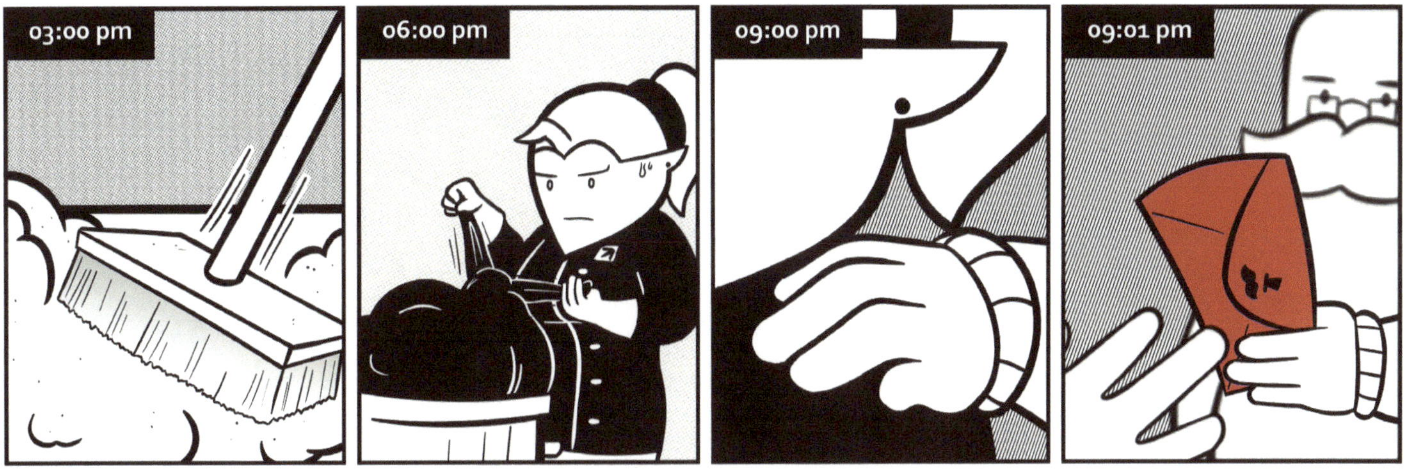
03:00 pm
06:00 pm
09:00 pm
09:01 pm

"The Remanding"

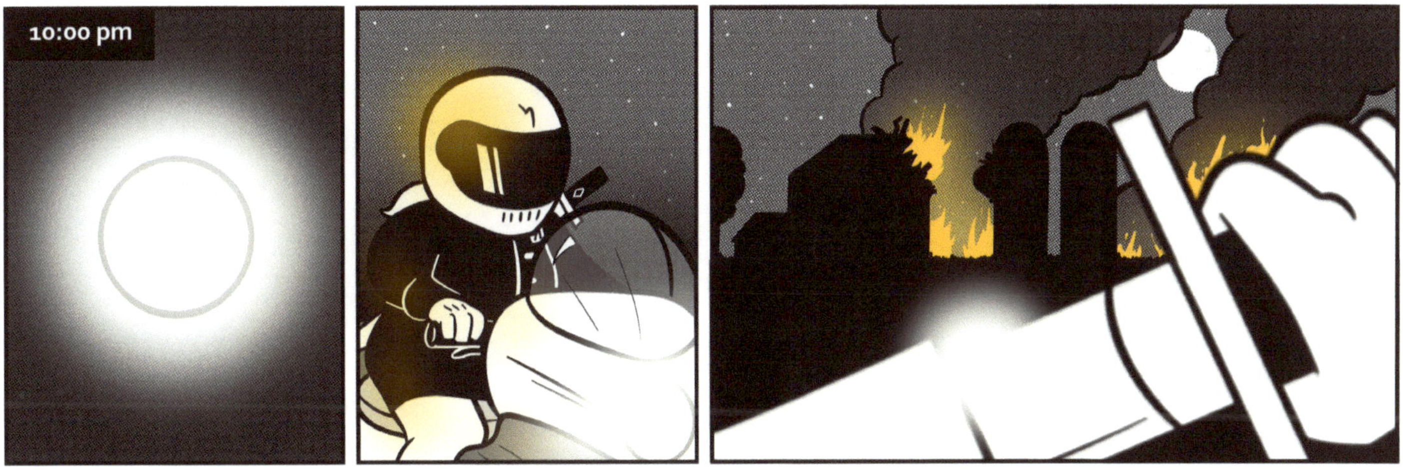
10:00 pm

"Slicing Pun"

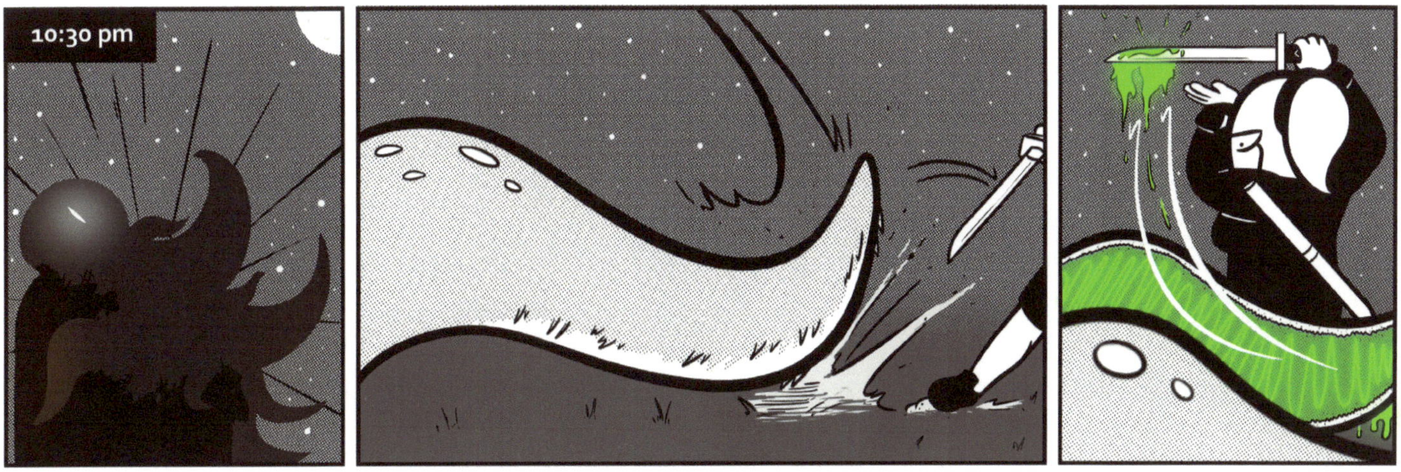
10:30 pm

"All In A Day's Work"

"Winding Down"

MAMMOTH

"Let Me Know"

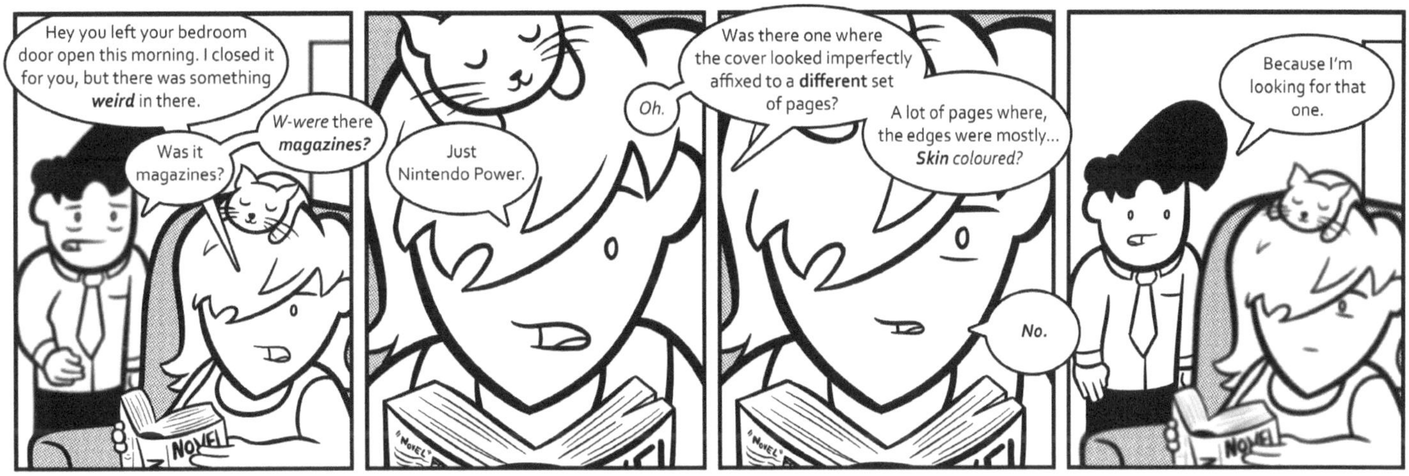
Hey you left your bedroom door open this morning. I closed it for you, but there was something *weird* in there.
Was it magazines?
W-were there ***magazines?***
Just Nintendo Power.
Oh.
Was there one where the cover looked imperfectly affixed to a **different** set of pages?
A lot of pages where, the edges were mostly... ***Skin*** *coloured?*
No.
Because I'm looking for that one.

"Seedless"

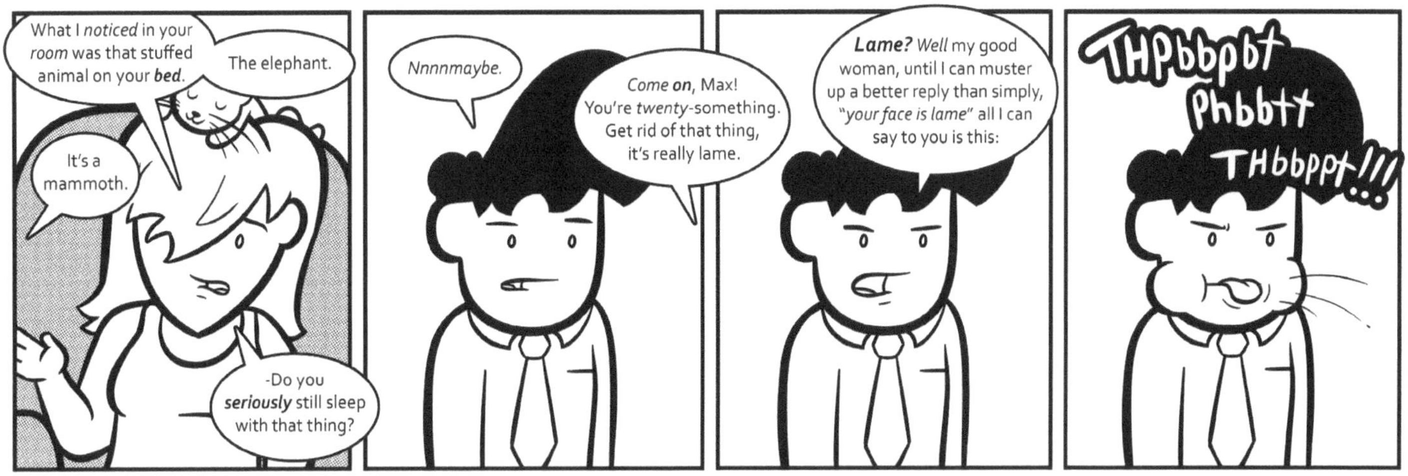
What I *noticed* in your *room* was that stuffed animal on your ***bed***.
The elephant.
It's a mammoth.
-Do you ***seriously*** still sleep with that thing?
Nnnnmaybe.
Come **on**, Max! You're *twenty*-something. Get rid of that thing, it's really lame.
Lame? *Well* my good woman, until I can muster up a better reply than simply, *"your face is lame"* all I can say to you is this:
THPbbpbt
Phbbtt
THbbppt!!!

"Conflixiation"

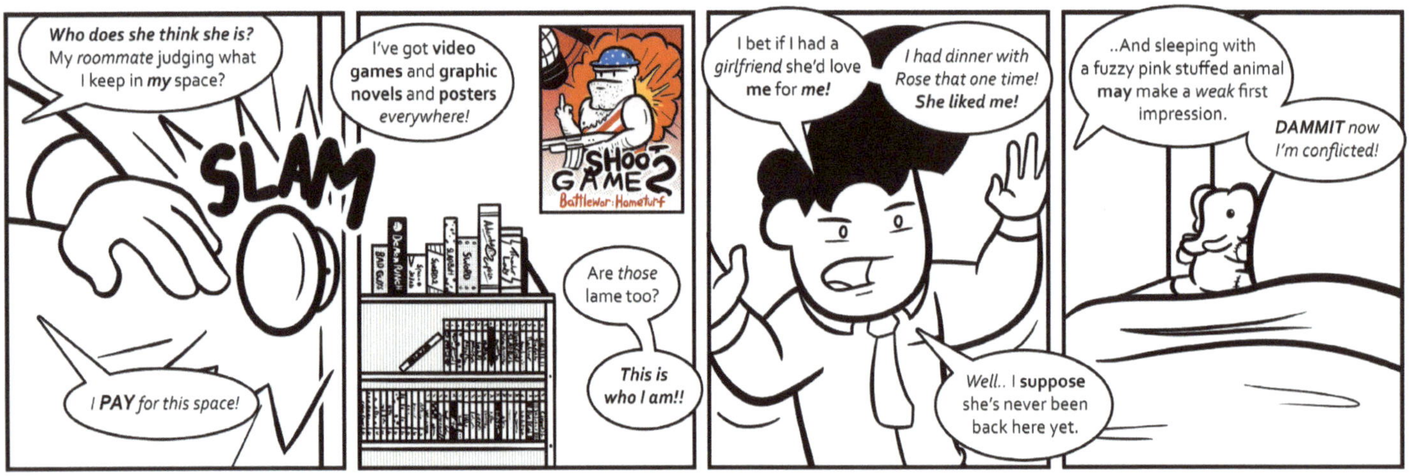

Who does she think she is? My *roommate* judging what I keep in ***my*** space?
SLAM
I **PAY** *for this space!*
I've got **video games** and **graphic novels** and **posters** *everywhere!*
SHOOT GAMES 2
Battlewar: Hometurf
Are *those* lame too?
This is who I am!!
I bet if I had a *girlfriend* she'd love **me** for ***me!***
I had dinner with Rose that one time! ***She liked me!***
Well.. I **suppose** she's never been back here yet.
..And sleeping with a fuzzy pink stuffed animal **may** make a *weak* first impression.
DAMMIT *now I'm conflicted!*

"On A Forgotten Laundry Throne"

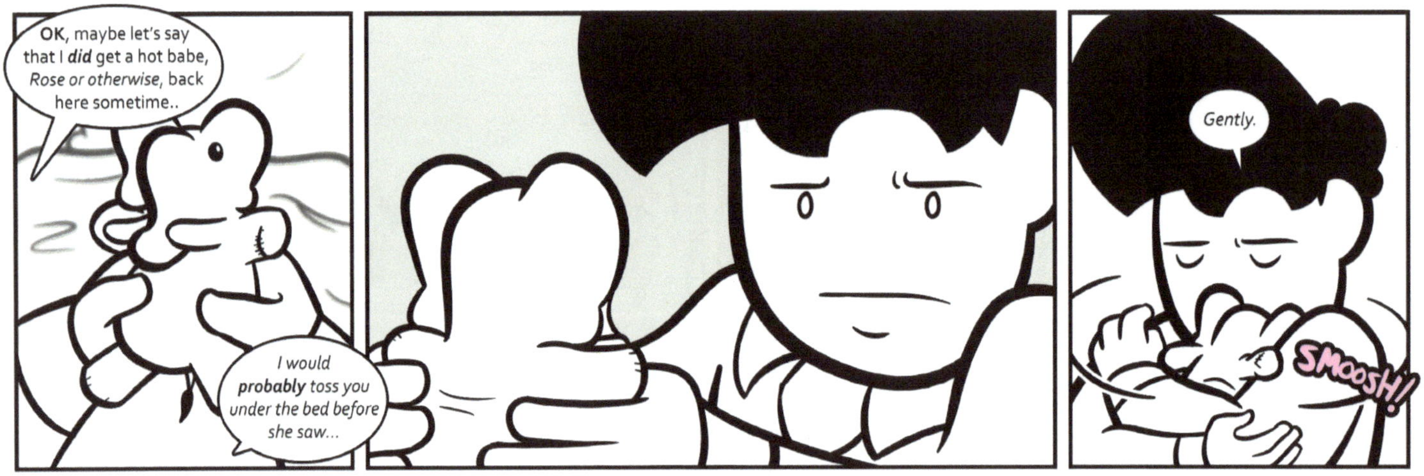

OK, maybe let's say that I ***did*** get a hot babe, *Rose or otherwise*, back here sometime..
I would ***probably*** *toss you under the bed before she saw...*
Gently.
SMOOSH!

"Sand Mammoth Cometh"

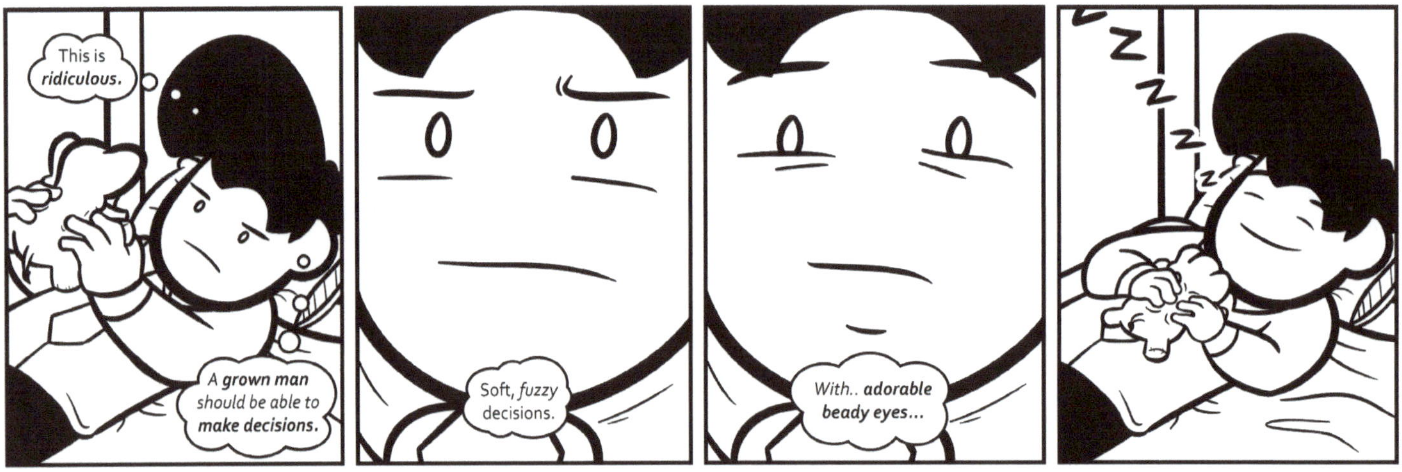

This is ***ridiculous.***
A ***grown man*** *should be able to* ***make decisions.***
Soft, *fuzzy* decisions.
With.. ***adorable beady eyes...***
Z Z Z Z Z

"Both Handy And Capable"

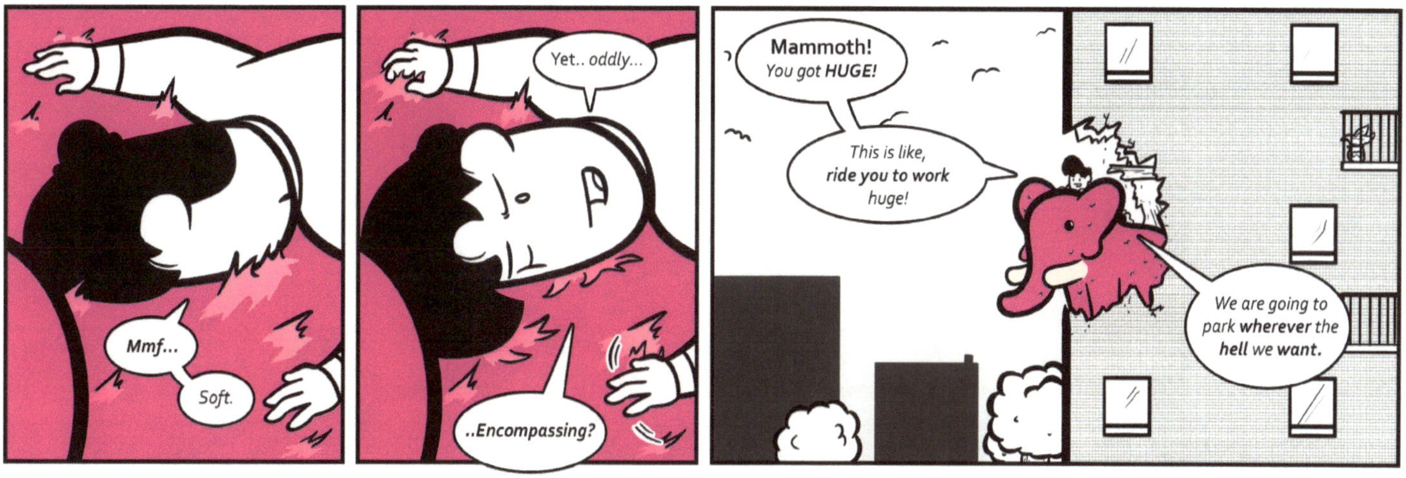

Mmf...
Soft.
Yet.. oddly...
..Encompassing?
Mammoth! You got HUGE!
This is like, ride you to work huge!
We are going to park wherever the hell we want.

"Pimp My Ride"

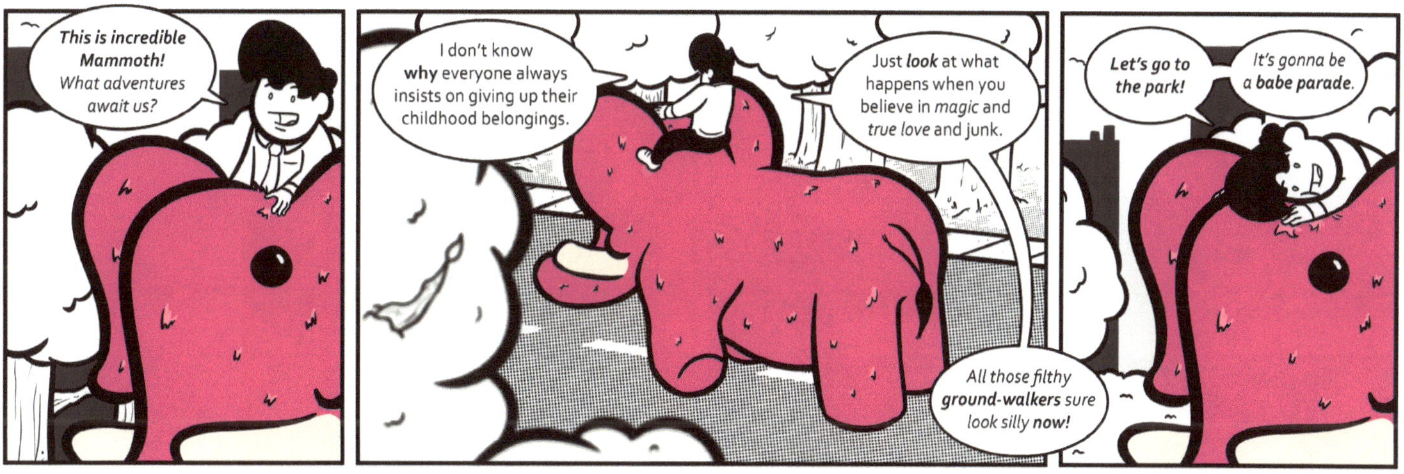

This is incredible Mammoth! What adventures await us?
I don't know why everyone always insists on giving up their childhood belongings.
Just look at what happens when you believe in magic and true love and junk.
All those filthy ground-walkers sure look silly now!
Let's go to the park!
It's gonna be a babe parade.

"We All Scream For Eye Beams"

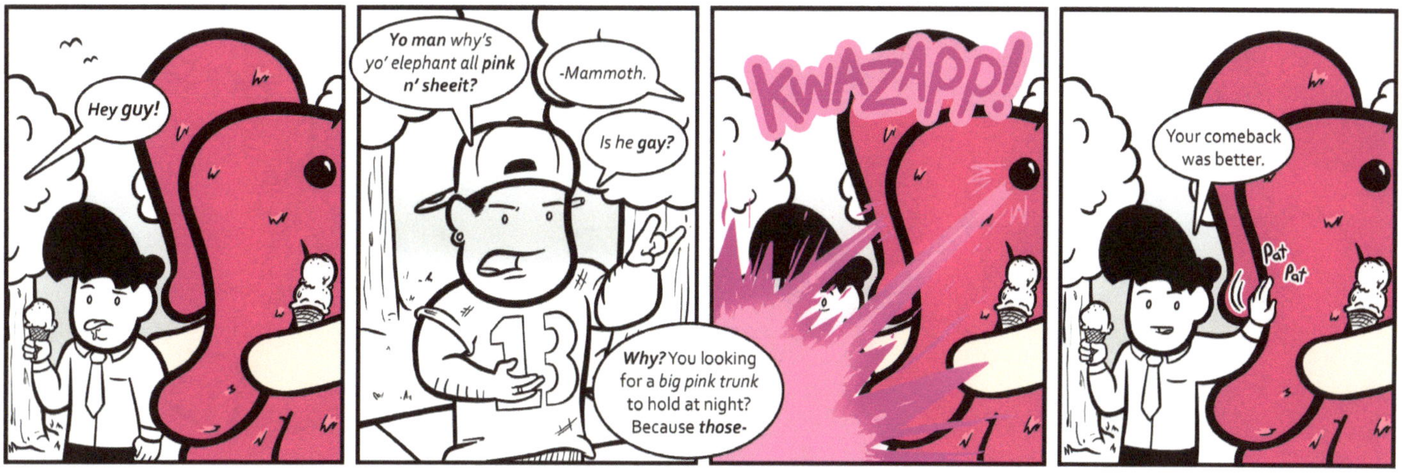

Hey guy!
Yo man why's yo' elephant all pink n' sheeit?
-Mammoth.
Is he gay?
Why? You looking for a big pink trunk to hold at night? Because those-
KWAZAPP!
Your comeback was better.
Pat Pat

"One Of The Team"

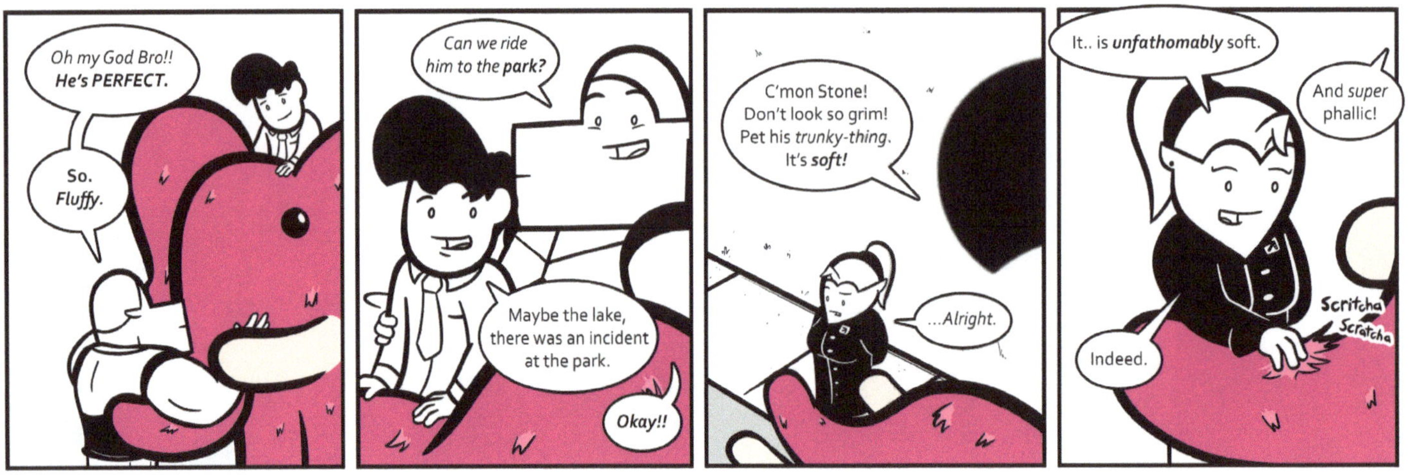

Oh my God Bro!! **He's PERFECT.**
So. *Fluffy*.
*Can we ride him to the **park?***
Maybe the lake, there was an incident at the park.
Okay!!
C'mon Stone! Don't look so grim! Pet his *trunky-thing*. It's *soft!*
...Alright.
It.. is ***unfathomably*** soft.
And *super* phallic!
Indeed.
Scritcha Scratcha

"But First Let's Visit School Naked"

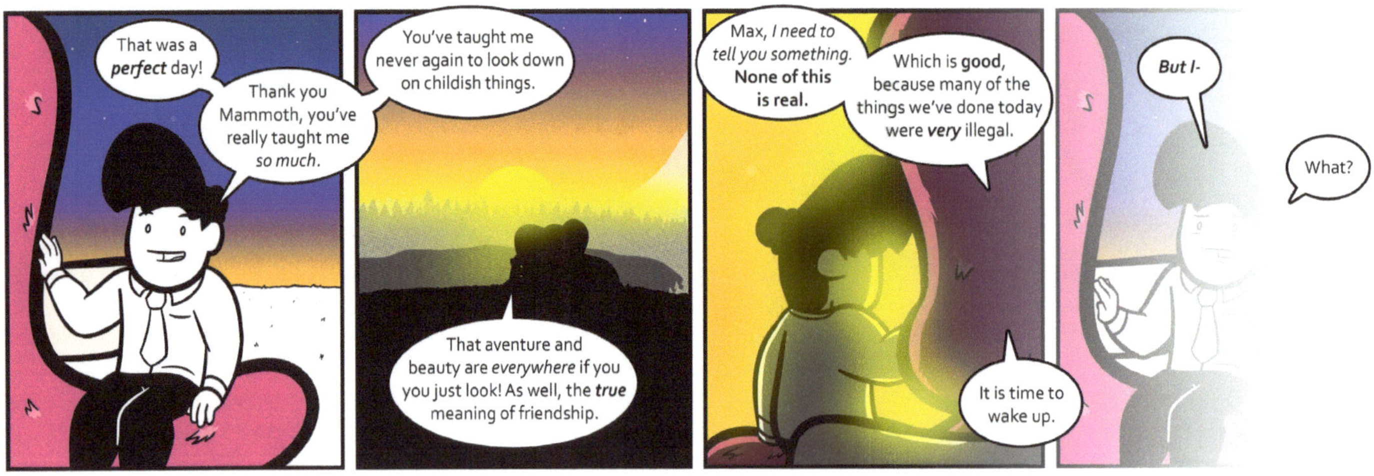

That was a ***perfect*** day!
Thank you Mammoth, you've really taught me *so much*.
You've taught me never again to look down on childish things.
That aventure and beauty are *everywhere* if you you just look! As well, the ***true*** meaning of friendship.
Max, *I need to tell you something.* **None of this is real.**
Which is **good**, because many of the things we've done today were ***very*** illegal.
It is time to wake up.
But I-
What?

"Sober Truth"

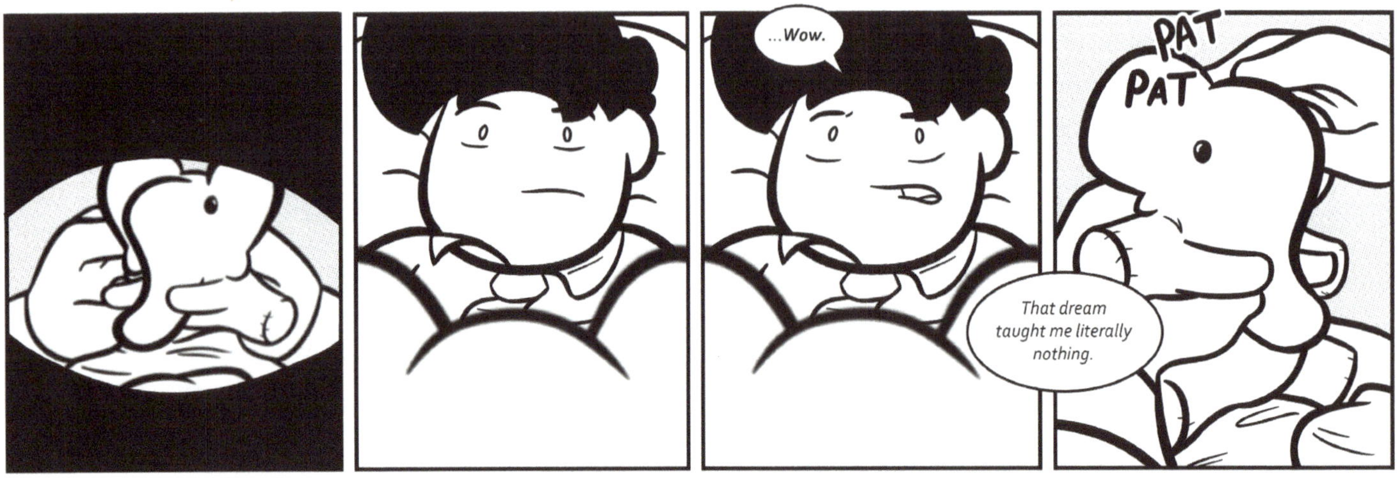

...Wow.
PAT PAT
That dream taught me literally nothing.

"Pachyderm Eyes"

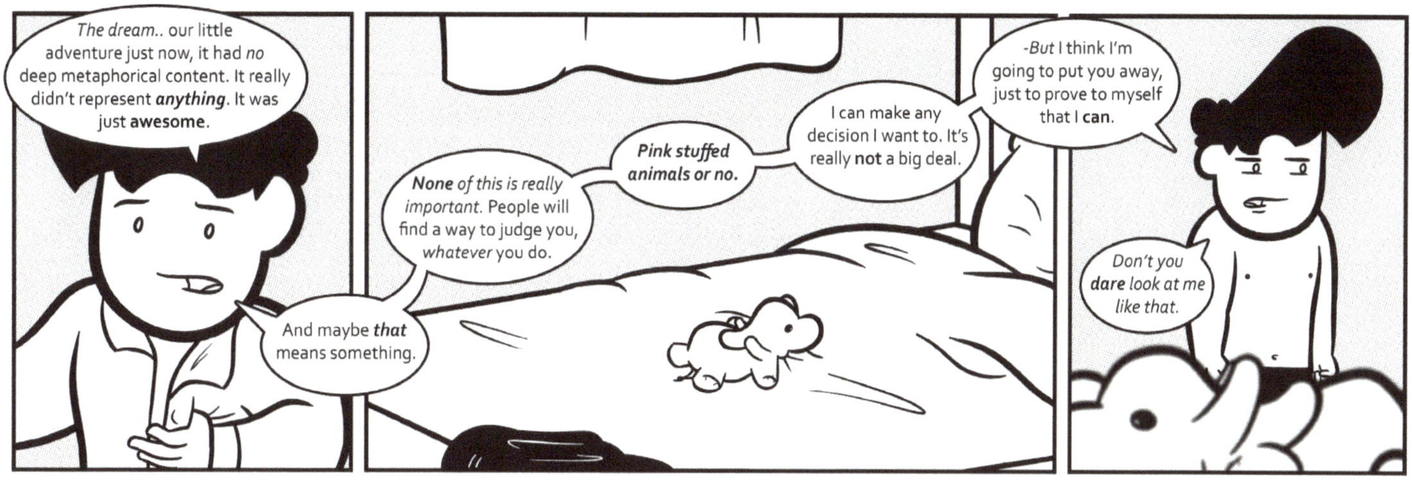

The dream.. our little adventure just now, it had *no* deep metaphorical content. It really didn't represent ***anything***. It was just **awesome**.
And maybe ***that*** means something.
None *of this is really important*. People will find a way to judge you, *whatever* you do.
Pink stuffed animals or no.
I can make any decision I want to. It's really **not** a big deal.
-*But* I think I'm going to put you away, just to prove to myself that I **can**.
Don't you ***dare*** *look at me like that.*

"Seriously Don't Ever Do That"

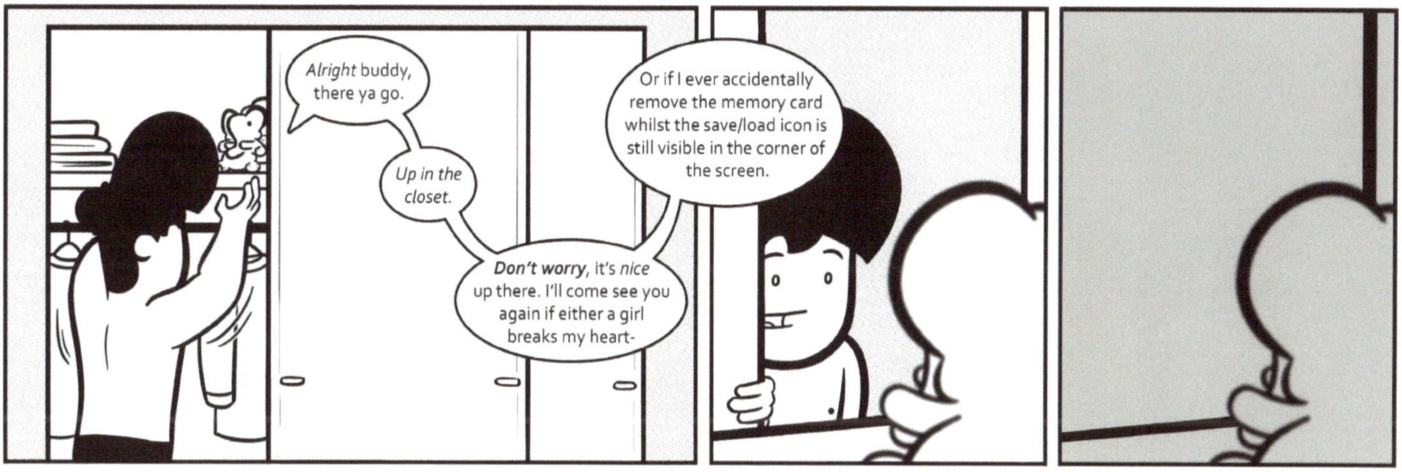

Alright buddy, there ya go.
Up in the closet.
Don't worry, it's *nice* up there. I'll come see you again if either a girl breaks my heart-
Or if I ever accidentally remove the memory card whilst the save/load icon is still visible in the corner of the screen.

"Larry Curly And Moe"

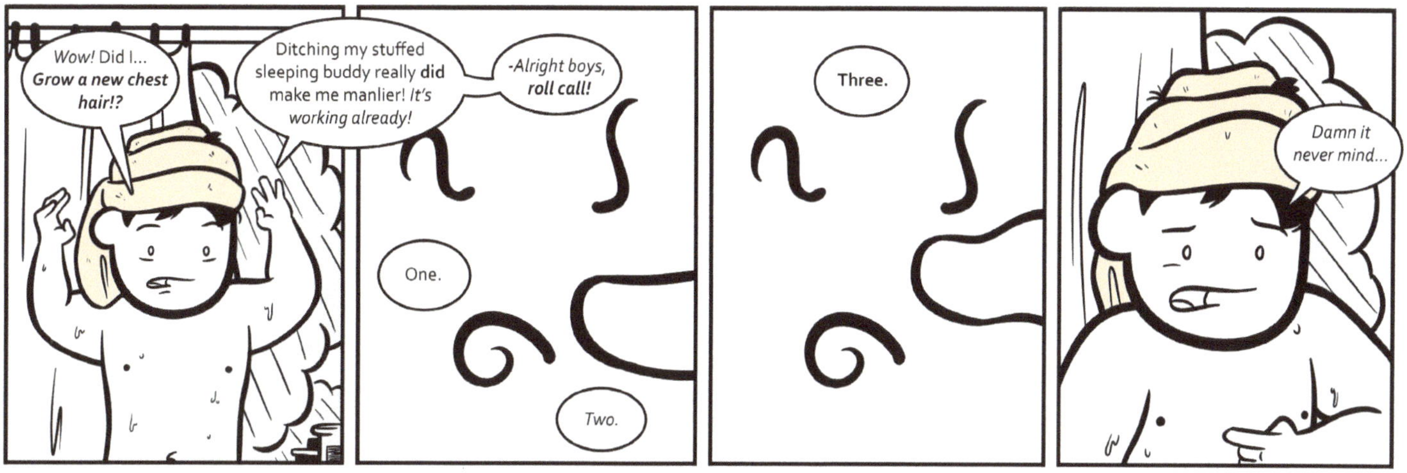

Wow! Did I... ***Grow a new chest hair!?***
Ditching my stuffed sleeping buddy really **did** make me manlier! *It's working already!*
-Alright boys, ***roll call!***
One.
Two.
Three.
Damn it never mind...

"Right Before The Best Part"

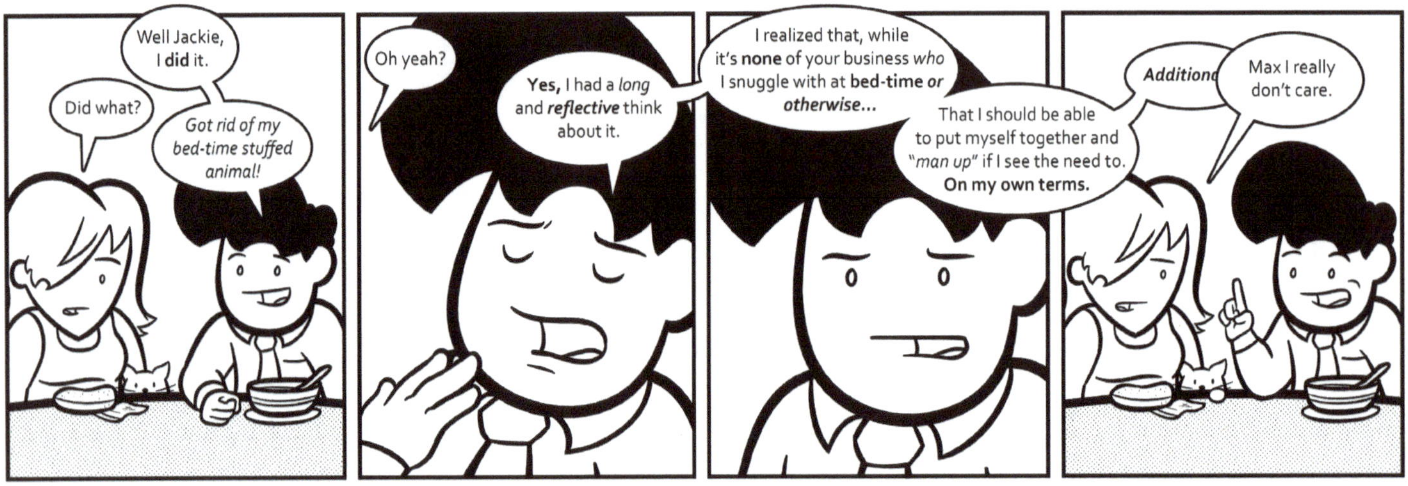
Well Jackie, I **did** it.
Did what?
Got rid of my bed-time stuffed animal!
Oh yeah?
Yes, I had a *long* and ***reflective*** think about it.
I realized that, while it's **none** of your business *who* I snuggle with at **bed-time *or otherwise...***
That I should be able to put myself together and "*man up*" if I see the need to. **On my own terms.**
Max I really don't care.

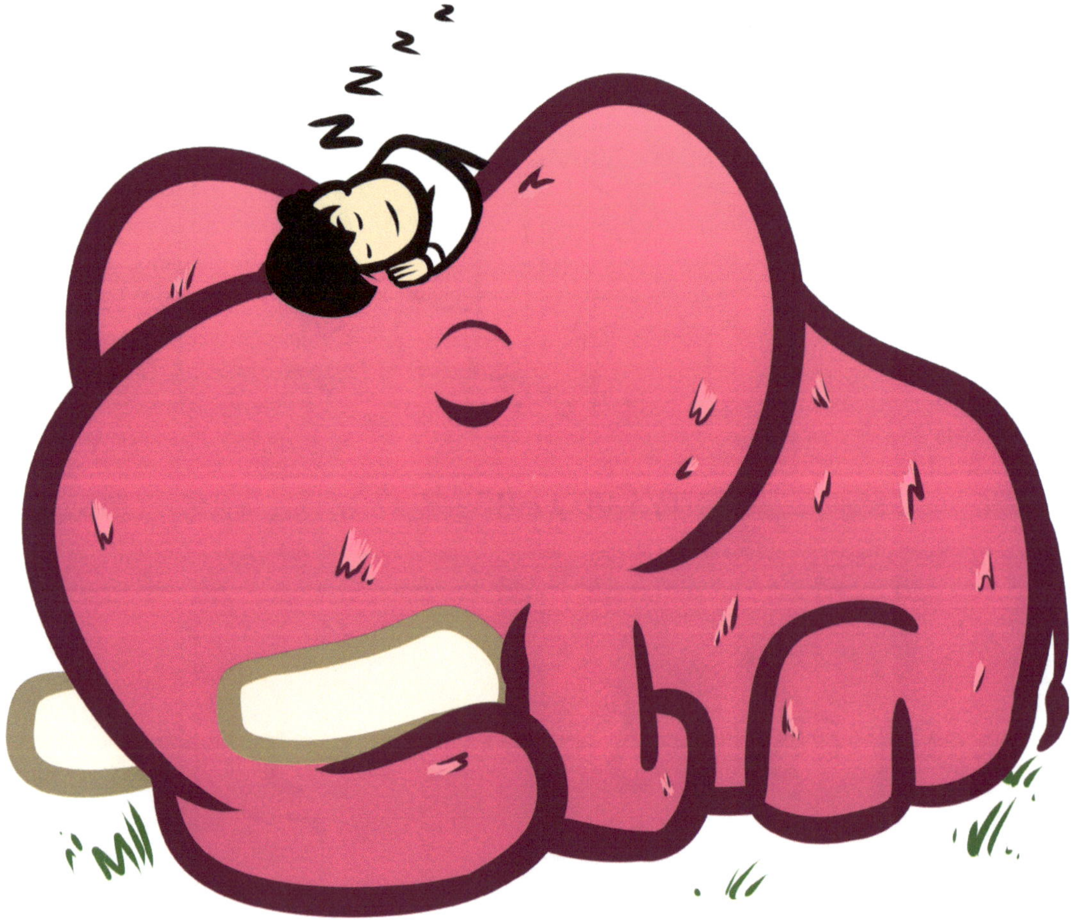
Z Z Z Z Z

CALCULO DOMINUM

"Feeling Hella Good"

Heh-heh.
No Doubt INTERCOM
SPEAK DONTSPEAK
Are you *ready*, super-hot secretary babe?
Click
Always *ready for you, agent Davison.*

"Good At Basketball"

But, Mr. Davison, this is, like, ***super inappropriate!*** *What if we get caught?*
You let **me** worry about that baby.
Oh.. Oh ***MY*** *Mr. Davison! Your hands are so* ***large.***
You know what they say about **large hands,** super hot secretary babe?
←Elevator
They're indicators linked to an increased likelihood of prostate cancer?
No the other thing.
Oooh!!

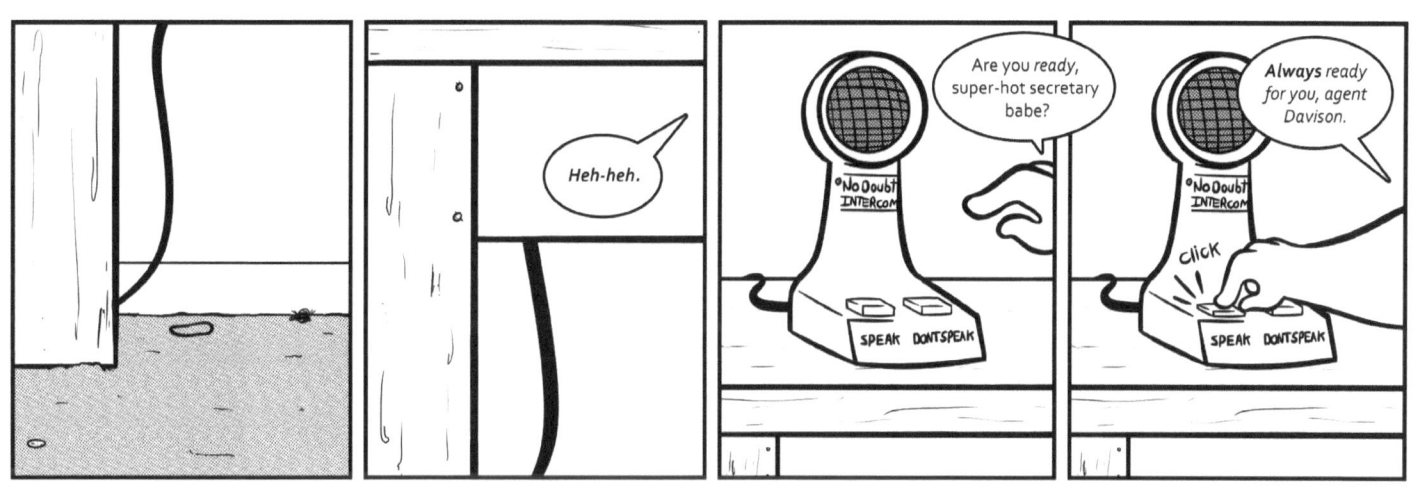

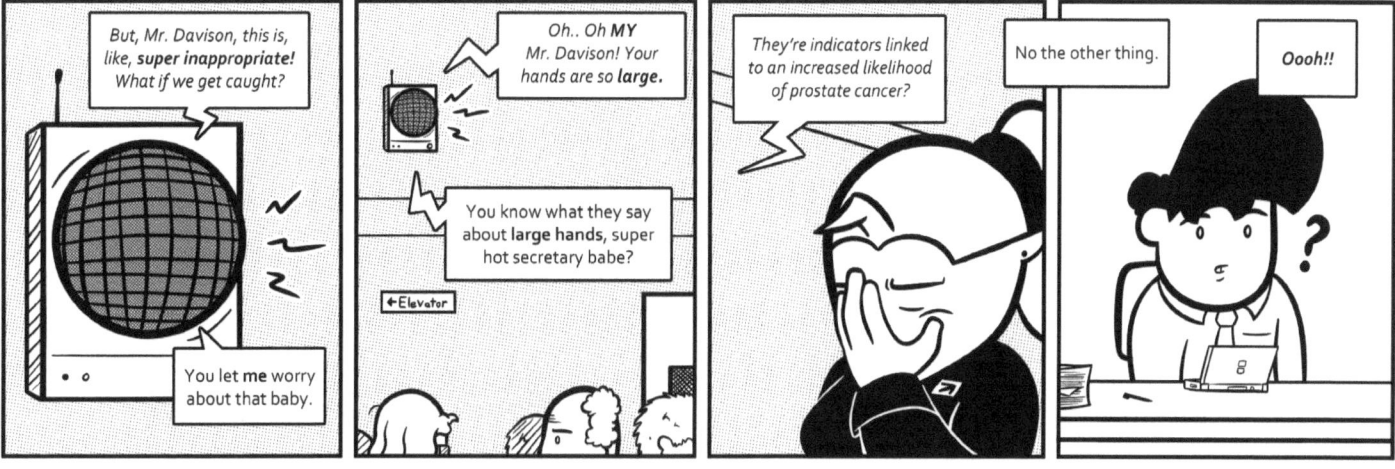

"The Intracacies Of Delicates"

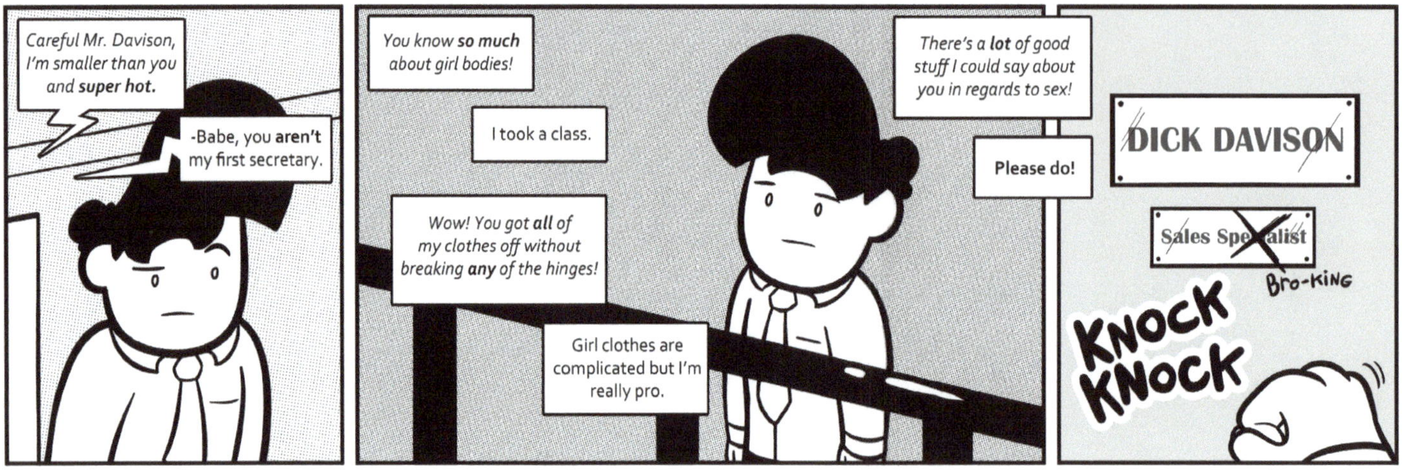
Careful Mr. Davison, I'm smaller than you and **super hot.**
-Babe, you **aren't** my first secretary.
You know ***so much*** *about girl bodies!*
I took a class.
Wow! You got ***all*** *of my clothes off without breaking* ***any*** *of the hinges!*
Girl clothes are complicated but I'm really pro.
There's a ***lot*** *of good stuff I could say about you in regards to sex!*
Please do!
DICK DAVISON
Sales Specialist
Bro-KING
KNOCK KNOCK

"Freudian Hemorrhage"

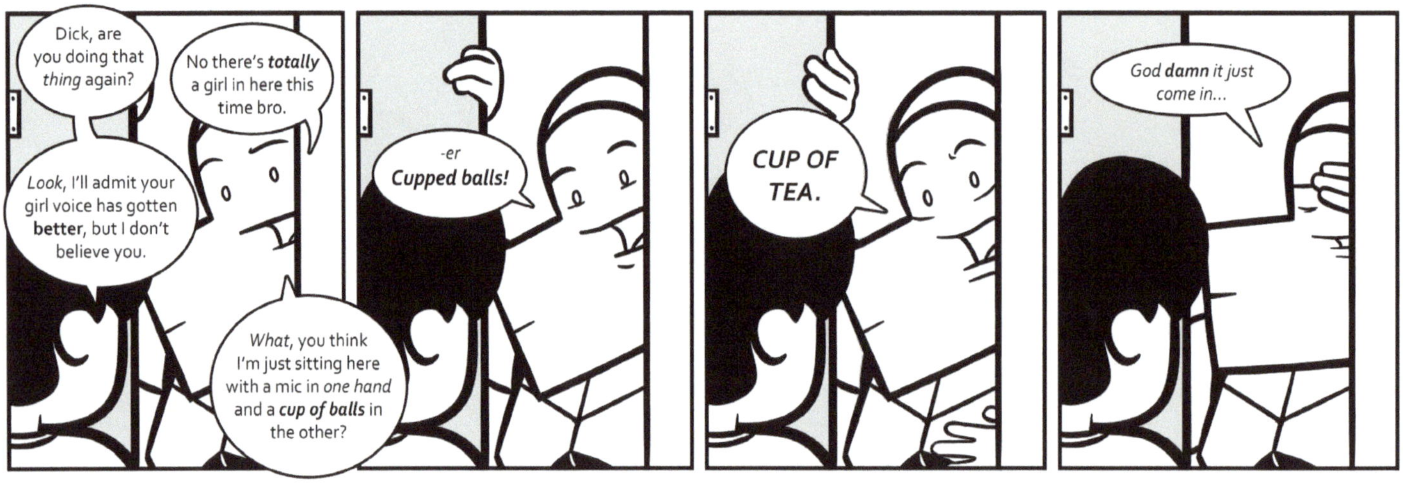
Dick, are you doing that *thing* again?
No there's ***totally*** a girl in here this time bro.
Look, I'll admit your girl voice has gotten **better**, but I don't believe you.
What, you think I'm just sitting here with a mic in *one hand* and a ***cup of balls*** in the other?
-er
Cupped balls!
CUP OF TEA.
God ***damn*** *it just come in...*

"What Could It Mean"

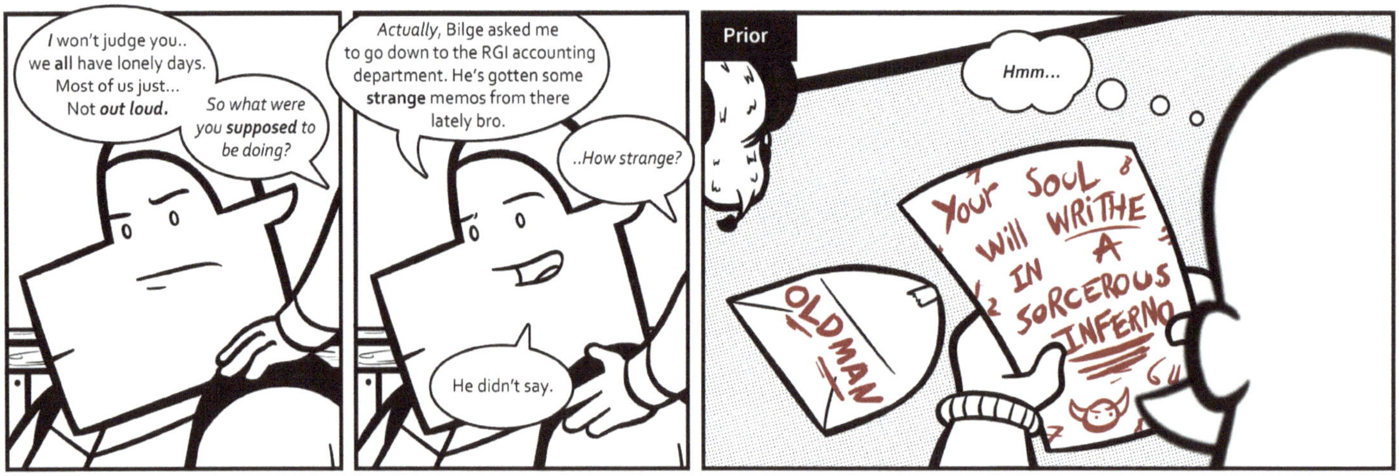
I won't judge you.. we **all** have lonely days. Most of us just... Not ***out loud.***
So what were you ***supposed*** *to be doing?*
Actually, Bilge asked me to go down to the RGI accounting department. He's gotten some **strange** memos from there lately bro.
..How strange?
He didn't say.
Prior
Hmm...
OLDMAN
Your Soul will WRITHE IN A SORCEROUS INFERNO

"Don't Tell PETA"

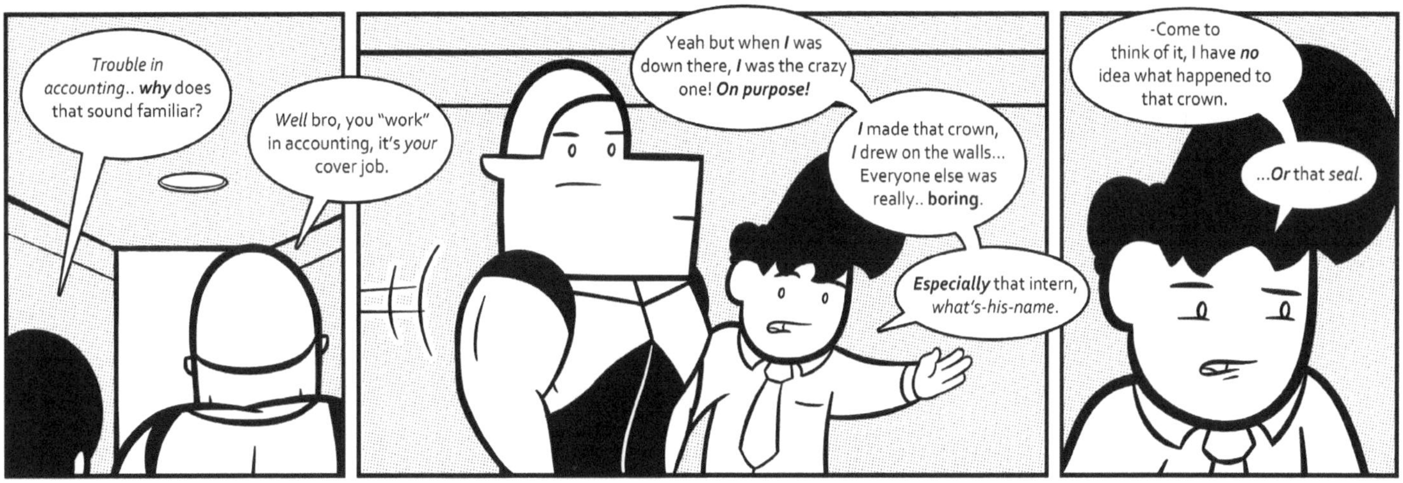
Trouble in accounting.. why does that sound familiar?
Well bro, you "work" in accounting, it's your cover job.
Yeah but when I was down there, I was the crazy one! On purpose!
I made that crown, I drew on the walls... Everyone else was really.. boring.
Especially that intern, what's-his-name.
-Come to think of it, I have no idea what happened to that crown.
...Or that seal.

"The Truth Meaning"

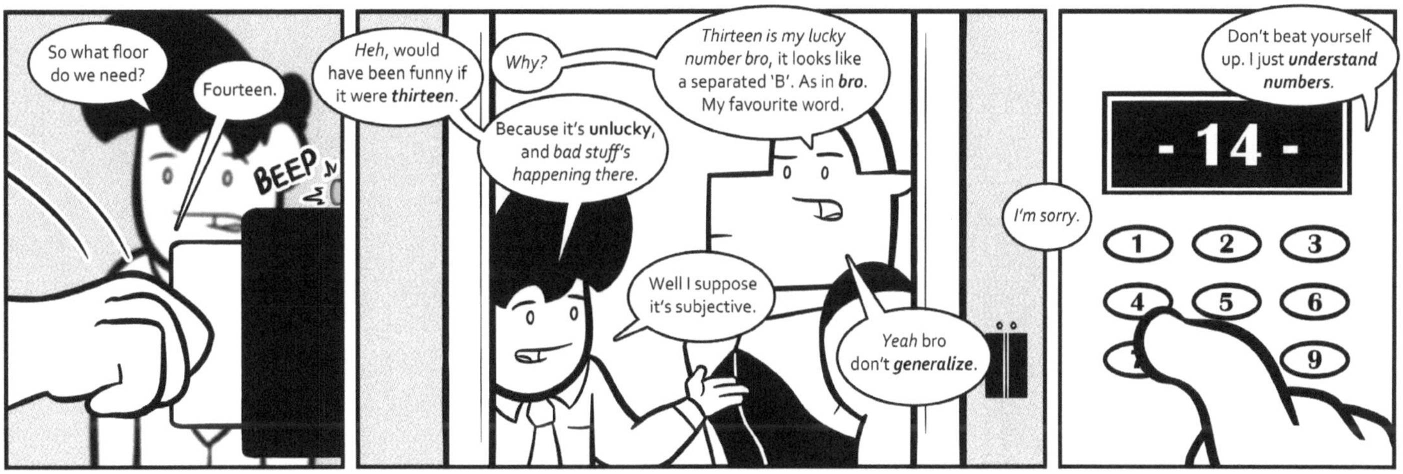
So what floor do we need?
Fourteen.
BEEP
Heh, would have been funny if it were thirteen.
Why?
Because it's unlucky, and bad stuff's happening there.
Thirteen is my lucky number bro, it looks like a separated 'B'. As in bro. My favourite word.
Well I suppose it's subjective.
Yeah bro don't generalize.
I'm sorry.
Don't beat yourself up. I just understand numbers.
- 14 -

"The Old Skiperoo"

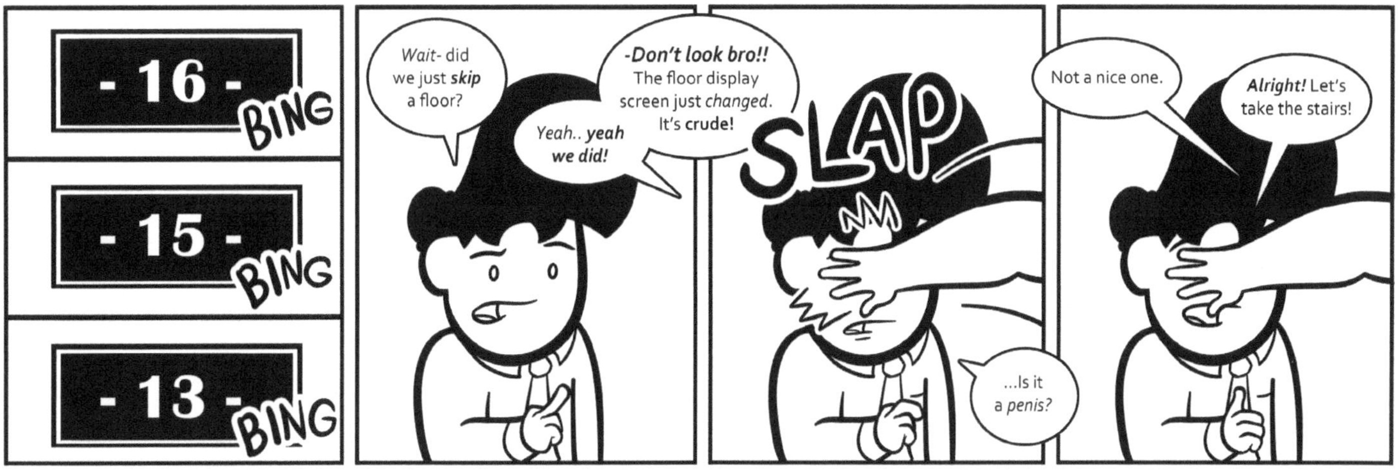
- 16 -
BING
- 15 -
BING
- 13 -
BING
Wait- did we just skip a floor?
Yeah.. yeah we did!
-Don't look bro!! The floor display screen just changed. It's crude!
SLAP
...Is it a penis?
Not a nice one.
Alright! Let's take the stairs!

"The Janitor Pretends It Isn't There"

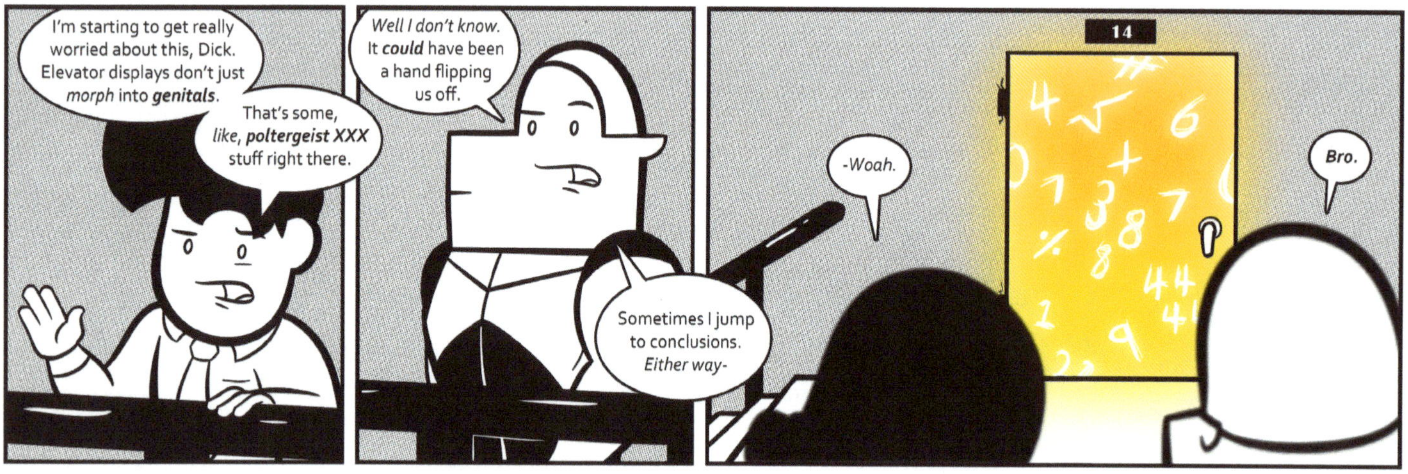

I'm starting to get really worried about this, Dick. Elevator displays don't just *morph* into **genitals**.
That's some, *like*, ***poltergeist XXX*** stuff right there.
Well I don't know. It ***could*** have been a hand flipping us off.
Sometimes I jump to conclusions. *Either way-*
14
-Woah.
Bro.

"Easy Enough To Guess"

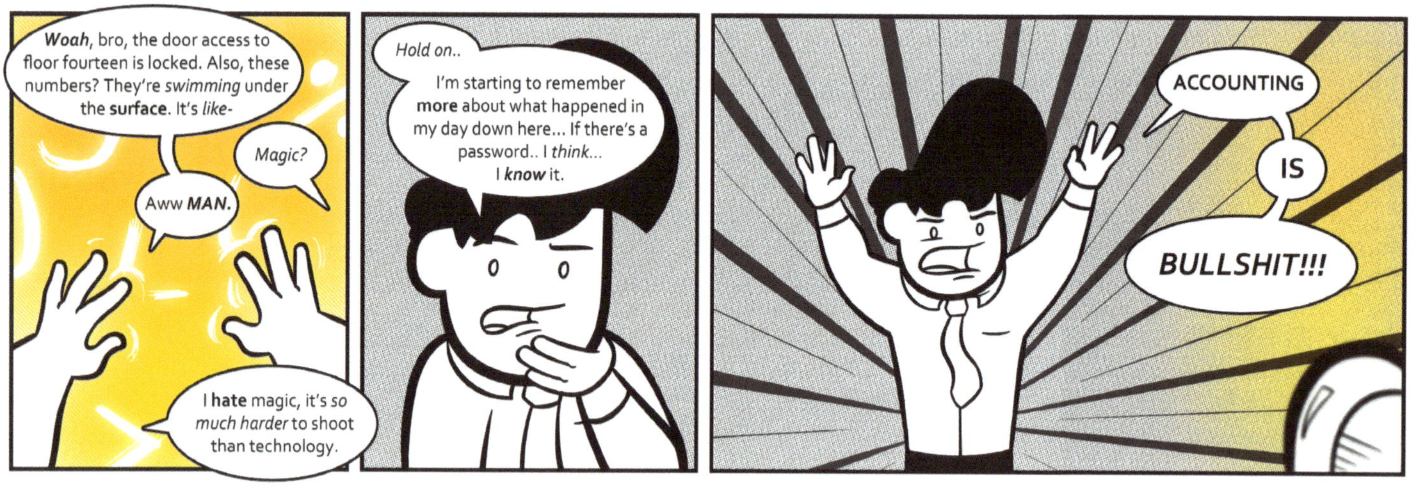

Woah, bro, the door access to floor fourteen is locked. Also, these numbers? They're *swimming* under the **surface**. It's *like-*
Magic?
Aww ***MAN.***
I **hate** magic, it's *so much harder* to shoot than technology.
Hold on..
I'm starting to remember **more** about what happened in my day down here... If there's a password.. I *think*... I ***know*** it.
ACCOUNTING
IS
BULLSHIT!!!

"Nose Game"

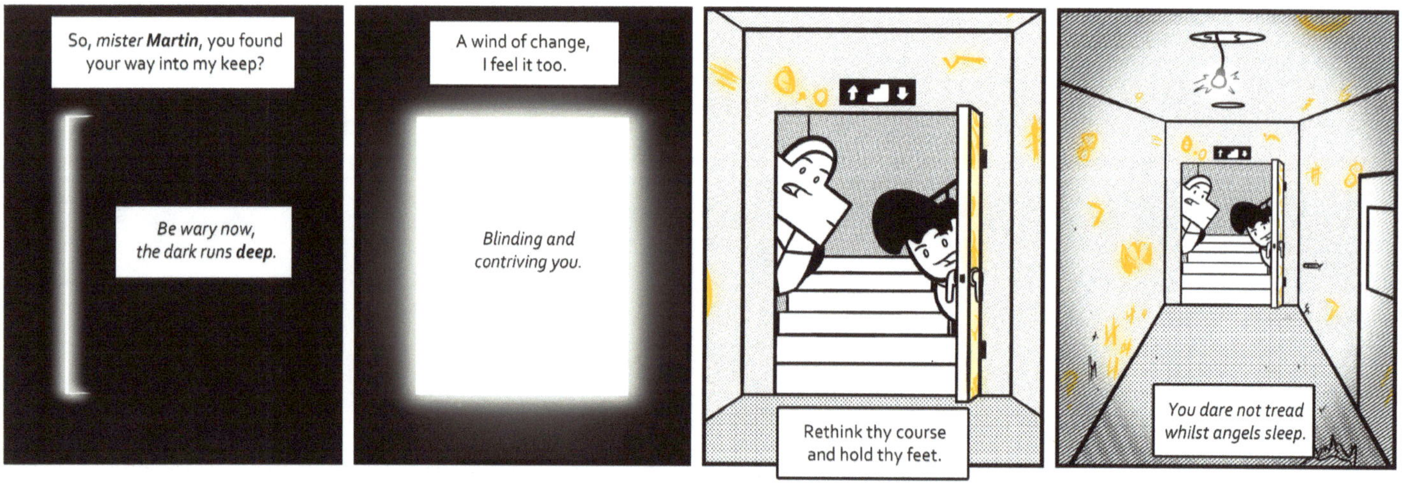

So, *mister* ***Martin***, you found your way into my keep?
Be wary now, the dark runs ***deep***.
A wind of change, I feel it too.
Blinding and contriving you.
Rethink thy course and hold thy feet.
You dare not tread whilst angels sleep.

"The Plural Is Abaci"

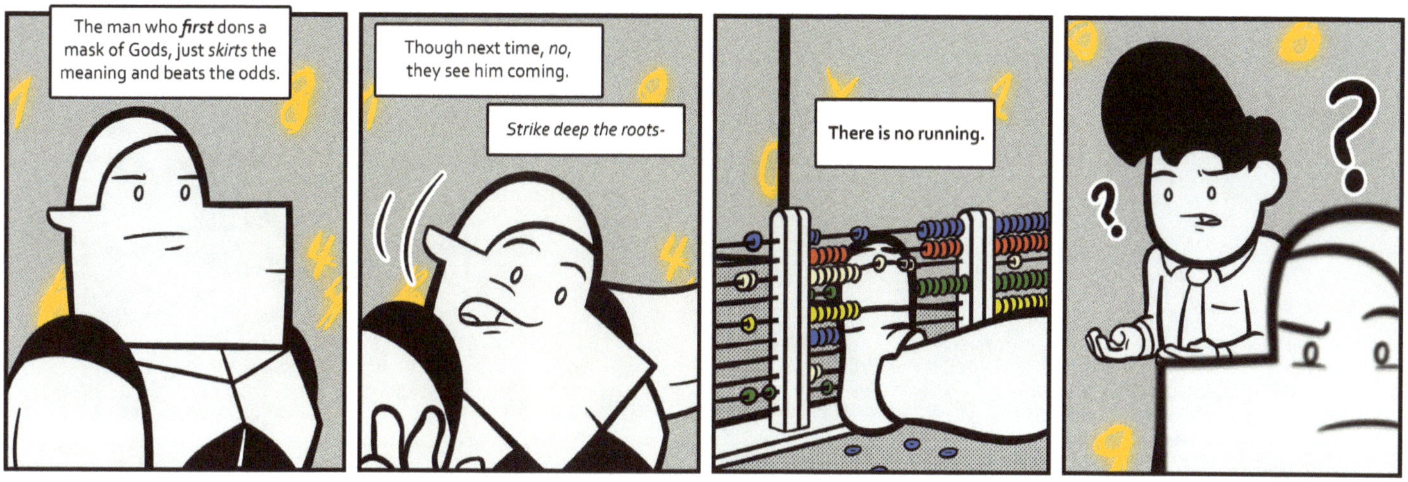

The man who *first* dons a mask of Gods, just *skirts* the meaning and beats the odds.
Though next time, *no*, they see him coming.
Strike deep the roots-
There is no running.
?
?

"Is He Doing It Out Of Anger Or Necessity"

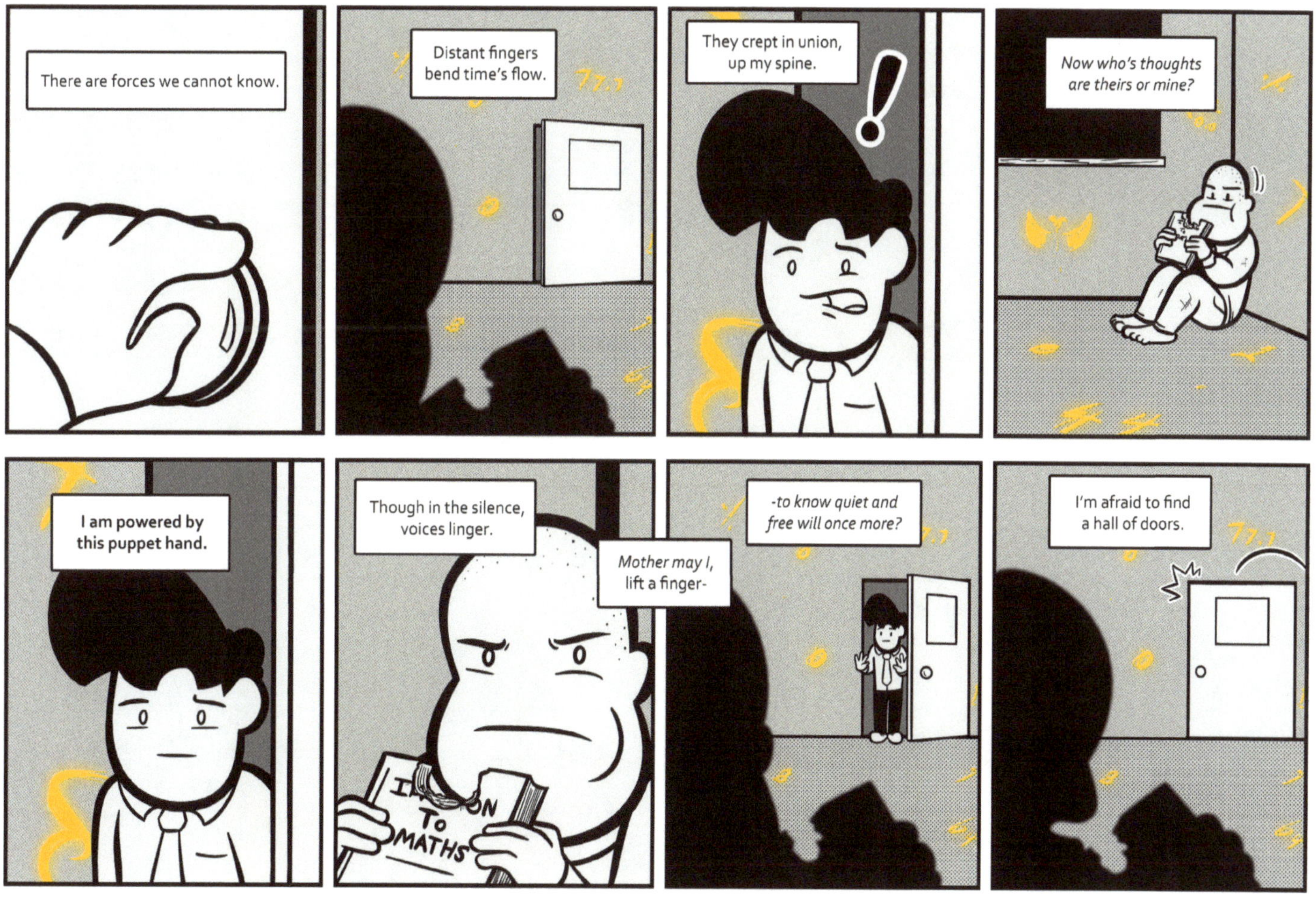

There are forces we cannot know.
Distant fingers bend time's flow.
They crept in union, up my spine.
!
Now who's thoughts are theirs or mine?
I am powered by this puppet hand.
Though in the silence, voices linger.
Mother may I, lift a finger-
-to know quiet and free will once more?
I'm afraid to find a hall of doors.

"Algebraic"

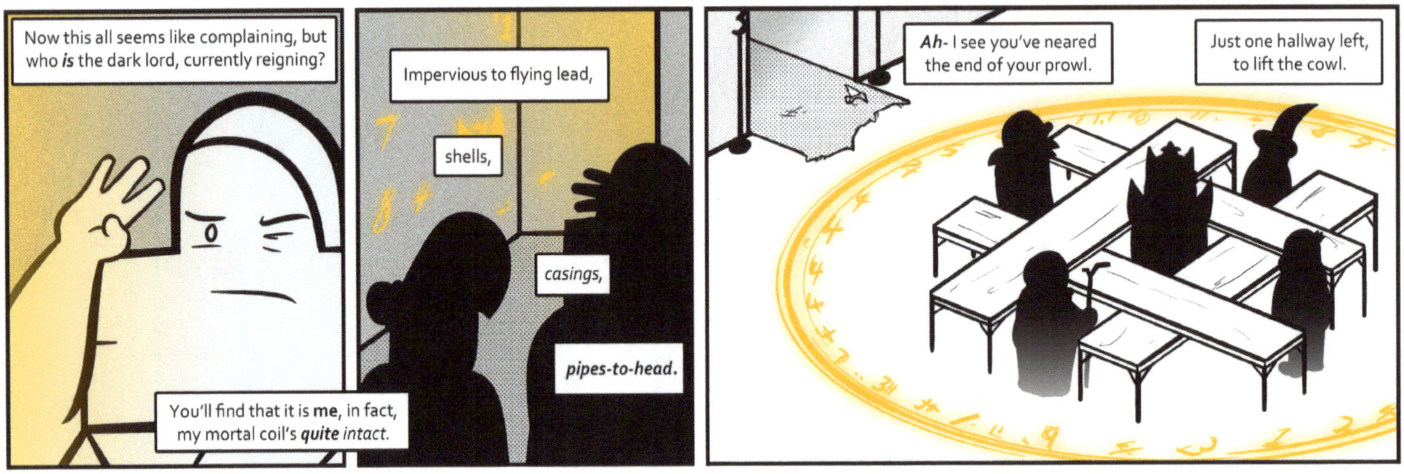

Now this all seems like complaining, but who *is* the dark lord, currently reigning?
You'll find that it is **me**, in fact, my mortal coil's ***quite** intact.*
Impervious to flying lead,
shells,
casings,
pipes-to-head.
Ah- I see you've neared the end of your prowl.
Just one hallway left, to lift the cowl.

"In Which We Question The Purpose Of Certain Narration"

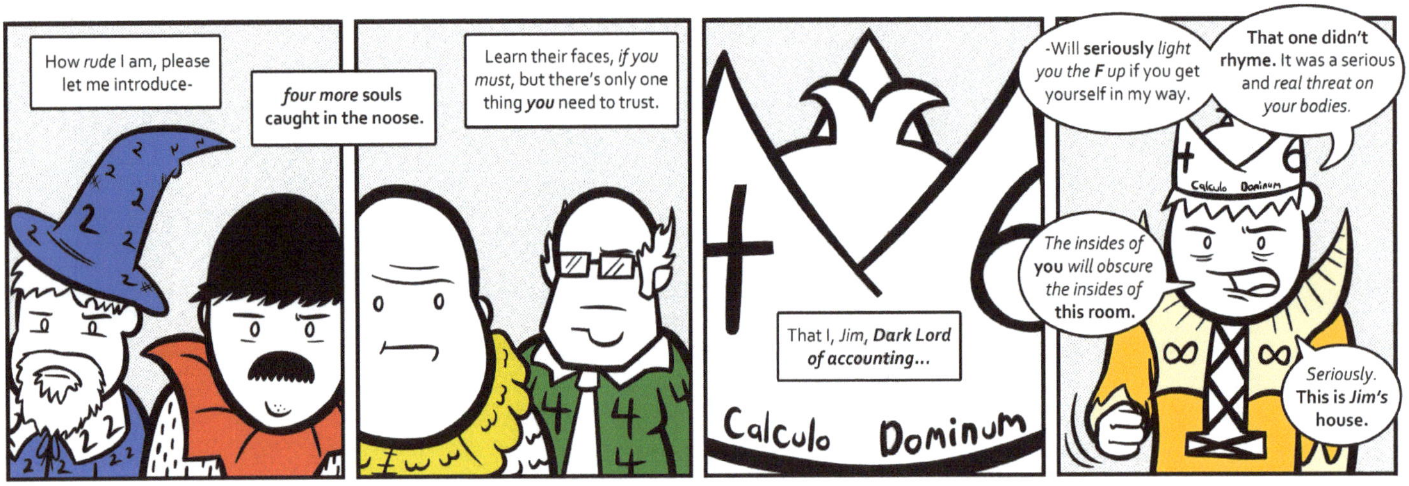

How *rude* I am, please let me introduce-
four more **souls caught in the noose.**
Learn their faces, *if you must,* but there's only one thing ***you*** need to trust.
That I, *Jim,* ***Dark Lord of accounting...***
Calculo Dominum
-Will **seriously** *light you the* ***F*** *up* if you get yourself in my way.
That one didn't rhyme. It was a serious and *real threat on your bodies.*
The insides of **you** *will obscure the insides of* **this room.**
Seriously. **This is** ***Jim's*** **house.**

"Seriously Not Cool Man"

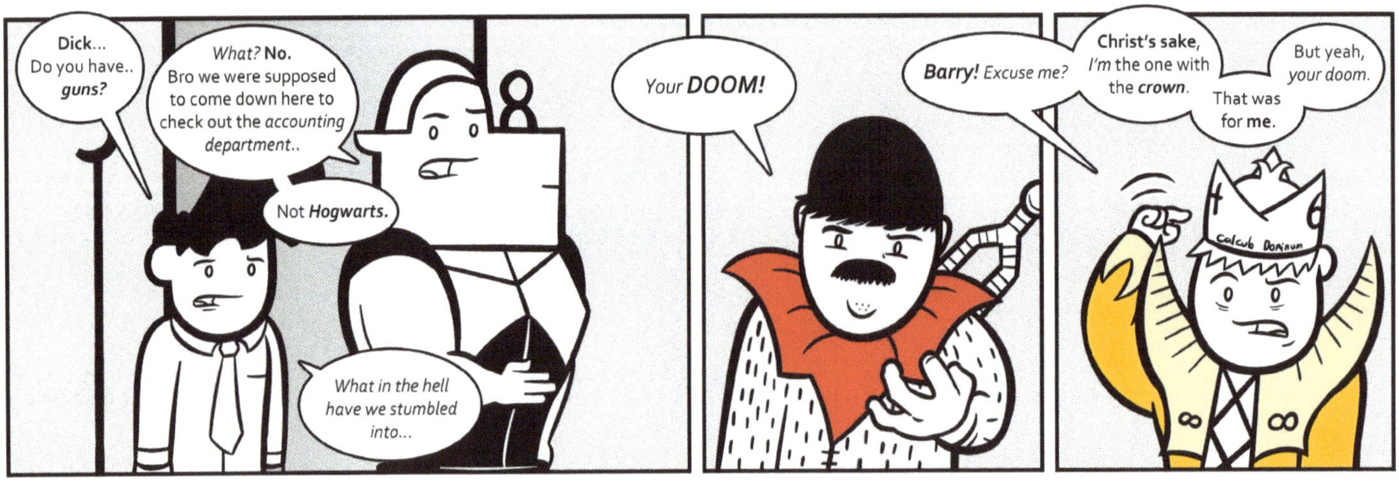

Dick... Do you have.. ***guns?***
What? **No.** Bro we were supposed to come down here to check out the *accounting department..*
Not ***Hogwarts.***
What in the hell have we stumbled into...
Your ***DOOM!***
Barry! *Excuse me?*
Christ's sake, *I'm* the one with the ***crown.***
That was for **me.**
But yeah, *your doom.*

"Killing Time With Unlimited Power"

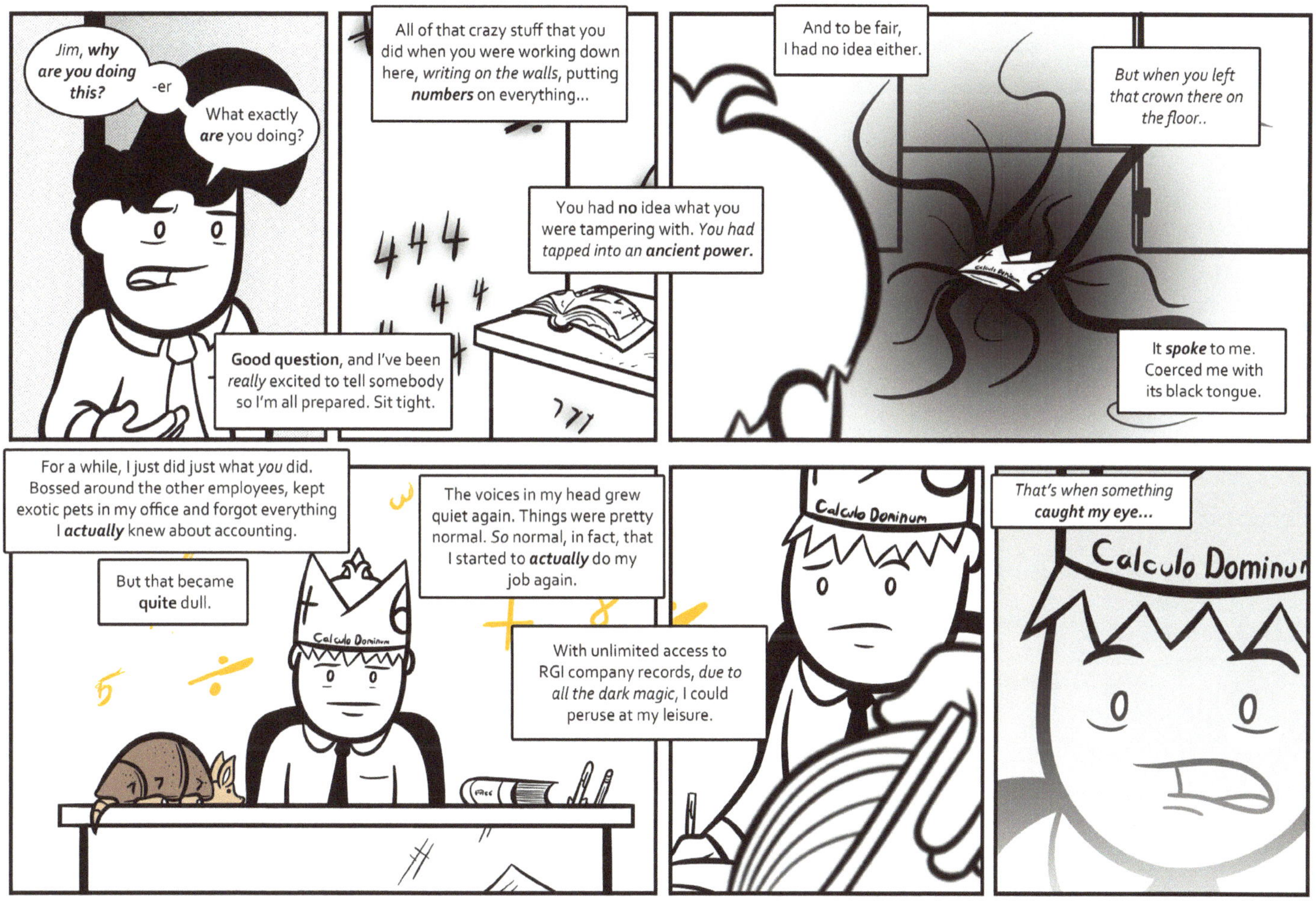

Jim, why are you doing this?
-er
What exactly are you doing?
Good question, and I've been really excited to tell somebody so I'm all prepared. Sit tight.
All of that crazy stuff that you did when you were working down here, writing on the walls, putting numbers on everything...
You had no idea what you were tampering with. You had tapped into an ancient power.
And to be fair, I had no idea either.
But when you left that crown there on the floor..
It spoke to me. Coerced me with its black tongue.
For a while, I just did just what you did. Bossed around the other employees, kept exotic pets in my office and forgot everything I actually knew about accounting.
But that became quite dull.
Calculo Dominum
The voices in my head grew quiet again. Things were pretty normal. So normal, in fact, that I started to actually do my job again.
With unlimited access to RGI company records, due to all the dark magic, I could peruse at my leisure.
Calculo Dominum
That's when something caught my eye...
Calculo Dominu

"Math Is The Best Way To Kill And Enslave People Just Trust Me"

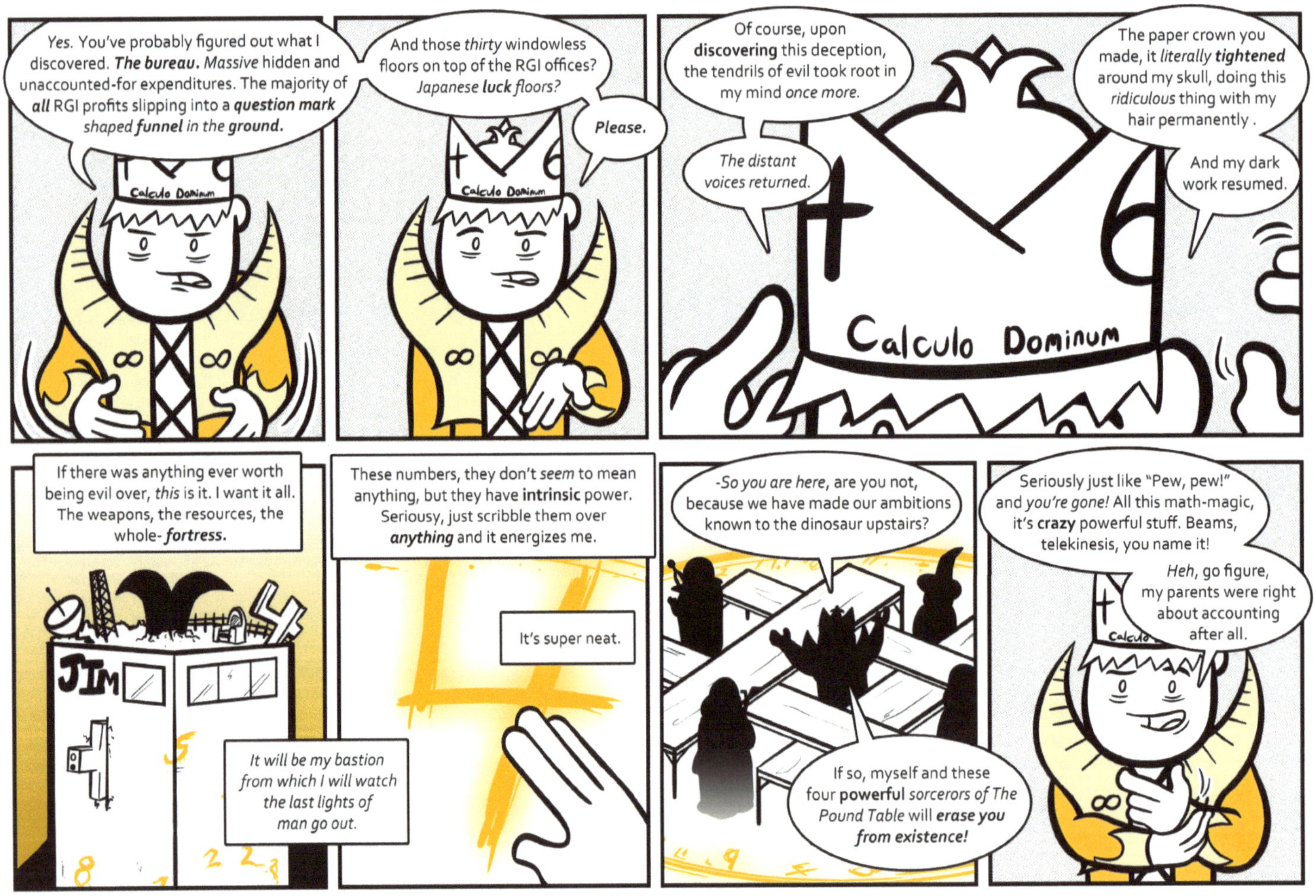
Yes. You've probably figured out what I discovered. The bureau. Massive hidden and unaccounted-for expenditures. The majority of all RGI profits slipping into a question mark shaped funnel in the ground.
Calculo Dominum
And those thirty windowless floors on top of the RGI offices? Japanese luck floors?
Please.
Calculo Dominum
Of course, upon discovering this deception, the tendrils of evil took root in my mind once more.
The distant voices returned.
The paper crown you made, it literally tightened around my skull, doing this ridiculous thing with my hair permanently .
And my dark work resumed.
Calculo Dominum
If there was anything ever worth being evil over, this is it. I want it all. The weapons, the resources, the whole- fortress.
JIM
It will be my bastion from which I will watch the last lights of man go out.
These numbers, they don't seem to mean anything, but they have intrinsic power. Seriousy, just scribble them over anything and it energizes me.
It's super neat.
-So you are here, are you not, because we have made our ambitions known to the dinosaur upstairs?
If so, myself and these four powerful sorcerors of The Pound Table will erase you from existence!
Seriously just like "Pew, pew!" and you're gone! All this math-magic, it's crazy powerful stuff. Beams, telekinesis, you name it!
Heh, go figure, my parents were right about accounting after all.

"He Has To Take The Bus"

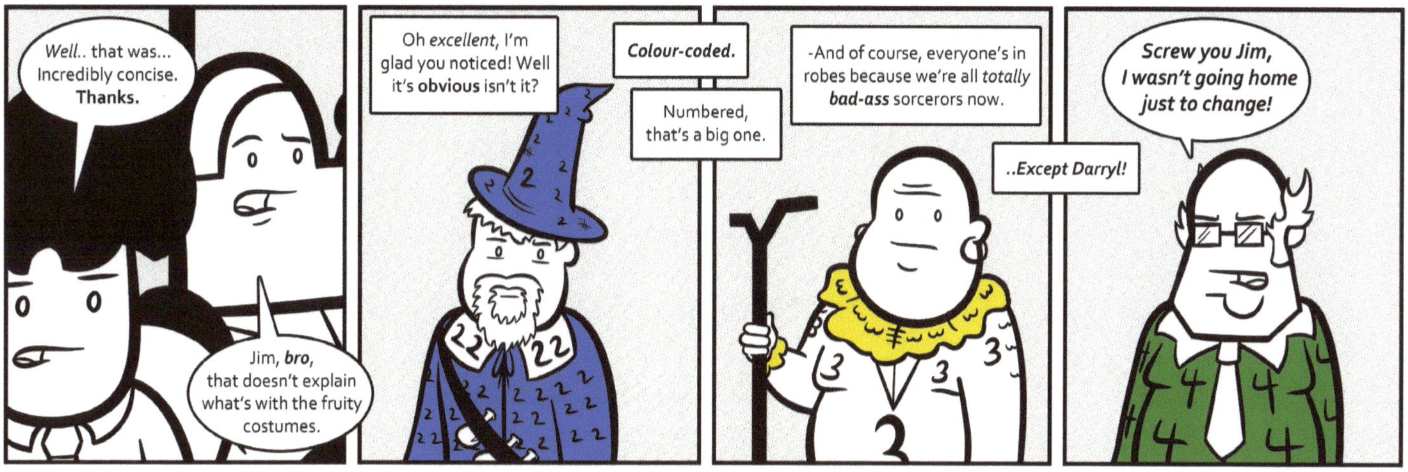

Well.. that was... Incredibly concise. **Thanks.**
Jim, ***bro***, that doesn't explain what's with the fruity costumes.
Oh *excellent*, I'm glad you noticed! Well it's **obvious** isn't it?
Colour-coded.
Numbered, that's a big one.
-And of course, everyone's in robes because we're all *totally* ***bad-ass*** sorcerors now.
..Except Darryl!
Screw you Jim, I wasn't going home just to change!

"You People Have No Respect For Theatrics"

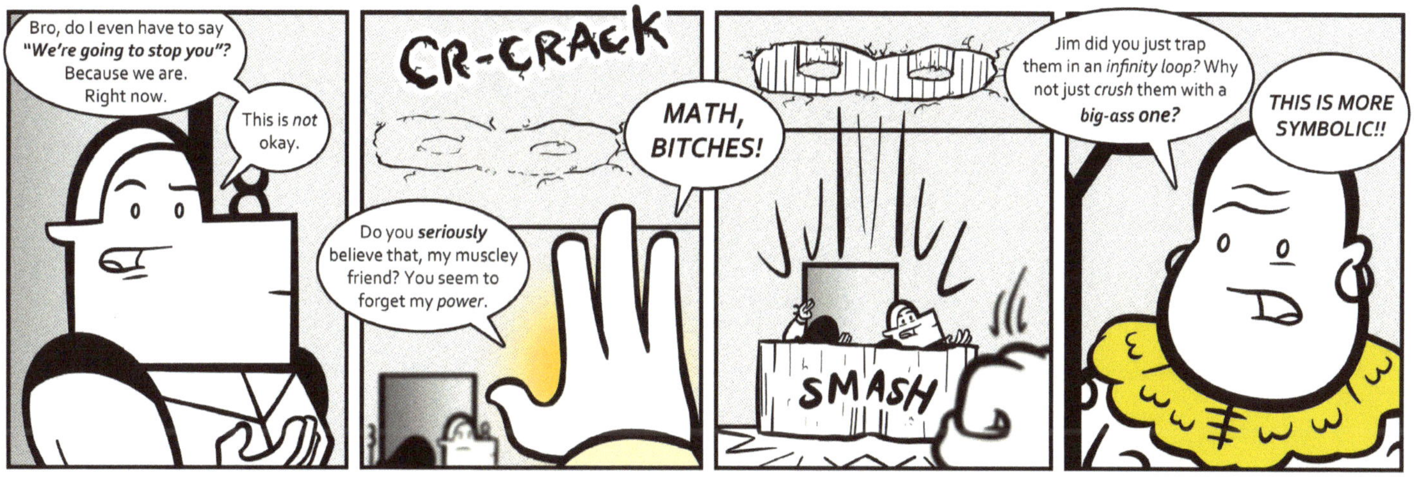

Bro, do I even have to say ***"We're going to stop you"?*** Because we are. Right now.
This is *not* okay.
CR-CRACK
Do you ***seriously*** believe that, my muscley friend? You seem to forget my *power*.
MATH, BITCHES!
SMASH
Jim did you just trap them in an *infinity loop?* Why not just *crush* them with a ***big-ass one?***
THIS IS MORE SYMBOLIC!!

"Sometimes You're In A Hurry"

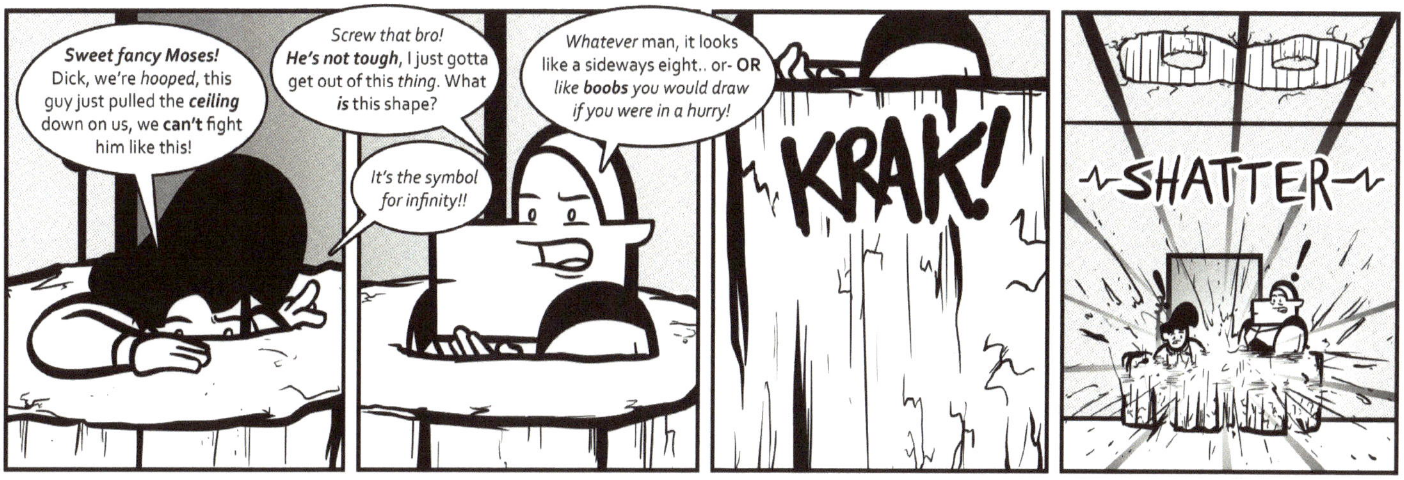

Sweet fancy Moses! Dick, we're *hooped*, this guy just pulled the ***ceiling*** down on us, we **can't** fight him like this!
Screw that bro! ***He's not tough***, I just gotta get out of this *thing*. What **is** this shape?
It's the symbol for infinity!!
Whatever man, it looks like a sideways eight.. or- **OR** *like* ***boobs*** *you would draw if you were in a hurry!*
KRAK!
SHATTER

"A Pattern Emerges"

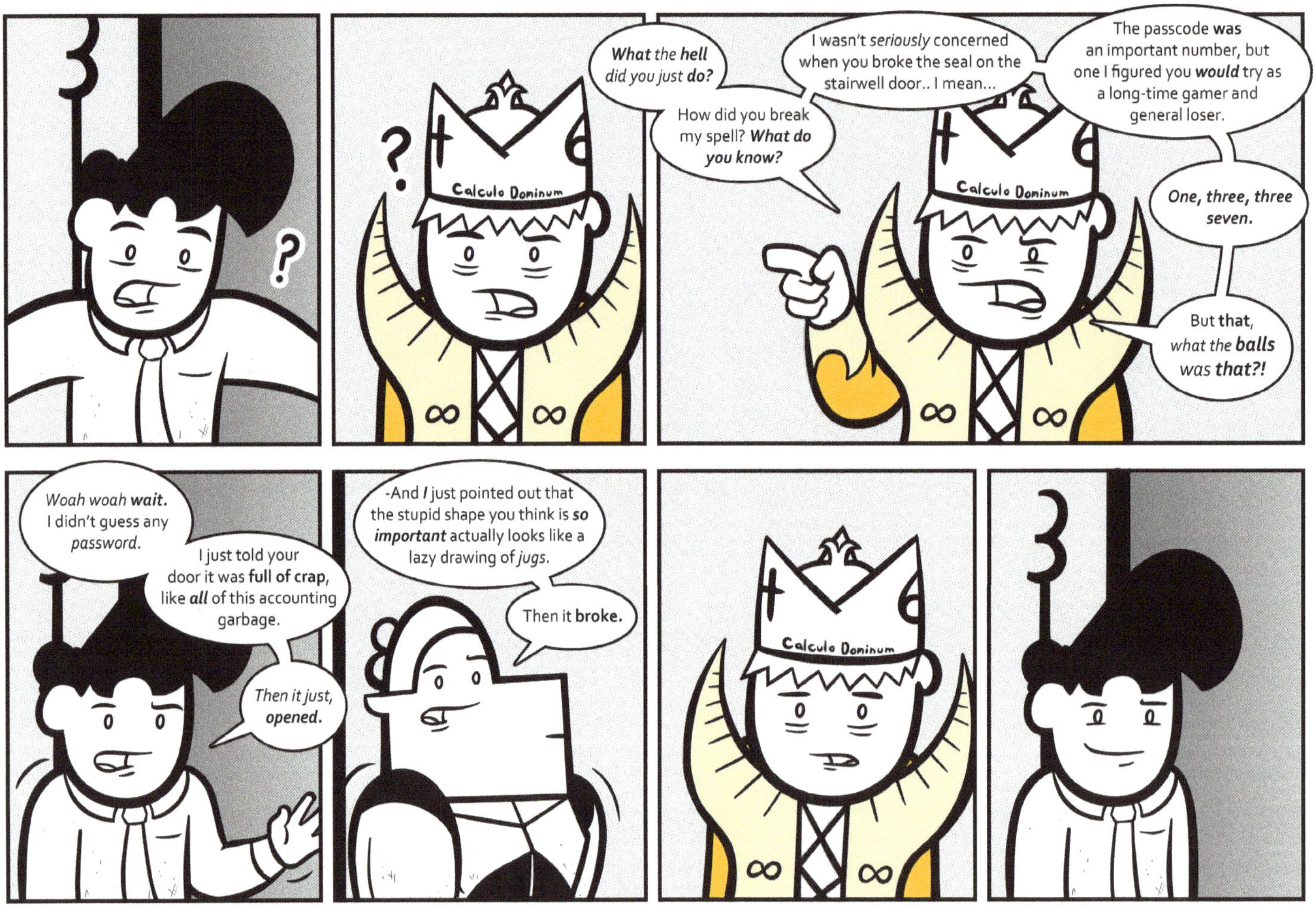
What the hell did you just do?
How did you break my spell? What do you know?
I wasn't seriously concerned when you broke the seal on the stairwell door.. I mean...
The passcode was an important number, but one I figured you would try as a long-time gamer and general loser.
One, three, three seven.
But that, what the balls was that?!
Woah woah wait. I didn't guess any password.
I just told your door it was full of crap, like all of this accounting garbage.
Then it just, opened.
-And I just pointed out that the stupid shape you think is so important actually looks like a lazy drawing of jugs.
Then it broke.
Calculo Dominum

"Rendered Seedless"

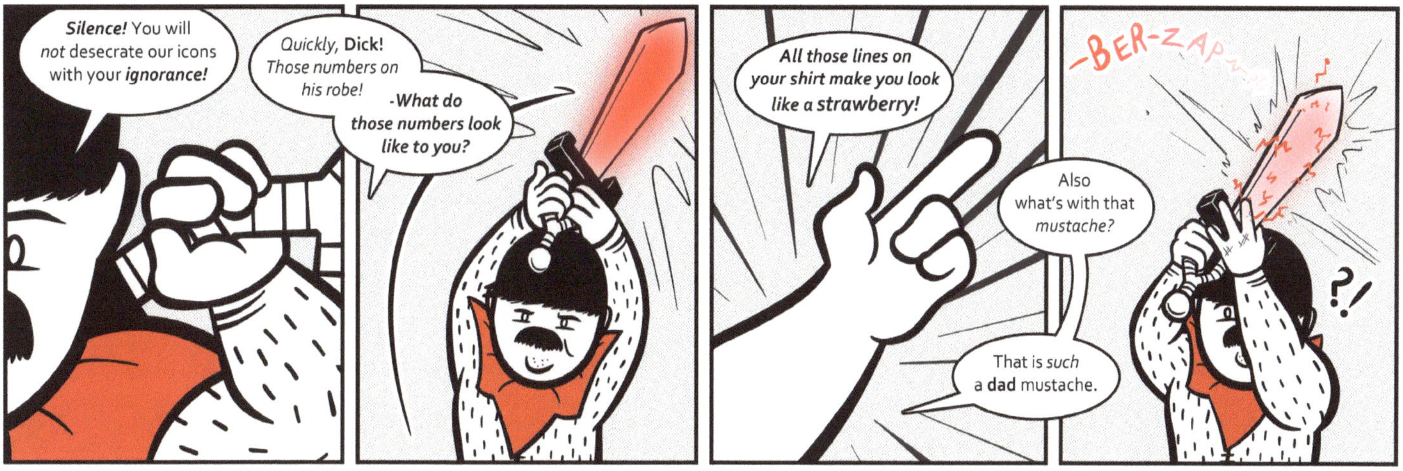

Silence! You will *not* desecrate our icons with your ***ignorance!***
Quickly, **Dick!** *Those numbers on his robe!*
-What do those numbers look like to you?
All those lines on your shirt make you look like a strawberry!
Also what's with that *mustache?*
That is *such* a **dad** mustache.
-BER-ZAP-
?!

"Hard Counter"

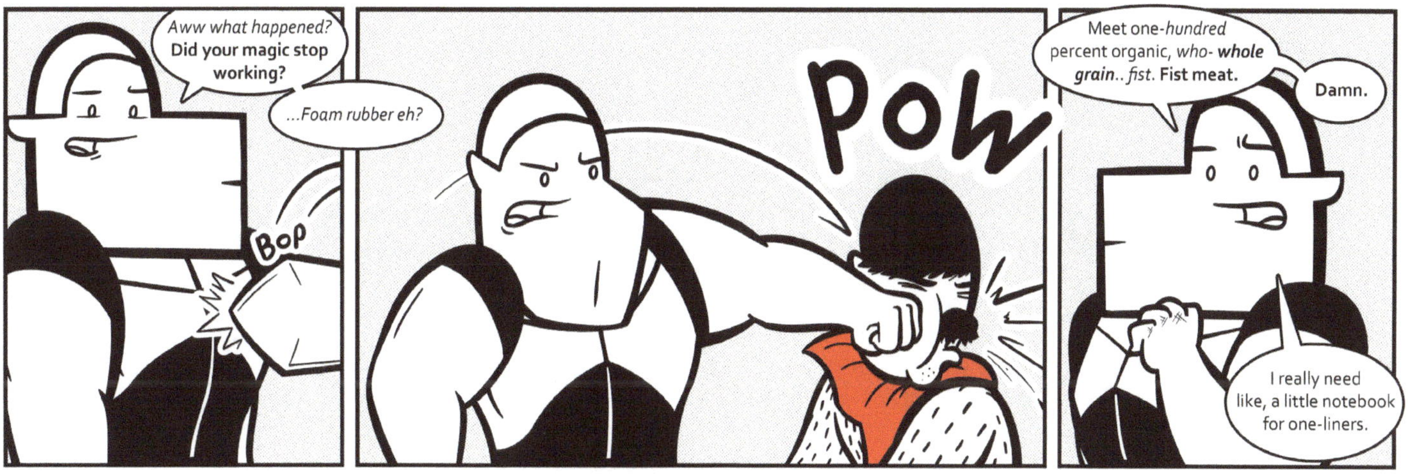

Aww what happened? **Did your magic stop working?**
...Foam rubber eh?
Bop
POW
Meet one-*hundred* percent organic, *who-* ***whole grain***.. *fist.* **Fist meat.**
Damn.
I really need like, a little notebook for one-liners.

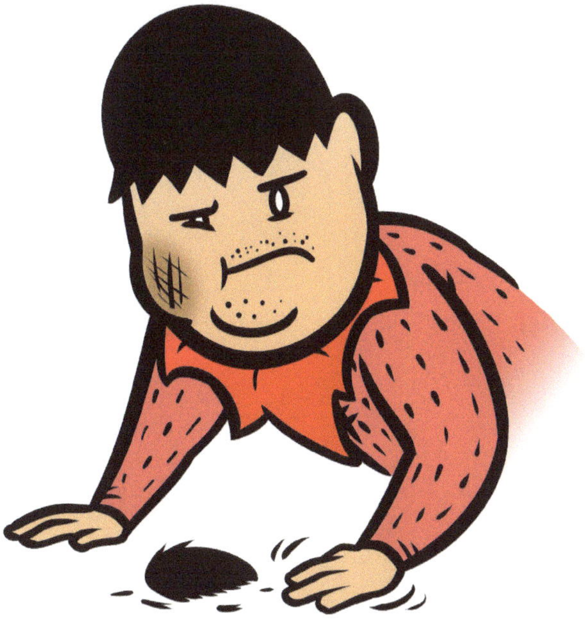

"Squishy Summoners"

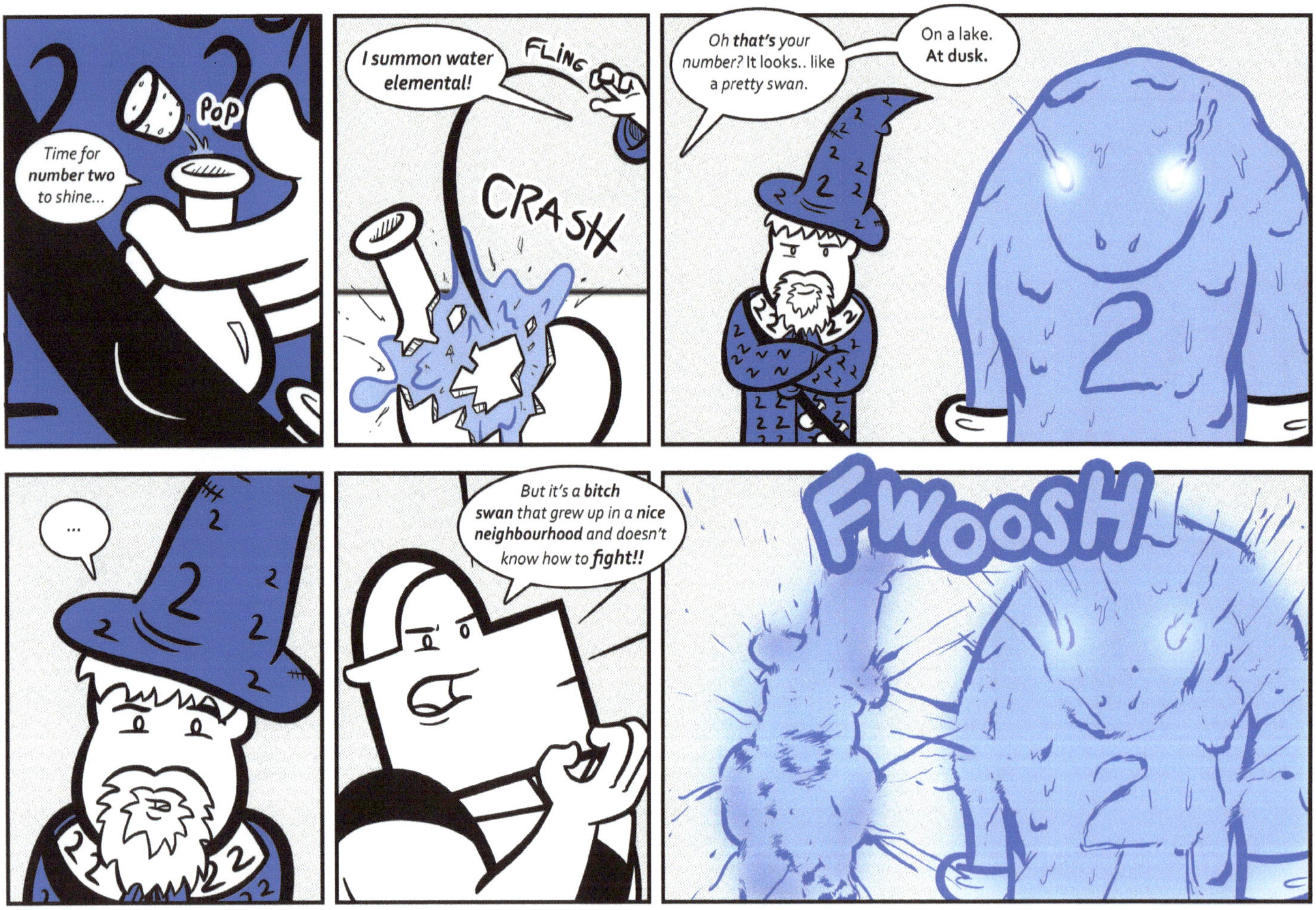
POP
Time for number two to shine...
I summon water elemental!
FLING
CRASH
Oh that's your number? It looks.. like a pretty swan.
On a lake. At dusk.
...
But it's a bitch swan that grew up in a nice neighbourhood and doesn't know how to fight!!
FWOOSH

"Don't Mix Lightning And Rods"

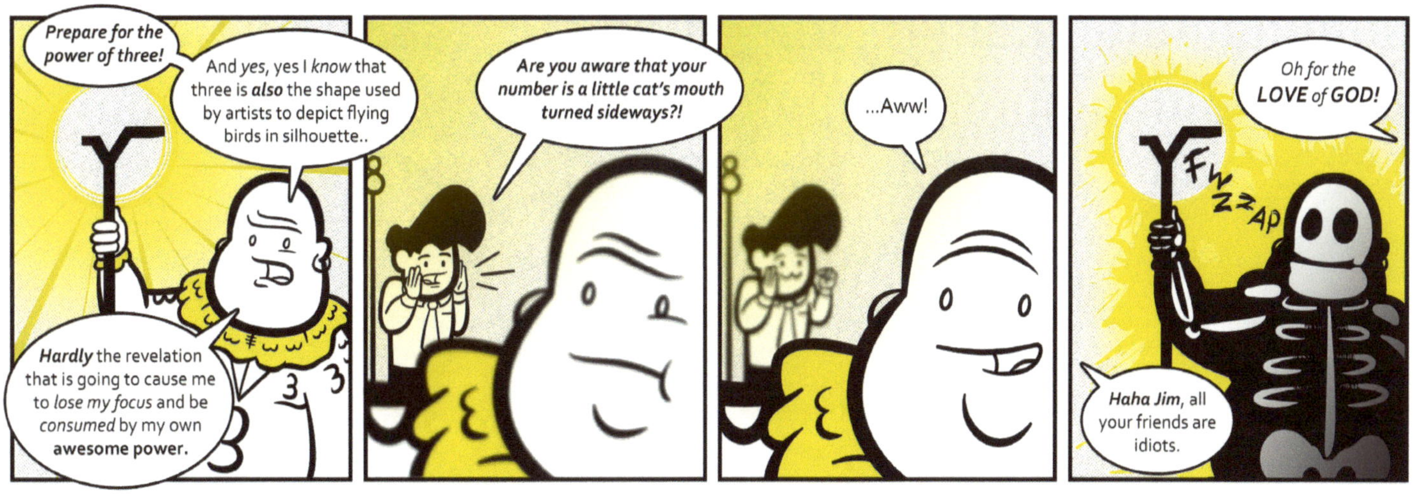
Prepare for the power of three!
And yes, yes I know that three is also the shape used by artists to depict flying birds in silhouette..
Hardly the revelation that is going to cause me to lose my focus and be consumed by my own awesome power.
Are you aware that your number is a little cat's mouth turned sideways?!
...Aww!
Oh for the LOVE of GOD!
FWZZZAP
Haha Jim, all your friends are idiots.

"One For Four"

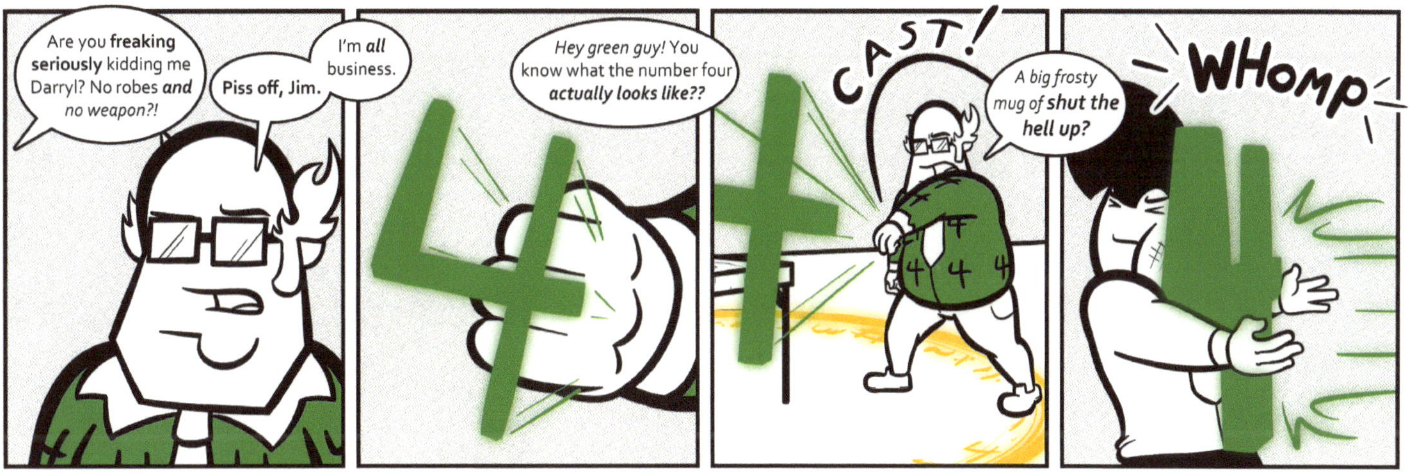
Are you freaking seriously kidding me Darryl? No robes and no weapon?!
Piss off, Jim.
I'm all business.
Hey green guy! You know what the number four actually looks like??
CAST!
A big frosty mug of shut the hell up?
WHOMP

"There Is Always Another Way"

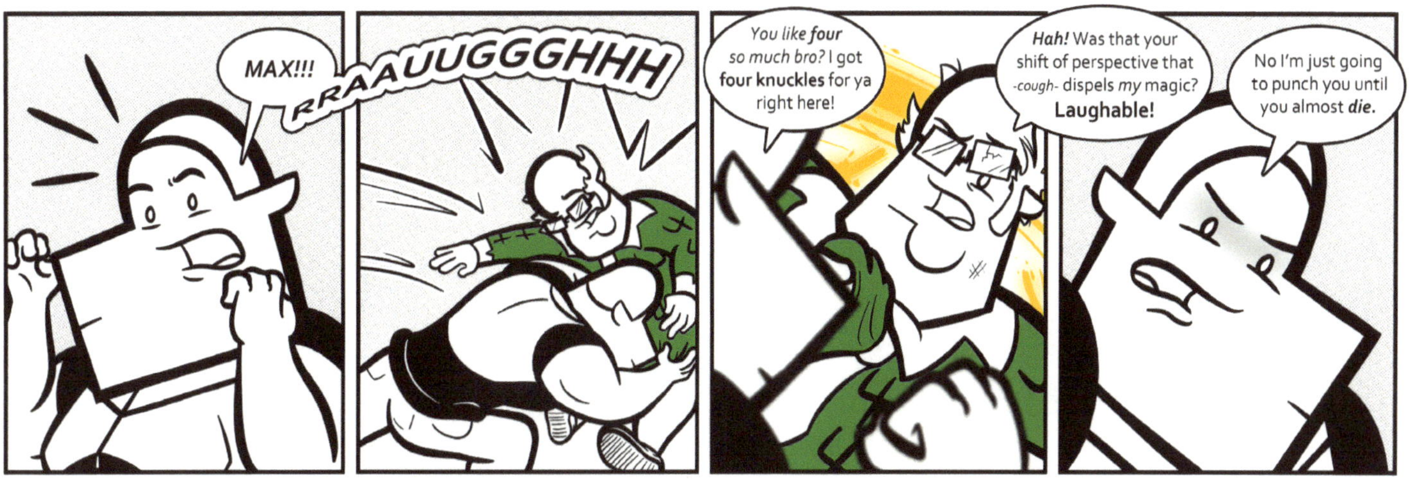
MAX!!!
RRAAUUGGGHHH
You like four so much bro? I got four knuckles for ya right here!
Hah! Was that your shift of perspective that -cough- dispels my magic? Laughable!
No I'm just going to punch you until you almost die.

"The Door That Was Always There"

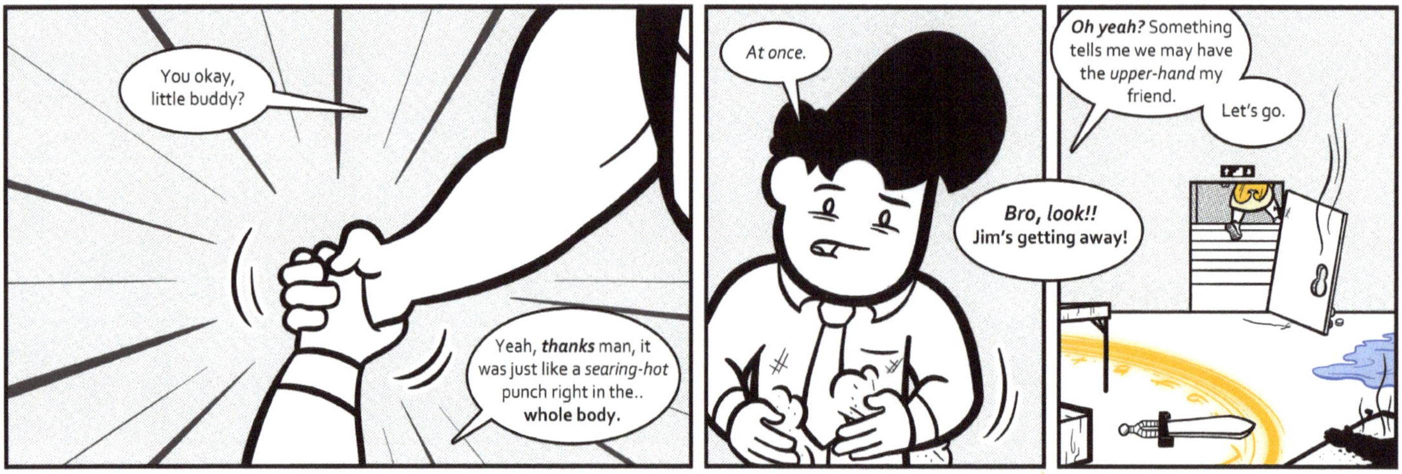

You okay, little buddy?
Yeah, *thanks* man, it was just like a *searing-hot* punch right in the.. **whole body.**
At once.
Bro, look!!
Jim's getting away!
Oh yeah? Something tells me we may have the *upper-hand* my friend.
Let's go.

"This Builiding Has So Many Hallways It's Ridiculous"

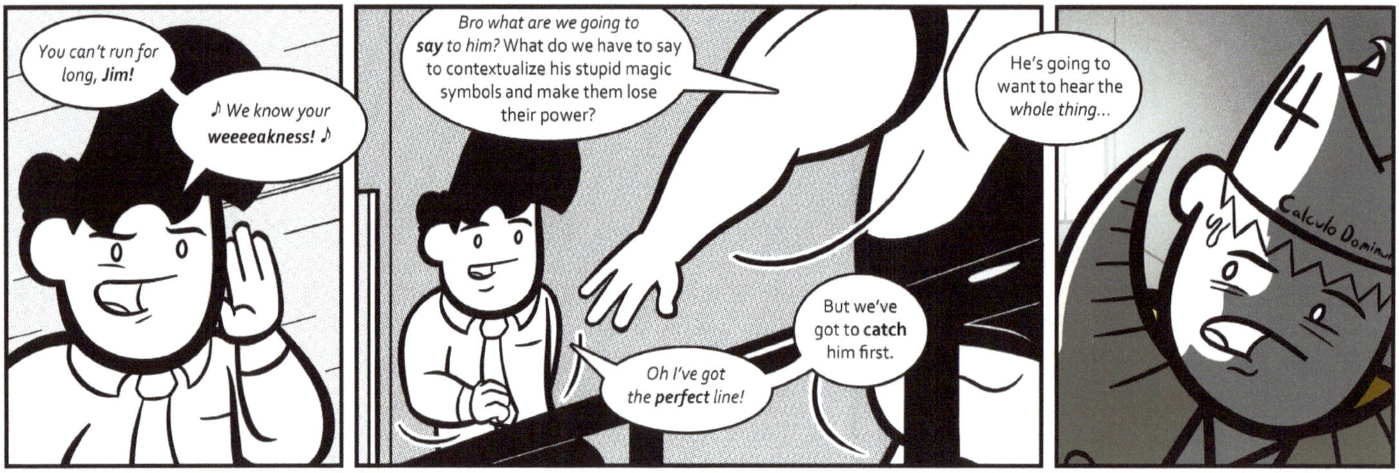

You can't run for long, ***Jim!***
♪ We know your ***weeeeakness!*** *♪*
Bro what are we going to ***say*** *to him?* What do we have to say to contextualize his stupid magic symbols and make them lose their power?
Oh I've got the ***perfect*** *line!*
But we've got to **catch** him first.
He's going to want to hear the *whole thing...*

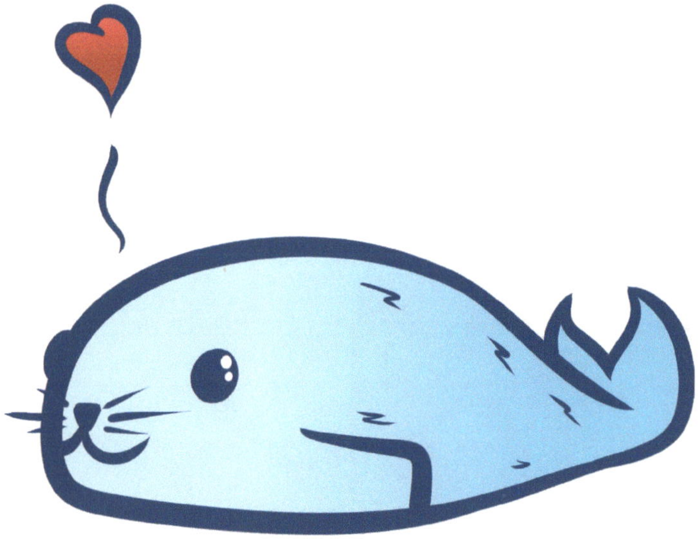

"Cut My Life Into Pieces"

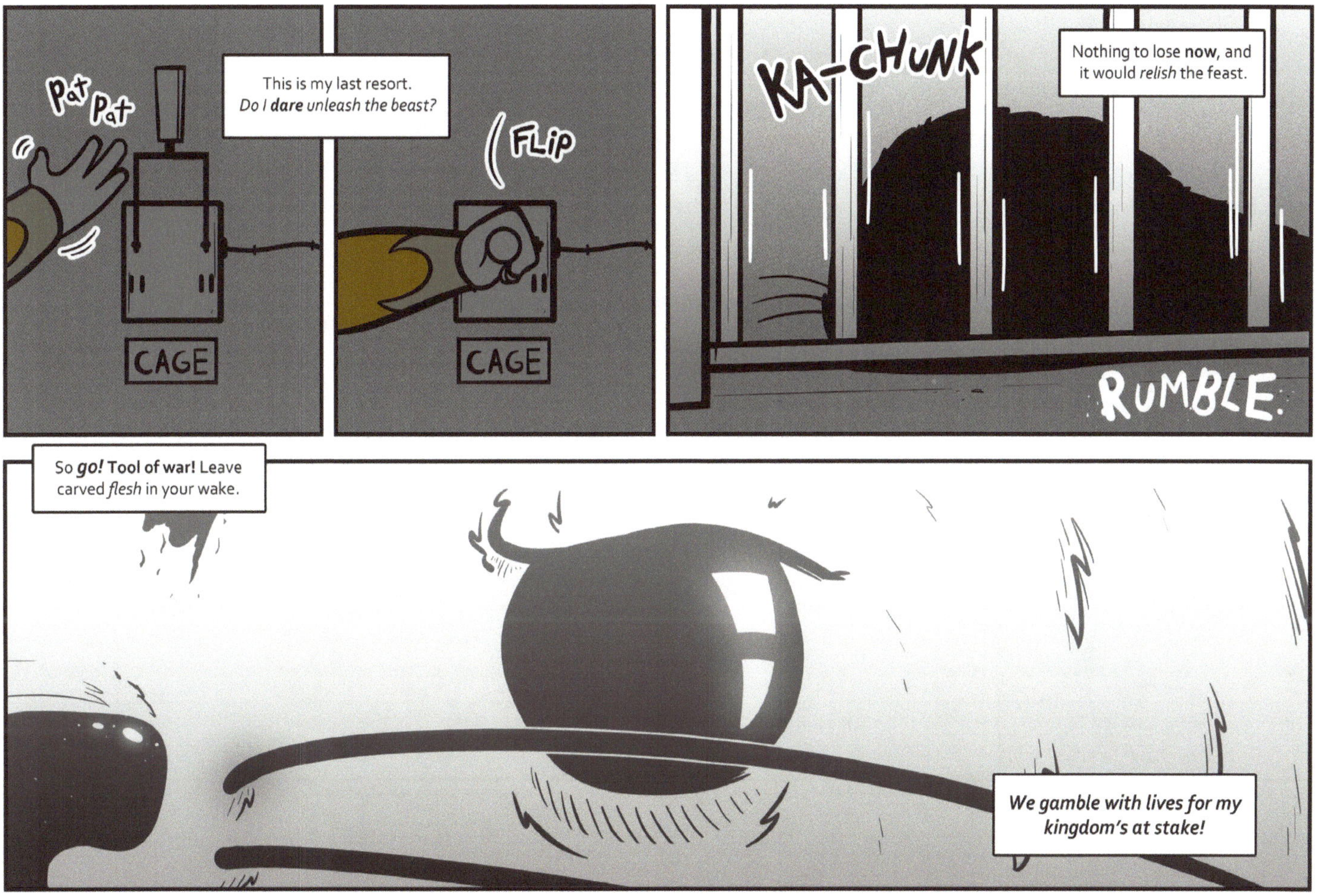
Pat Pat
This is my last resort. *Do I **dare** unleash the beast?*
FLIP
CAGE
CAGE
KA-CHUNK
Nothing to lose **now**, and it would *relish* the feast.
RUMBLE
So ***go!*** **Tool of war!** Leave carved *flesh* in your wake.
We gamble with lives for my kingdom's at stake!

"Reunited At Last"

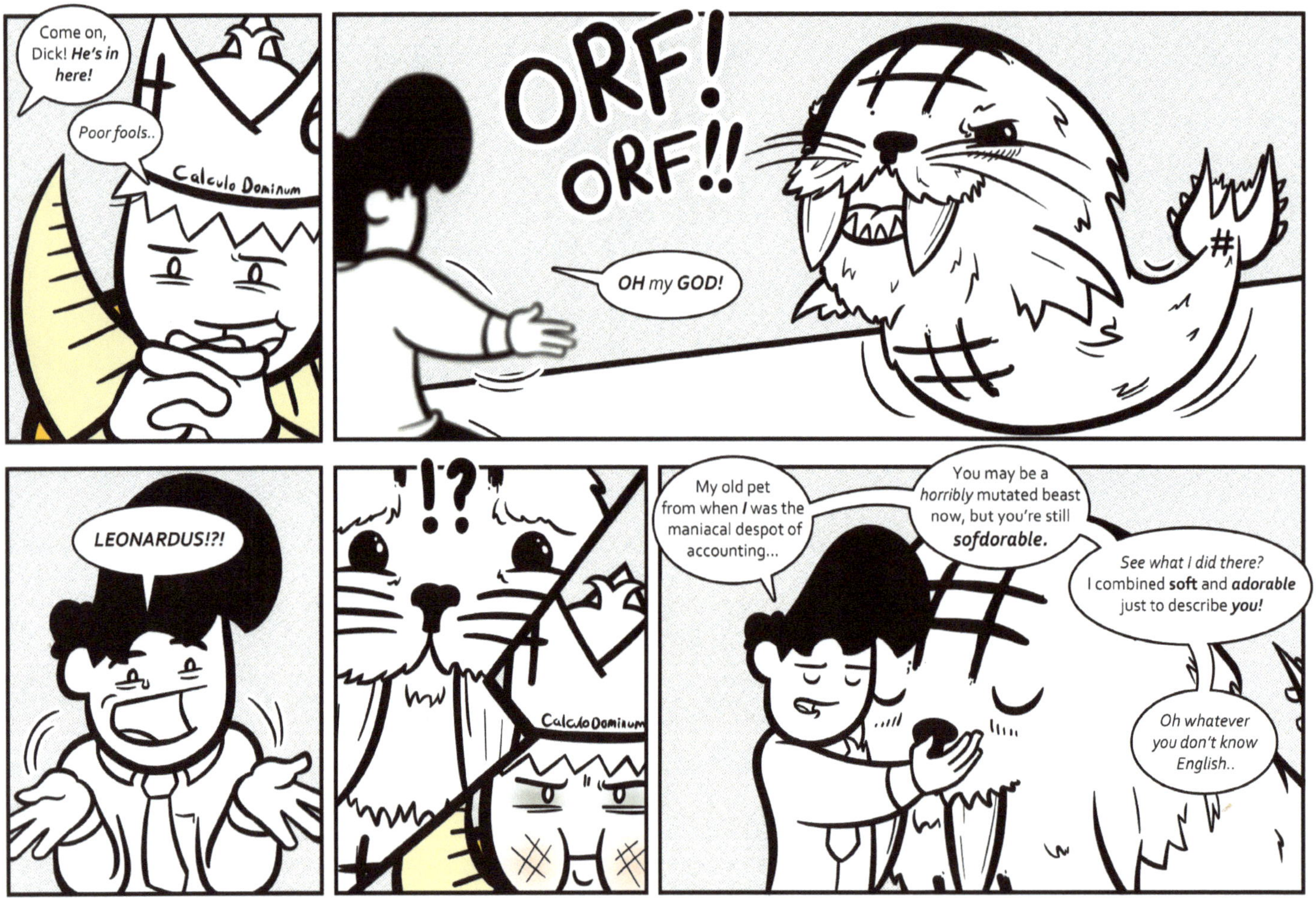

Come on, Dick! ***He's in here!***
Poor fools..
Calculo Dominum
ORF! ORF!!
OH** my **GOD!
LEONARDUS!?!
!?
Calculo Dominum
My old pet from when ***I*** was the maniacal despot of accounting...
You may be a *horribly* mutated beast now, but you're still ***sofdorable.***
See what I did there? I combined **soft** and ***adorable*** just to describe ***you!***
Oh whatever you don't know English..

"Over-Pronunciation"

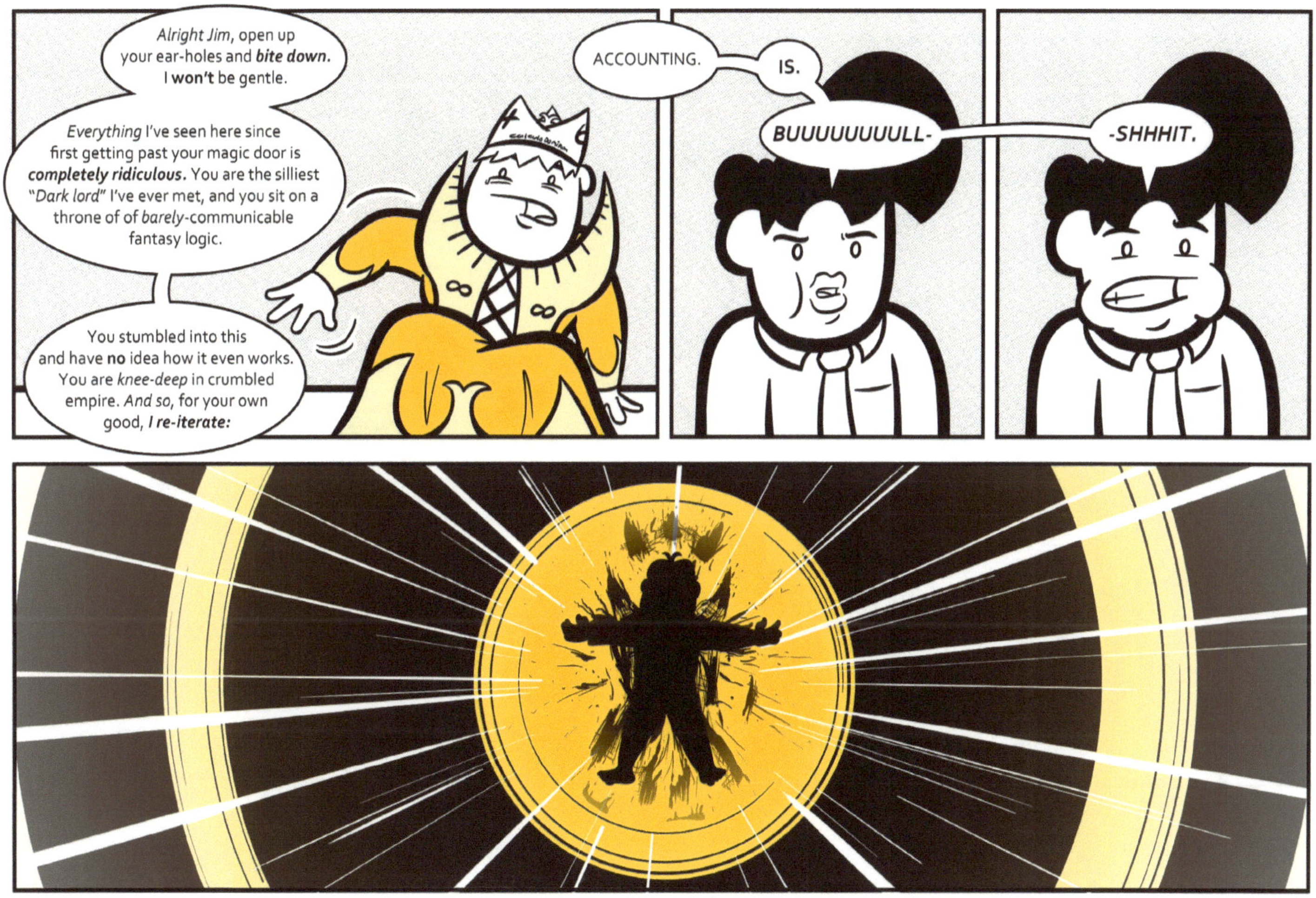
Alright Jim, open up your ear-holes and ***bite down.*** I **won't** be gentle.
Everything I've seen here since first getting past your magic door is ***completely ridiculous.*** You are the silliest "*Dark lord*" I've ever met, and you sit on a throne of of *barely*-communicable fantasy logic.
You stumbled into this and have **no** idea how it even works. You are *knee-deep* in crumbled empire. *And so*, for your own good, ***I re-iterate:***
ACCOUNTING.
IS.
BUUUUUUUULL-
-SHHHIT.

"An Immovable Friendship And A Brostoppable Force"

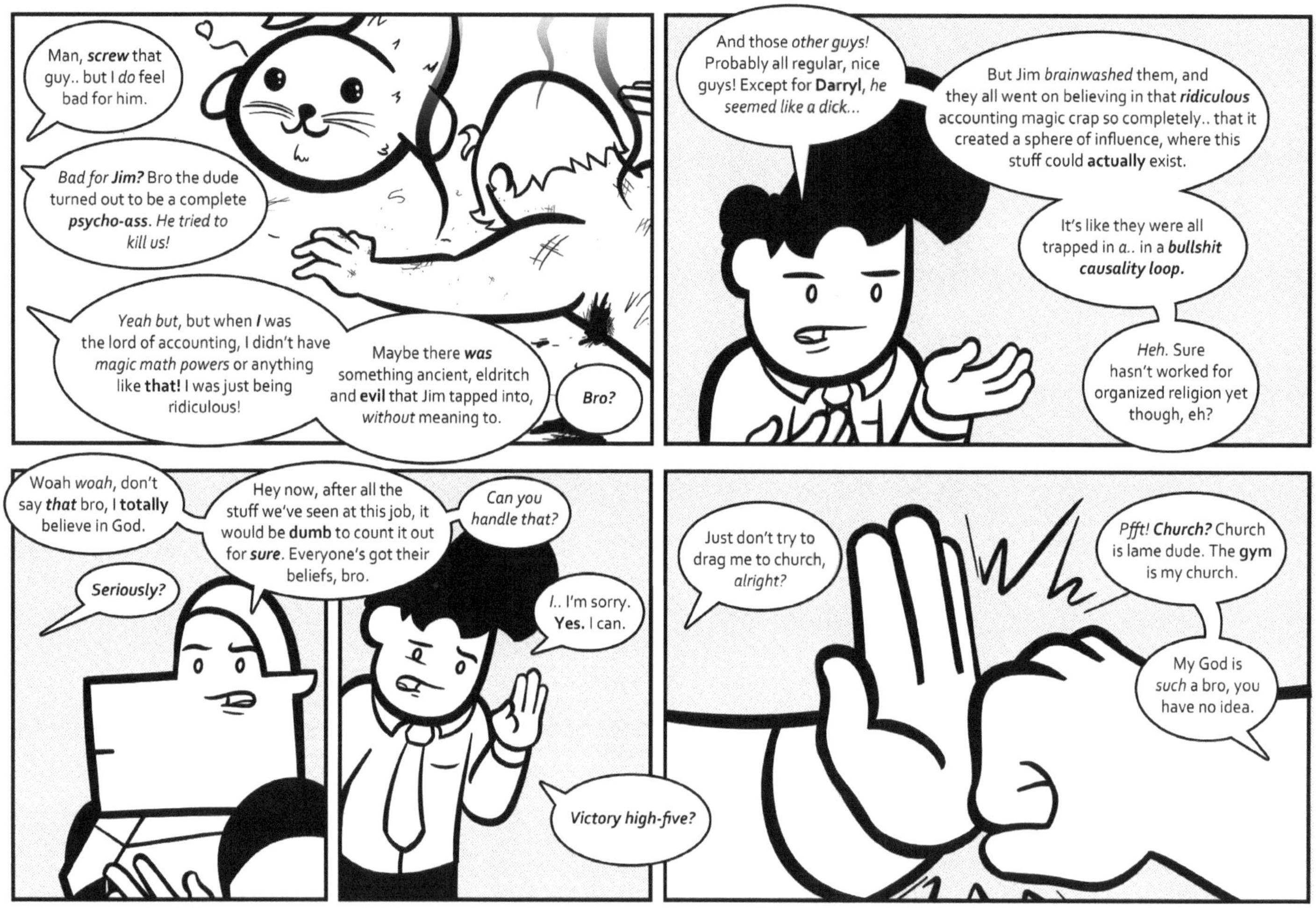

Man, *screw* that guy.. but I *do* feel bad for him.
*Bad for **Jim?*** Bro the dude turned out to be a complete ***psycho-ass**. He tried to kill us!*
Yeah but, but when ***I*** was the lord of accounting, I didn't have *magic math powers* or anything like **that!** I was just being ridiculous!
Maybe there ***was*** something ancient, eldritch and **evil** that Jim tapped into, *without* meaning to.
Bro?
And those *other guys!* Probably all regular, nice guys! Except for **Darryl**, *he seemed like a dick...*
But Jim *brainwashed* them, and they all went on believing in that ***ridiculous*** accounting magic crap so completely.. that it created a sphere of influence, where this stuff could **actually** exist.
It's like they were all trapped in *a*.. in a ***bullshit causality loop.***
Heh. Sure hasn't worked for organized religion yet though, eh?
Woah *woah*, don't say ***that*** bro, I **totally** believe in God.
Seriously?
Hey now, after all the stuff we've seen at this job, it would be **dumb** to count it out for ***sure***. Everyone's got their beliefs, bro.
Can you handle that?
I.. I'm sorry. **Yes.** I can.
Victory high-five?
Just don't try to drag me to church, *alright?*
*Pfft! **Church?*** Church is lame dude. The **gym** is my church.
My God is *such* a bro, you have no idea.

"Plot Relevant To Be Precise"

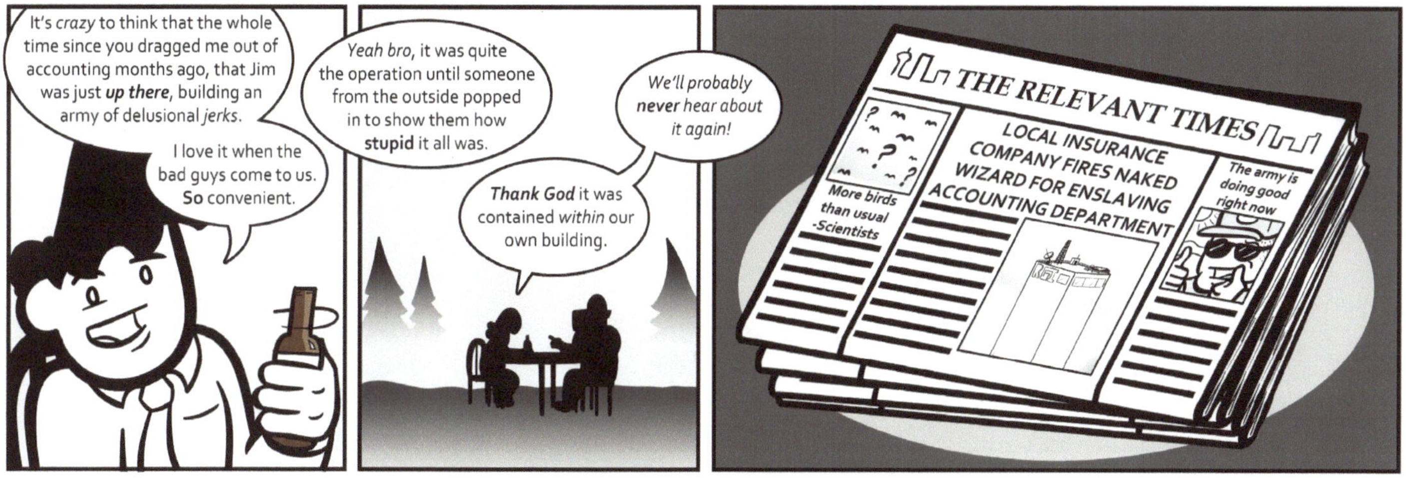
It's *crazy* to think that the whole time since you dragged me out of accounting months ago, that Jim was just ***up there***, building an army of delusional *jerks*.
I love it when the bad guys come to us. **So** convenient.
Yeah bro, it was quite the operation until someone from the outside popped in to show them how **stupid** it all was.
Thank God it was contained *within* our own building.
We'll probably ***never*** *hear about it again!*
THE RELEVANT TIMES
LOCAL INSURANCE COMPANY FIRES NAKED WIZARD FOR ENSLAVING ACCOUNTING DEPARTMENT
More birds than usual -Scientists
The army is doing good right now

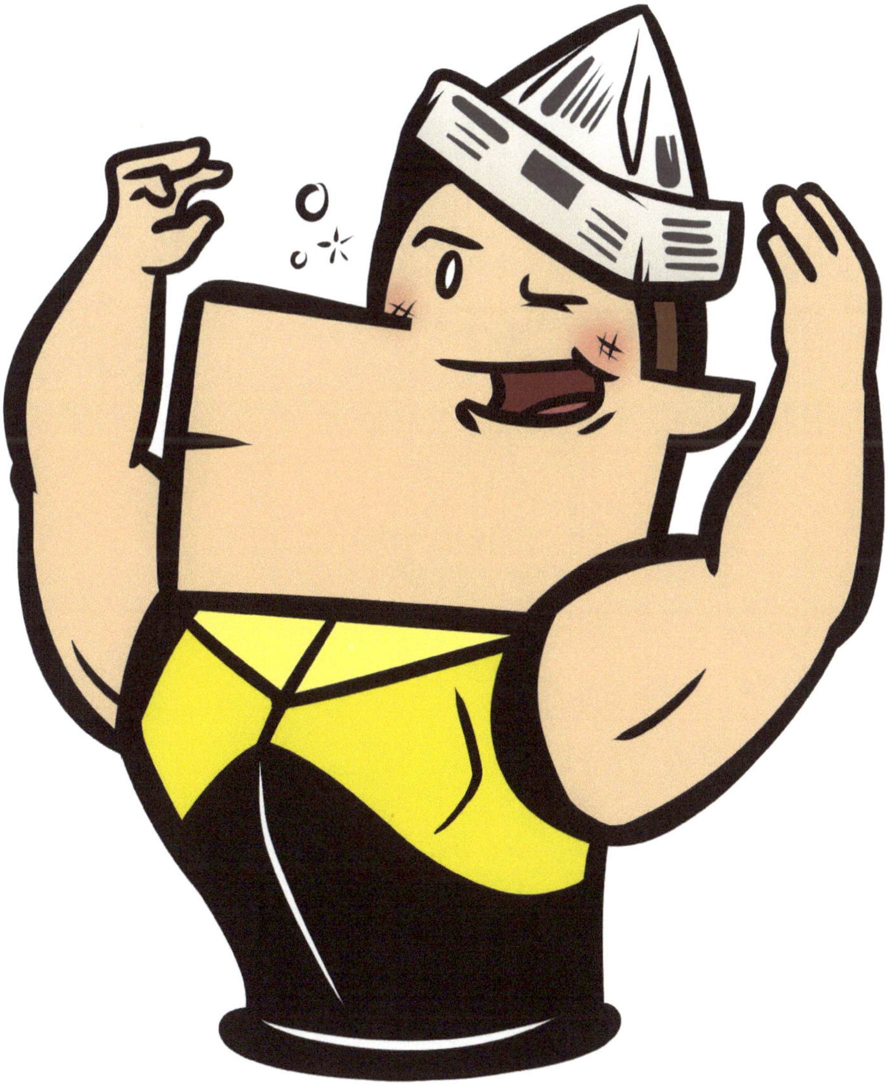

FORGET ME NOT

"The Sleepless Night"

"Whatcha Thinkin' About"

-Accept?-
INCOMING EMERGENCY MESSAGE
AGENT STONE
ABM - Agent N.Stone
Stone: Hey sent @ 9:01 pm
ABM - Agent N.Stone
Stone: Hey sent @ 9:01 pm
Stone: What's up? ;) sent @ 9:01 pm
ABM - Agent N.Stone
Stone: Hey sent @ 9:01 pm
Stone: What's up? sent @ 9:01 pm
Stone is typing a message...

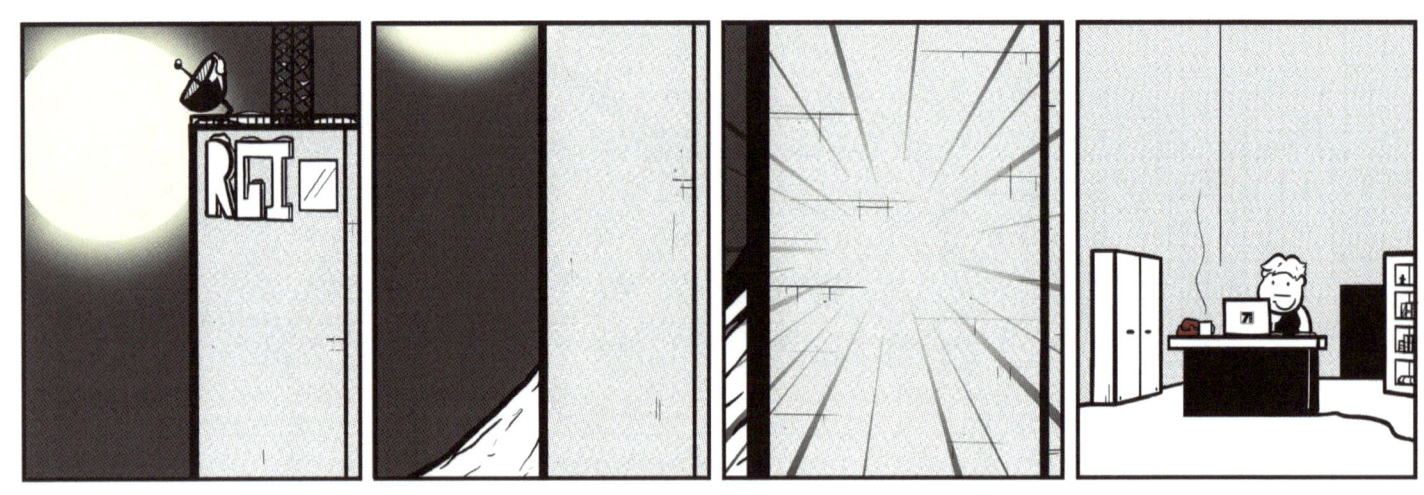

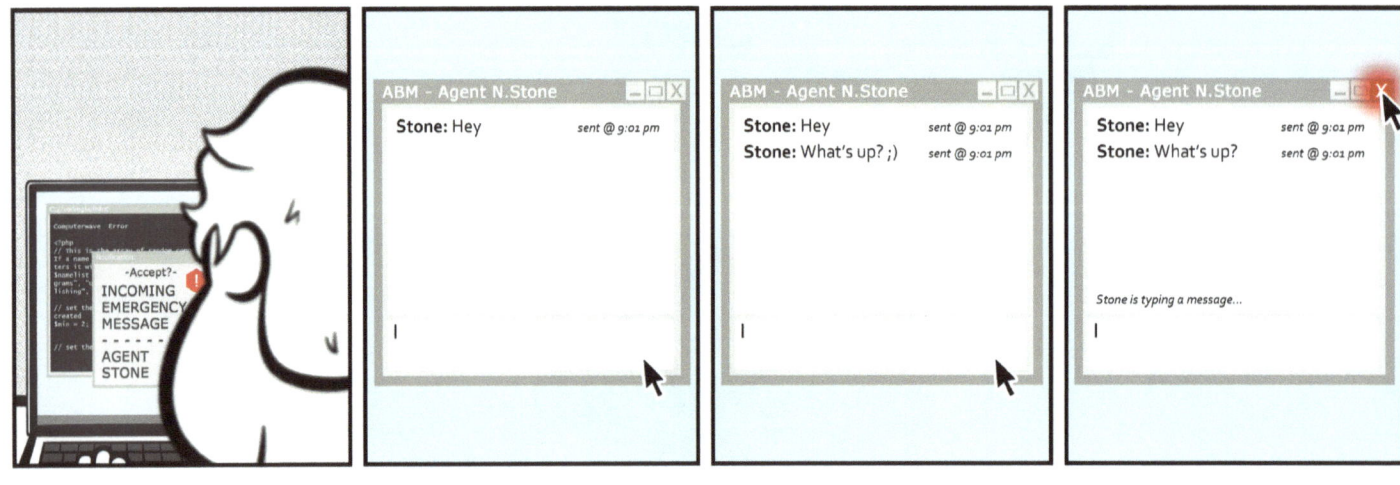

"Persistence"

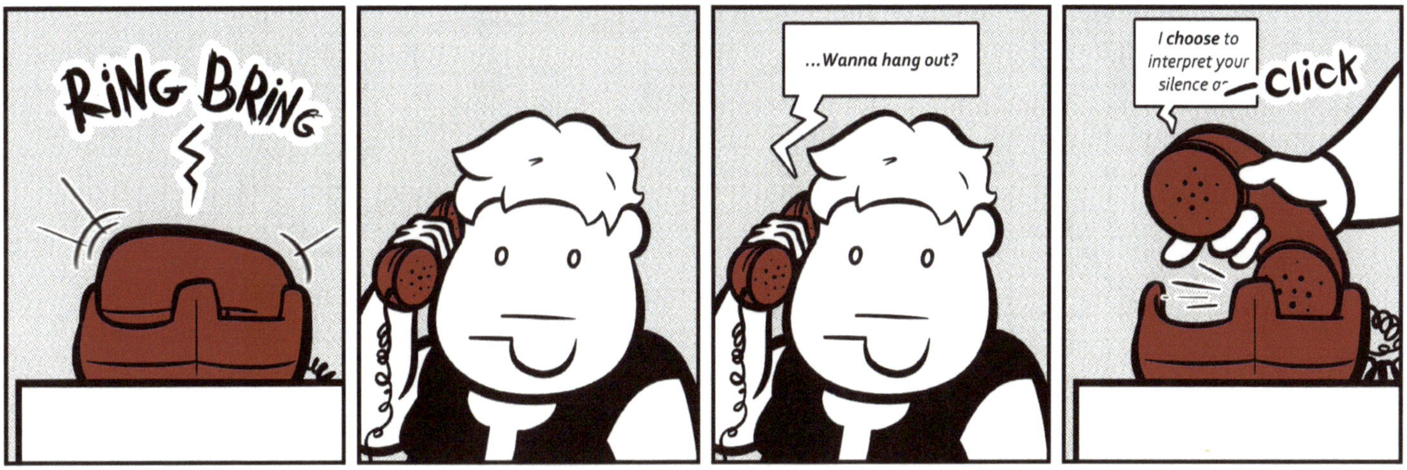
RiNG BRiNG
...Wanna hang out?
I choose to interpret your silence
Click

"Dialtone"

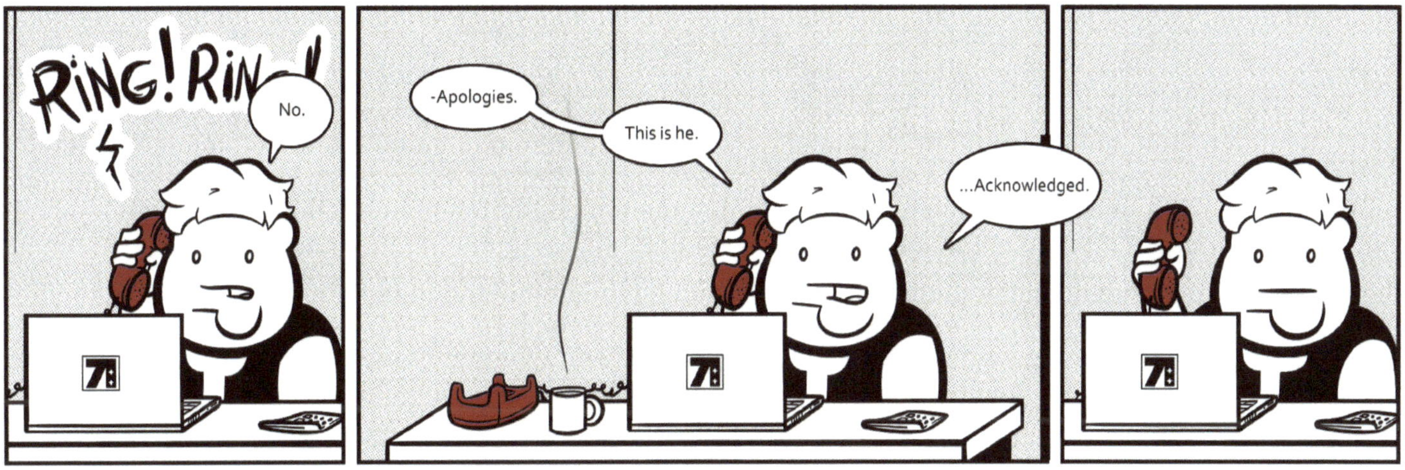
RiNG! RiN
No.
-Apologies.
This is he.
...Acknowledged.

"Boiling Point"

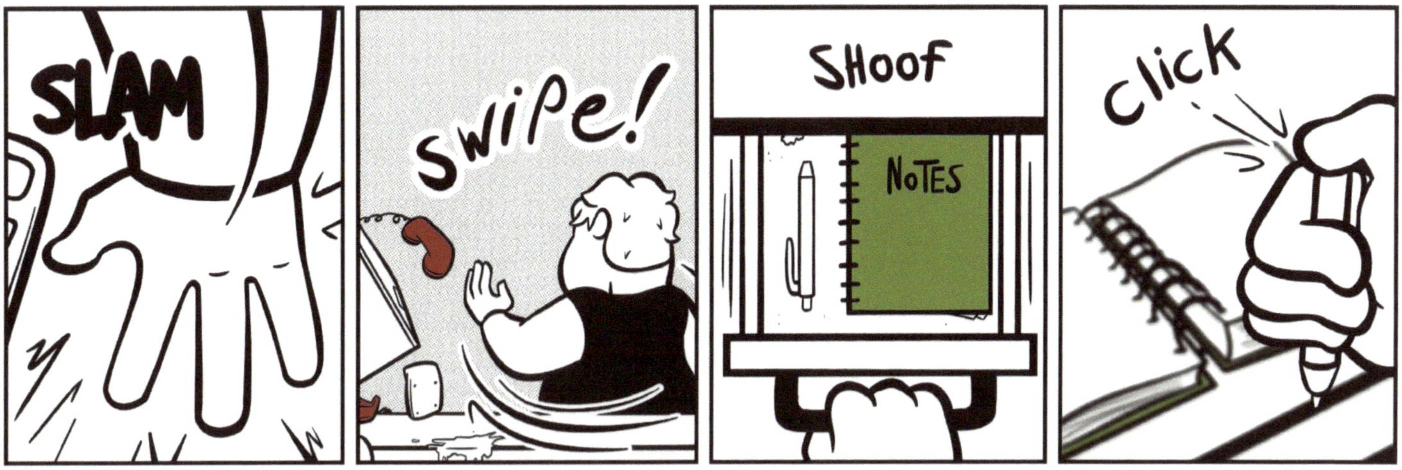
SLAM
swipe!
SHOOF
NOTES
click

"Bundle Up"

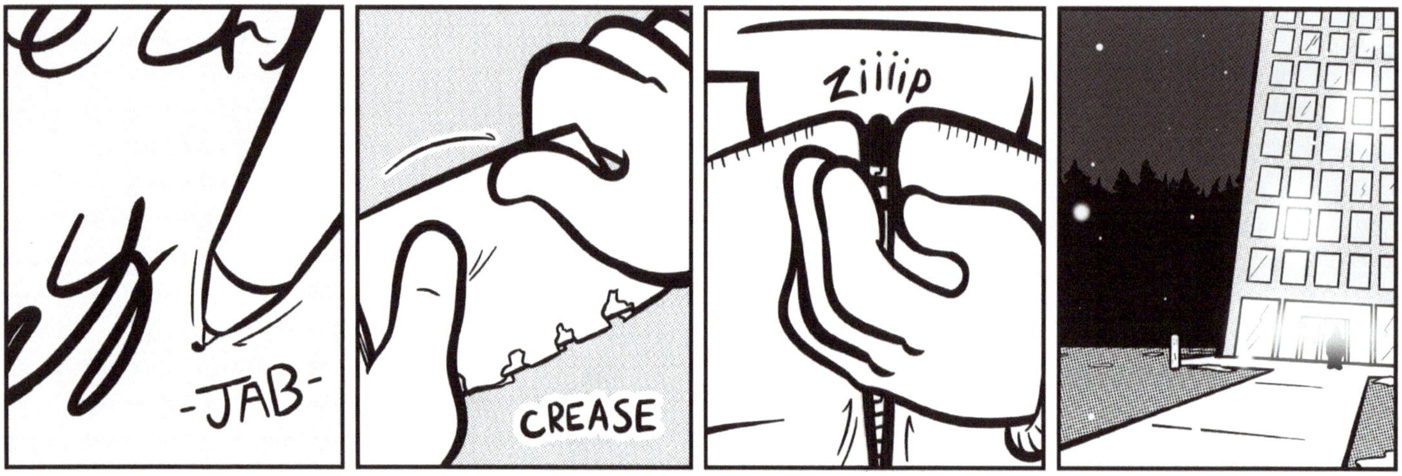
-JAB-
CREASE
ziiiip

"Just Put Your Name On The List"

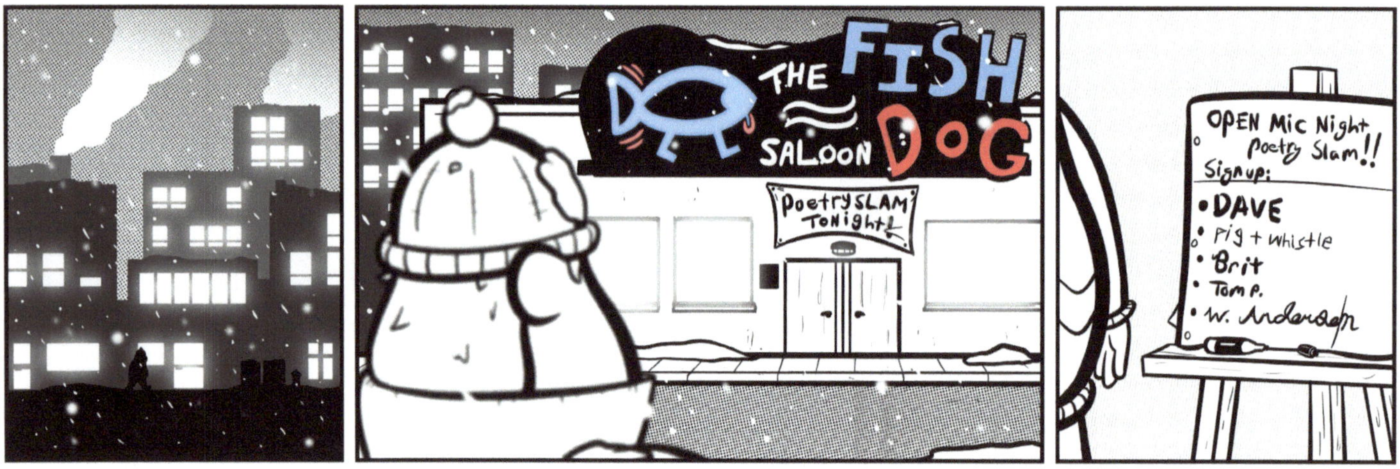
THE FISH DOG SALOON
PoetrySLAM TONight!
OPEN Mic Night Poetry Slam!!
Signup:
DAVE
Pig + whistle
Brit
Tom P.

"Do A Little Turn"

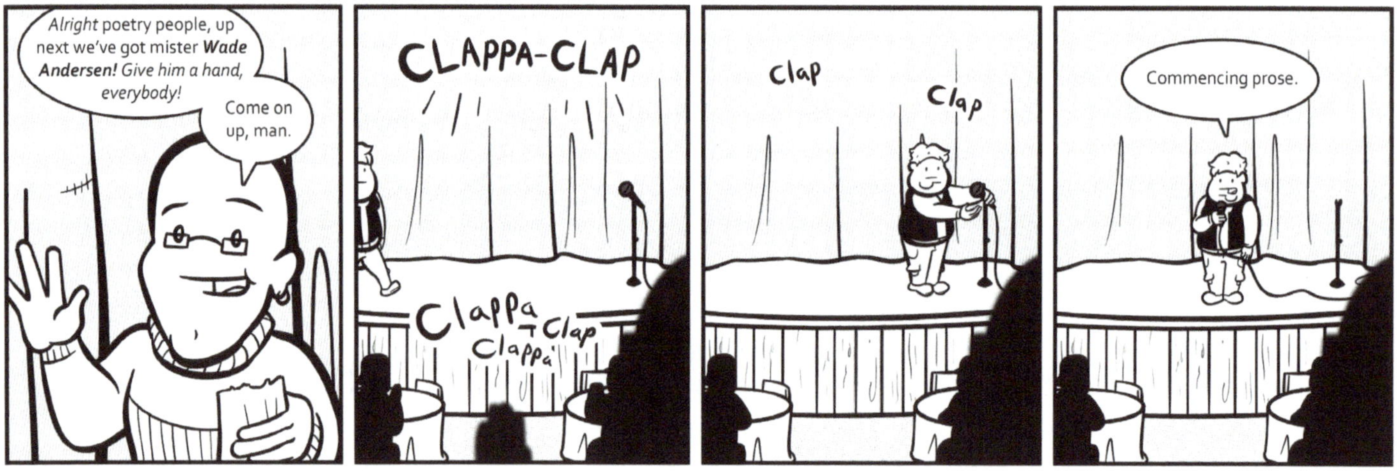
Alright poetry people, up next we've got mister ***Wade Andersen!*** *Give him a hand, everybody!*
Come on up, man.
CLAPPA-CLAP
Clappa Clap Clappa
Clap
Clap
Commencing prose.

"Prose"

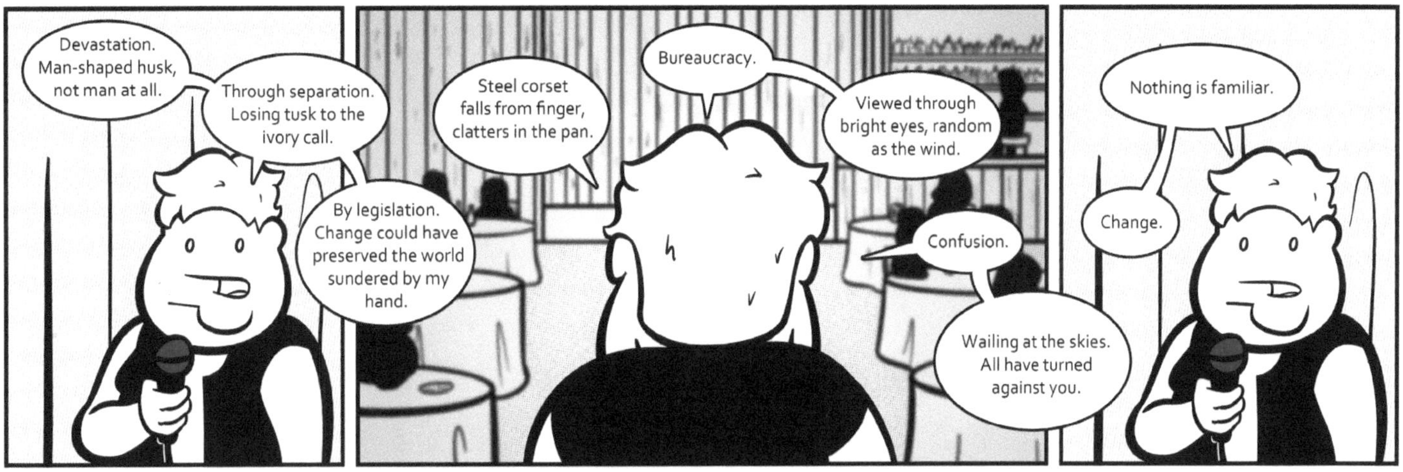

Devastation. Man-shaped husk, not man at all.
Through separation. Losing tusk to the ivory call.
By legislation. Change could have preserved the world sundered by my hand.
Steel corset falls from finger, clatters in the pan.
Bureaucracy.
Viewed through bright eyes, random as the wind.
Confusion.
Wailing at the skies. All have turned against you.
Nothing is familiar.
Change.

"Prose Addendum"

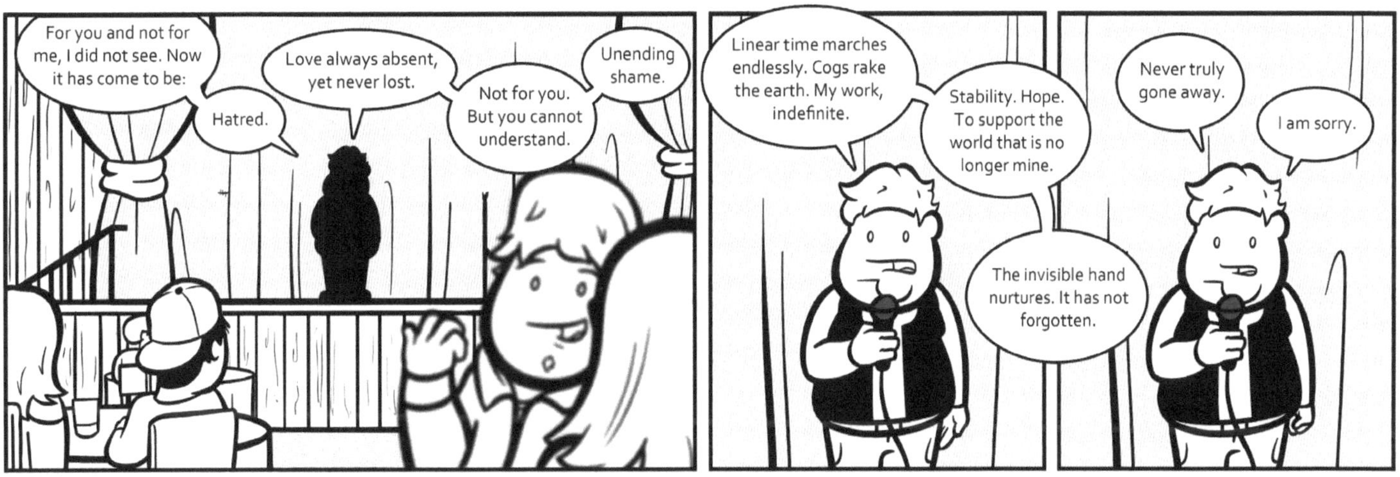

For you and not for me, I did not see. Now it has come to be:
Hatred.
Love always absent, yet never lost.
Not for you. But you cannot understand.
Unending shame.
Linear time marches endlessly. Cogs rake the earth. My work, indefinite.
Stability. Hope. To support the world that is no longer mine.
The invisible hand nurtures. It has not forgotten.
Never truly gone away.
I am sorry.

"Notwithstanding Validation"

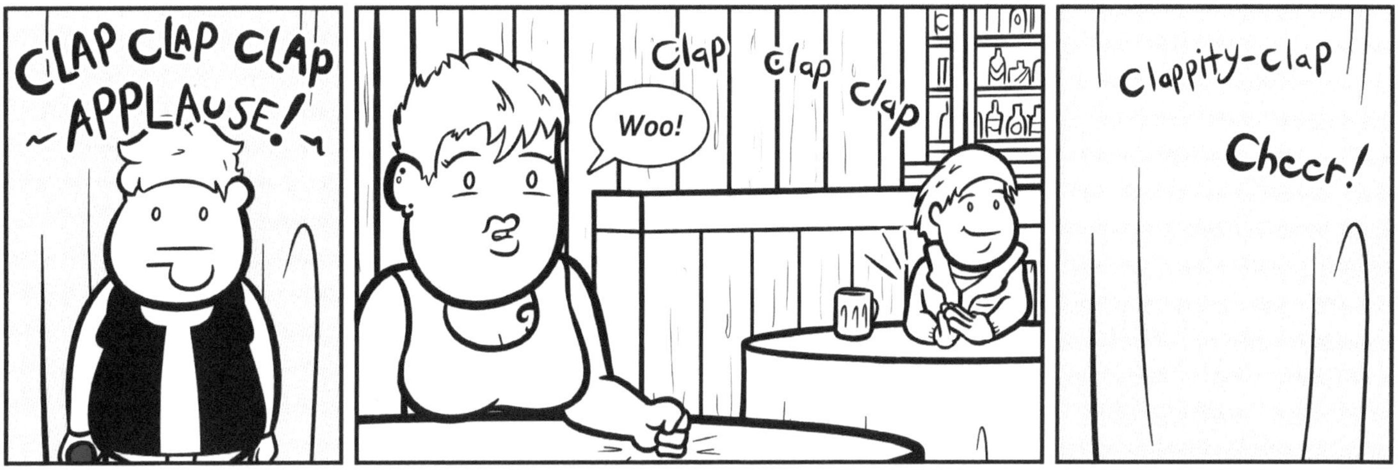

CLAP CLAP CLAP
~APPLAUSE!~
Clap clap clap
Woo!
Clappity-clap
Cheer!

"So Deep They In China By Now"

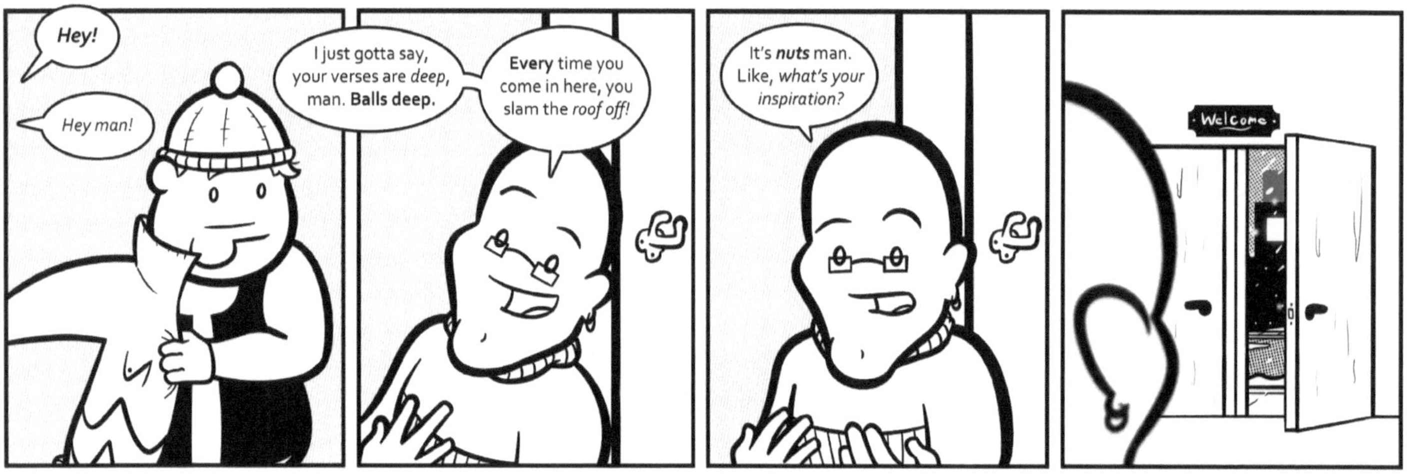
Hey!
Hey man!
I just gotta say, your verses are *deep*, man. **Balls deep.**
Every time you come in here, you slam the *roof off!*
It's ***nuts*** man. Like, *what's your inspiration?*
Welcome

"Rain Nor Sleet Nor Snow"

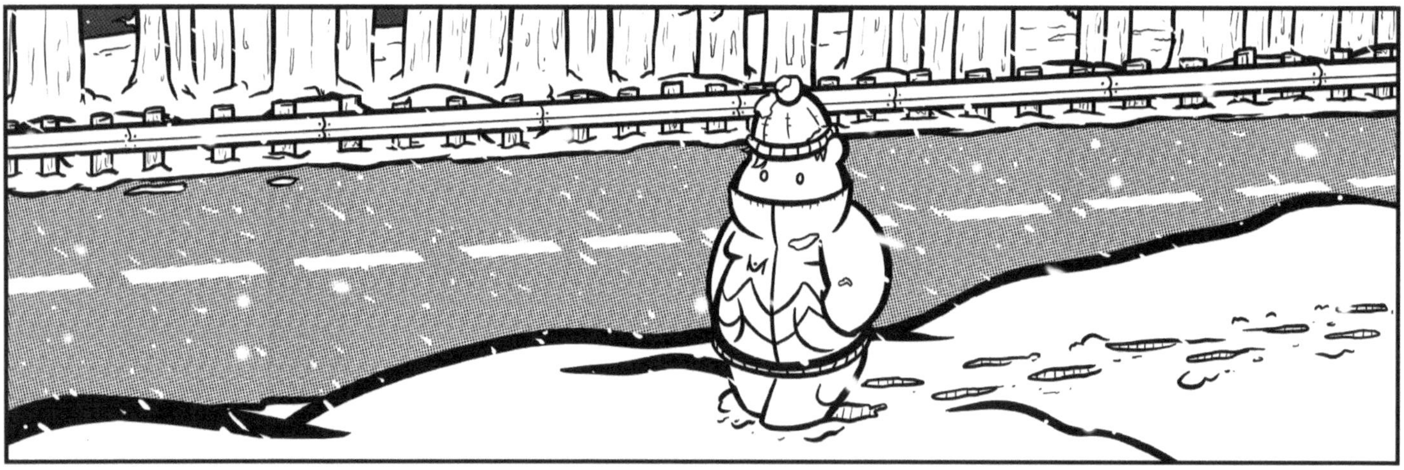

"Pensitivity"

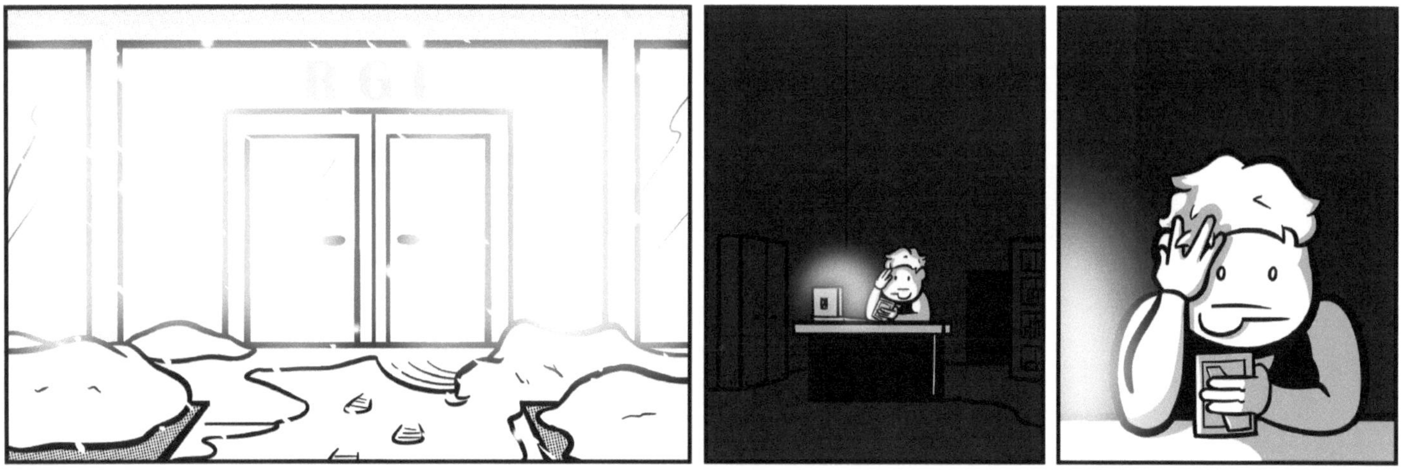

"Inspiration"

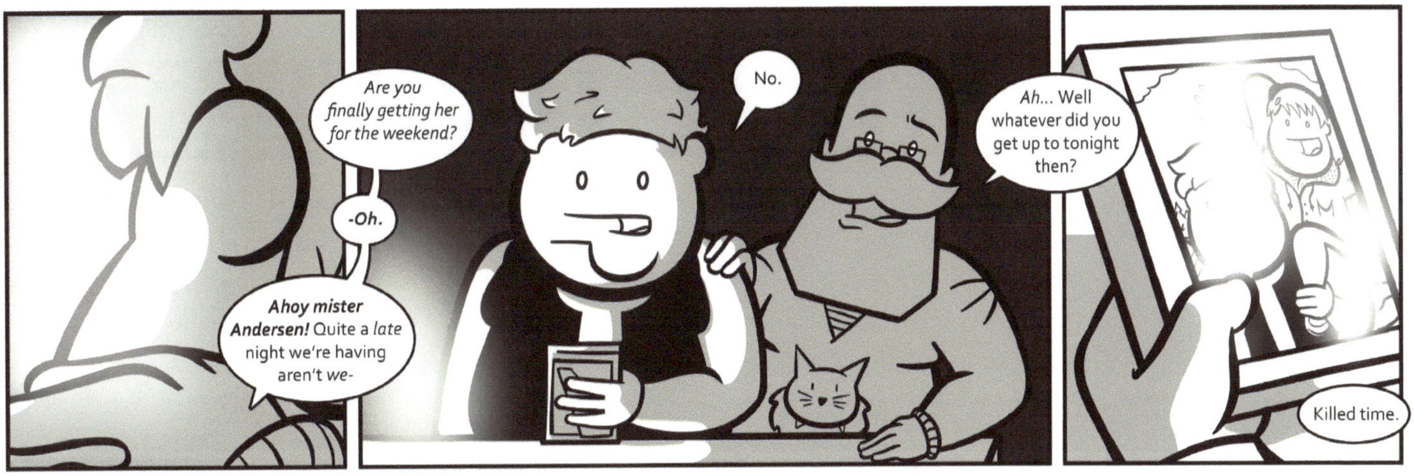
Ahoy mister Andersen! Quite a late night we're having aren't we-
-Oh.
Are you finally getting her for the weekend?
No.
Ah... Well whatever did you get up to tonight then?
Killed time.

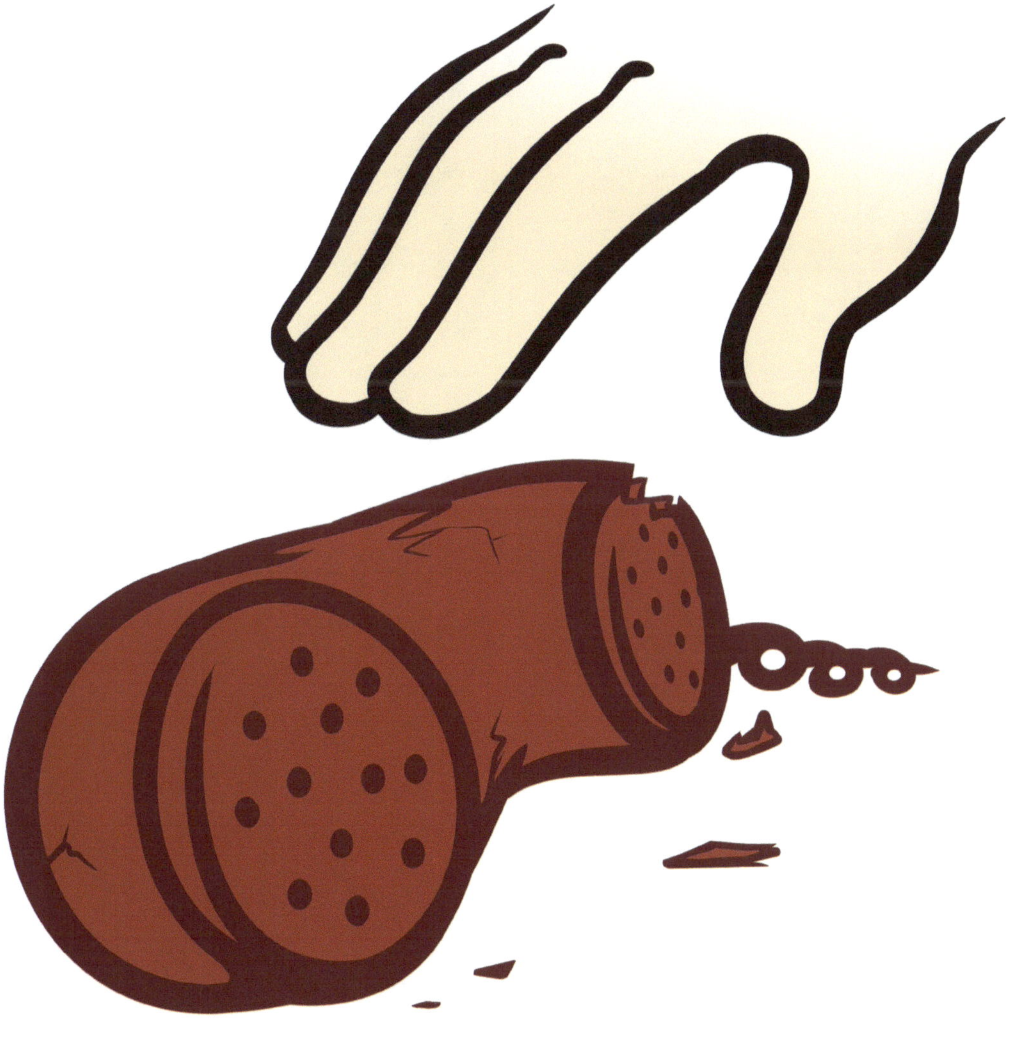

THE WHITE HARVEST

"Ivory Fields Forever"

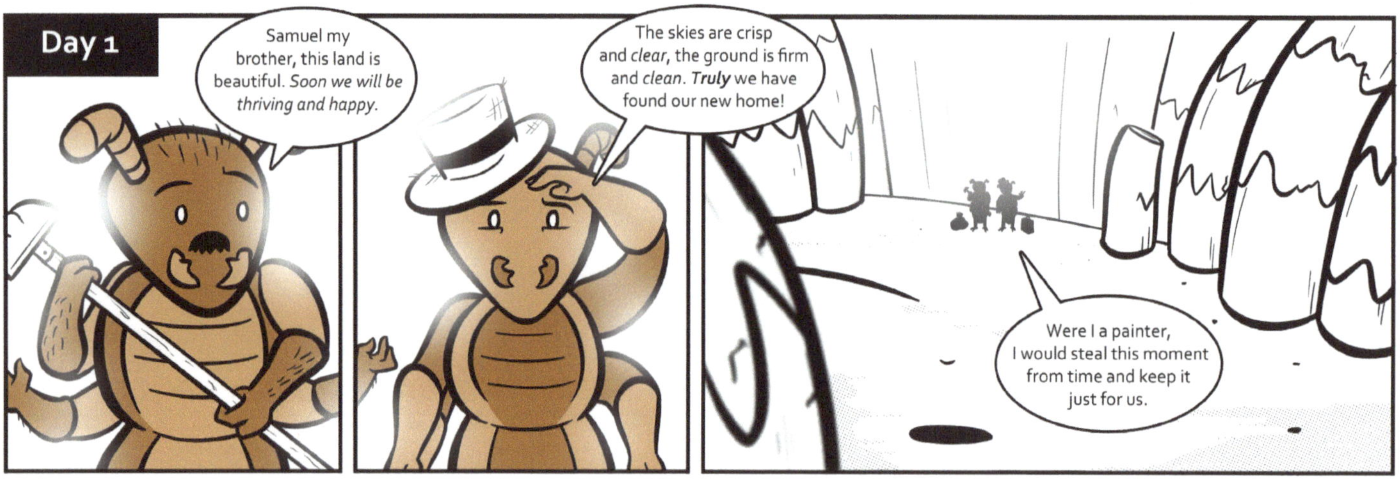
Day 1
Samuel my brother, this land is beautiful. *Soon we will be thriving and happy.*
The skies are crisp and *clear*, the ground is firm and *clean*. ***Truly*** we have found our new home!
Were I a painter, I would steal this moment from time and keep it just for us.

"And All The Angels Have My Face"

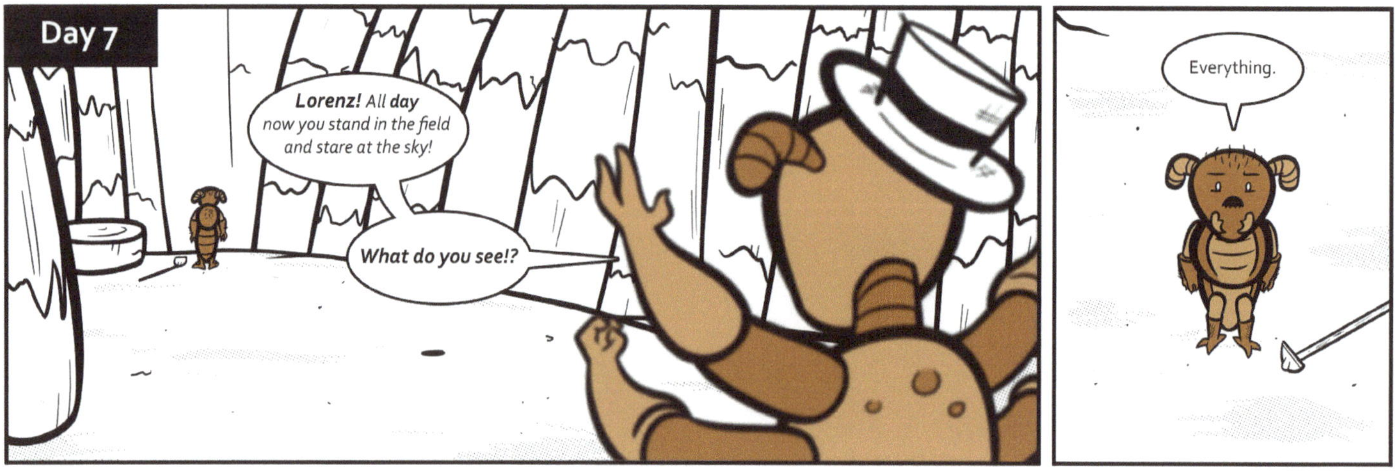
Day 7
Lorenz! *All **day** now you stand in the field and stare at the sky!*
What do you see!?
Everything.

"A Close Shave"

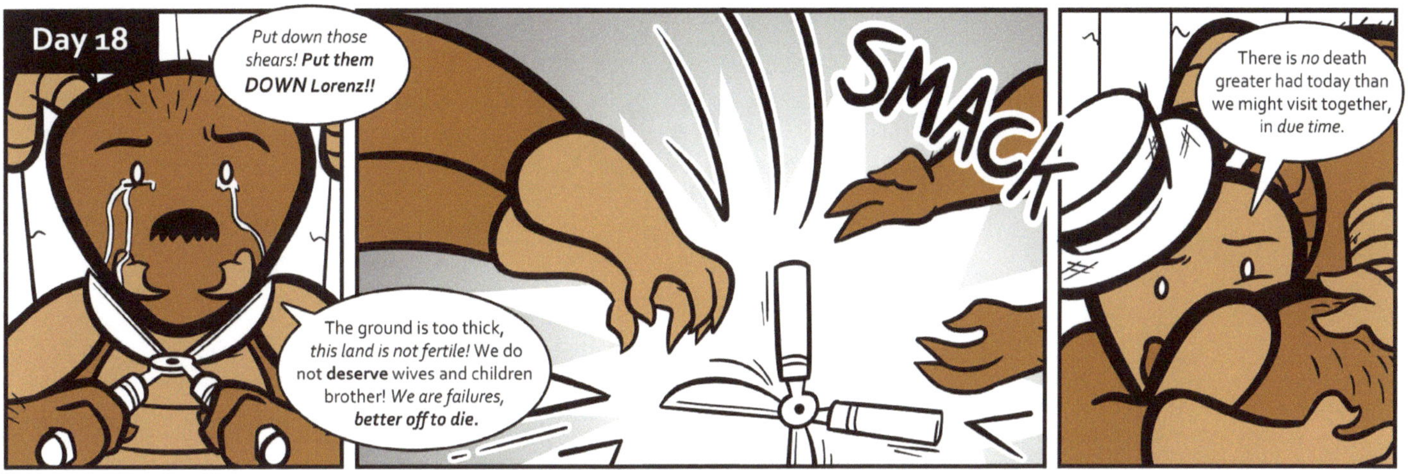

Day 18
Put down those shears! ***Put them DOWN Lorenz!!***
The ground is too thick, *this land is not fertile!* We do not **deserve** wives and children brother! *We are failures,* ***better off to die.***
SMACK
There is *no* death greater had today than we might visit together, in *due time.*

"Submission"

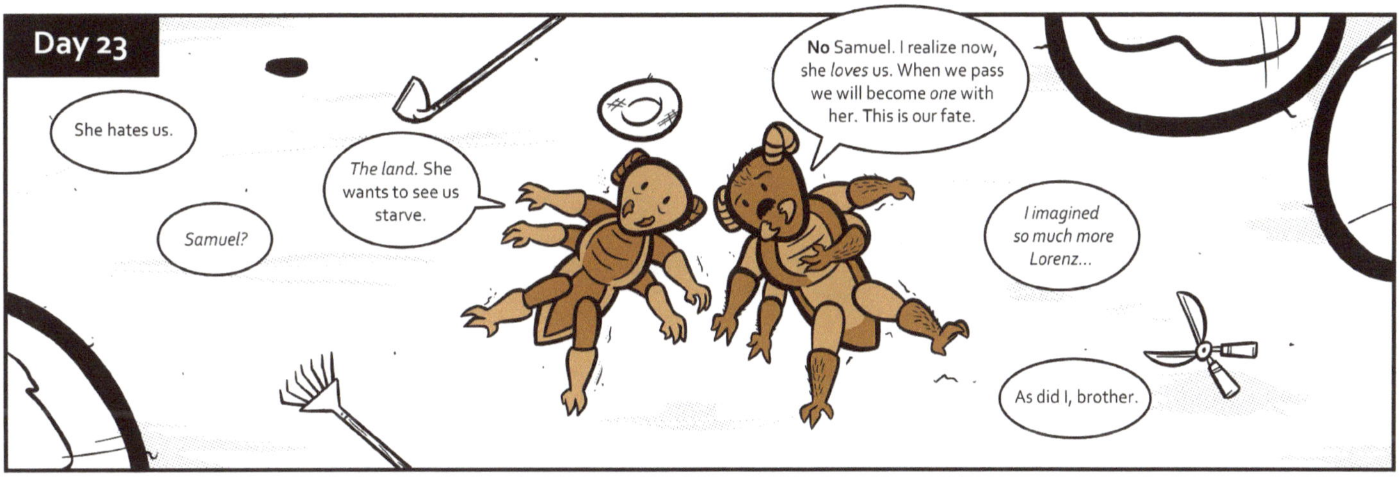

Day 23
She hates us.
Samuel?
The land. She wants to see us starve.
No Samuel. I realize now, she *loves* us. When we pass we will become *one* with her. This is our fate.
I imagined so much more Lorenz...
As did I, brother.

"Insecta Agricola"

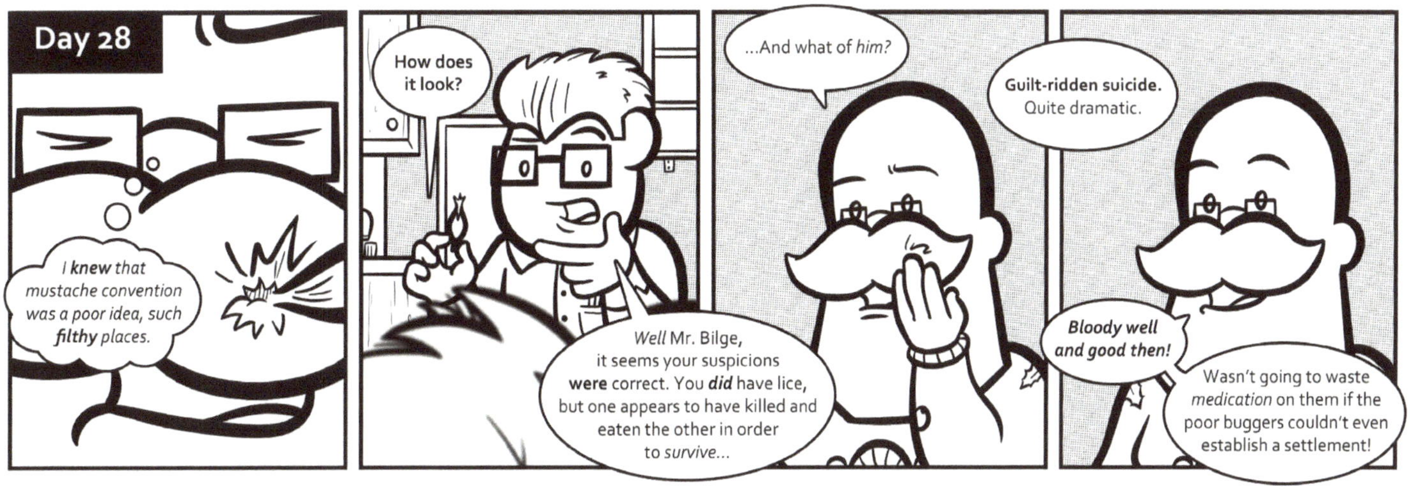

Day 28
I ***knew*** *that mustache convention was a poor idea, such* ***filthy*** *places.*
How does it look?
Well Mr. Bilge, it seems your suspicions **were** correct. You ***did*** have lice, but one appears to have killed and eaten the other in order to *survive...*
...And what of *him?*
Guilt-ridden suicide. Quite dramatic.
Bloody well and good then!
Wasn't going to waste *medication* on them if the poor buggers couldn't even establish a settlement!

EXODUS

"Hurdling The Firearm"

YAWWWNNN
Hmm.. *a message from Rose?*
Oh my ***God*** maybe this means we're dating now!!

"Keywords"

CLICK
Dear Max, no doubt at *this* point, we are ***both*** aware that we haven't spoken since the night we went to dinner. That was nearly a week ago. **You know why** that is.
You ran away and left me at the restaurant that night.
After we beat up those two thugs that were chasing your friend, **I** tried to make you **admit** that your real job had something to do with **it.** You laughed it off, but when I persisted you took a handful of **flour** out of your pants pocket, threw it in the air, and ***ran away*** with your co-worker. It was the *worst* smoke-bomb manoeuvre I've **ever** seen.
Look, if you really ***can't*** tell me what you do for a living, I can deal with that. Also, you're an **idiot**. But. We do have a great time together and I ***don't*** leave things un-addressed. So **I'm** saying that I *might* still be **interested in dating.**
But you've got to figure out what *you* want and how this is going to work. **Talk to you soon.**
P.S. It *was* fun knocking that guy out with the trashcan lid. I hope he didn't die.
...
We're ***totally*** *dating.*

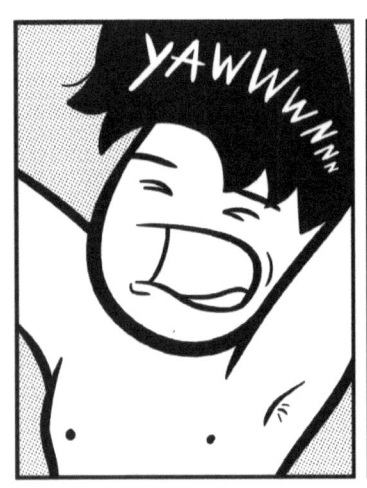

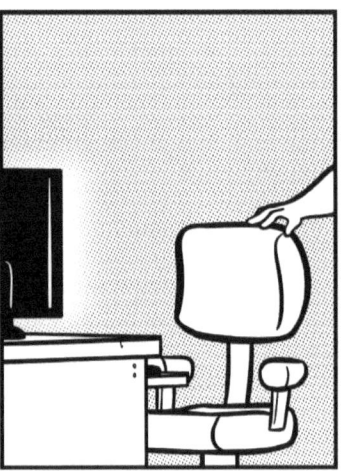

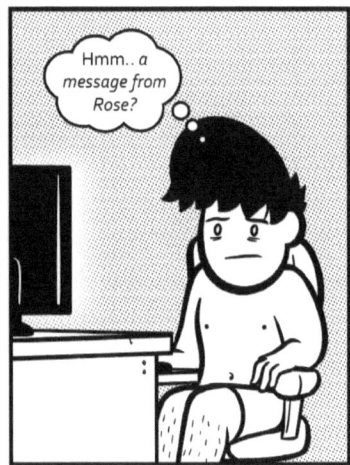

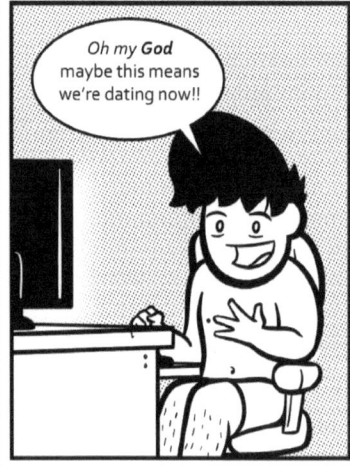

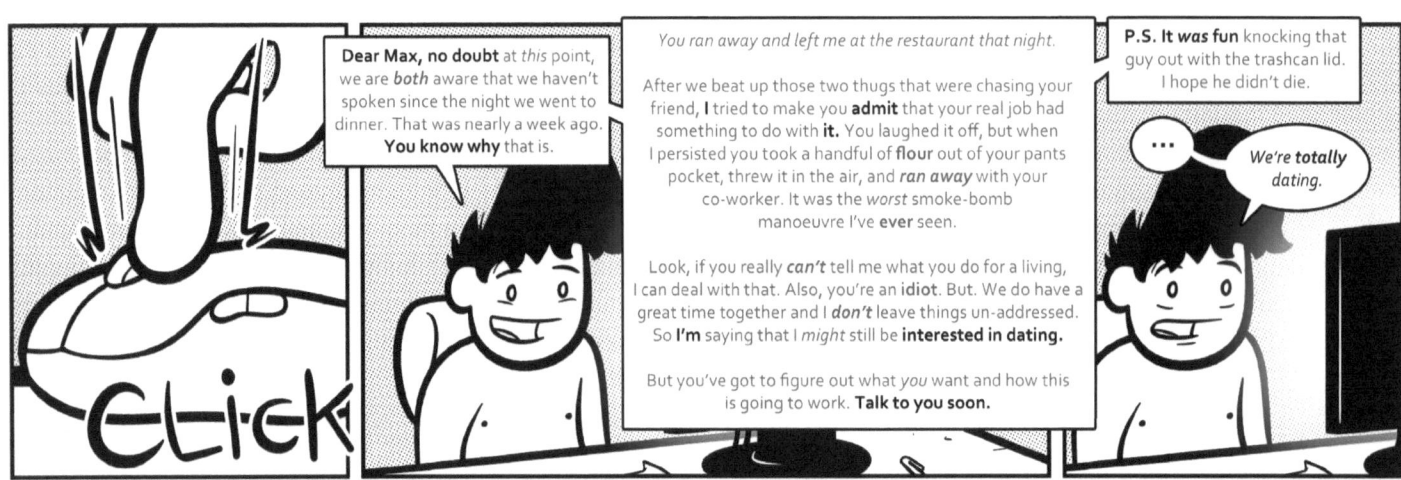

"The Boxes Are Shy"

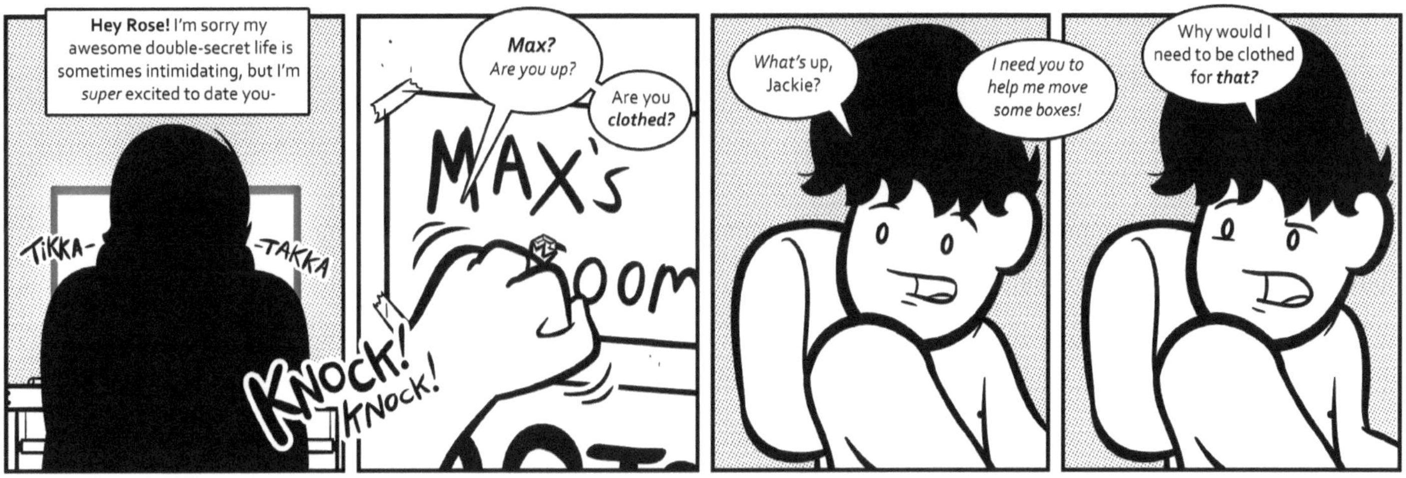
Hey Rose! I'm sorry my awesome double-secret life is sometimes intimidating, but I'm *super* excited to date you-
TIKKA-
-TAKKA
KNOCK!
KNOCK!
MAX's ROOM
Max? *Are you up?*
Are you ***clothed?***
What's up, Jackie?
I need you to help me move some boxes!
Why would I need to be clothed for ***that?***

"Only Photographic Evidence Remained"

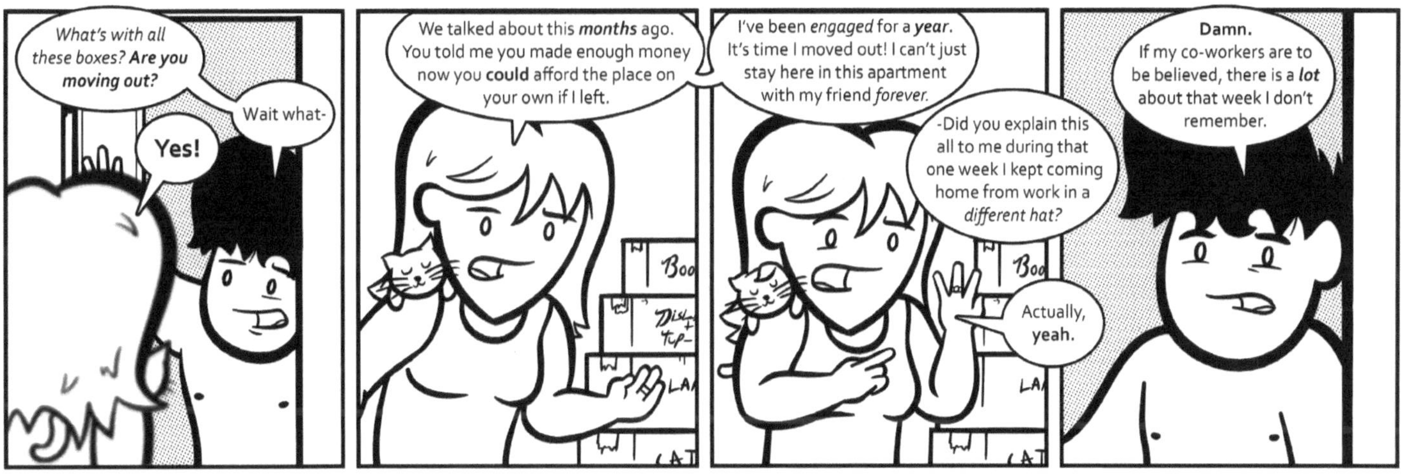
*What's with all these boxes? **Are you moving out?***
Yes!
Wait what-
We talked about this ***months*** ago. You told me you made enough money now you **could** afford the place on your own if I left.
I've been *engaged* for a ***year***. It's time I moved out! I can't just stay here in this apartment with my friend *forever*.
-Did you explain this all to me during that one week I kept coming home from work in a *different hat?*
Actually, **yeah.**
Damn.
If my co-workers are to be believed, there is a ***lot*** about that week I don't remember.

"From The Heart To The Neck"

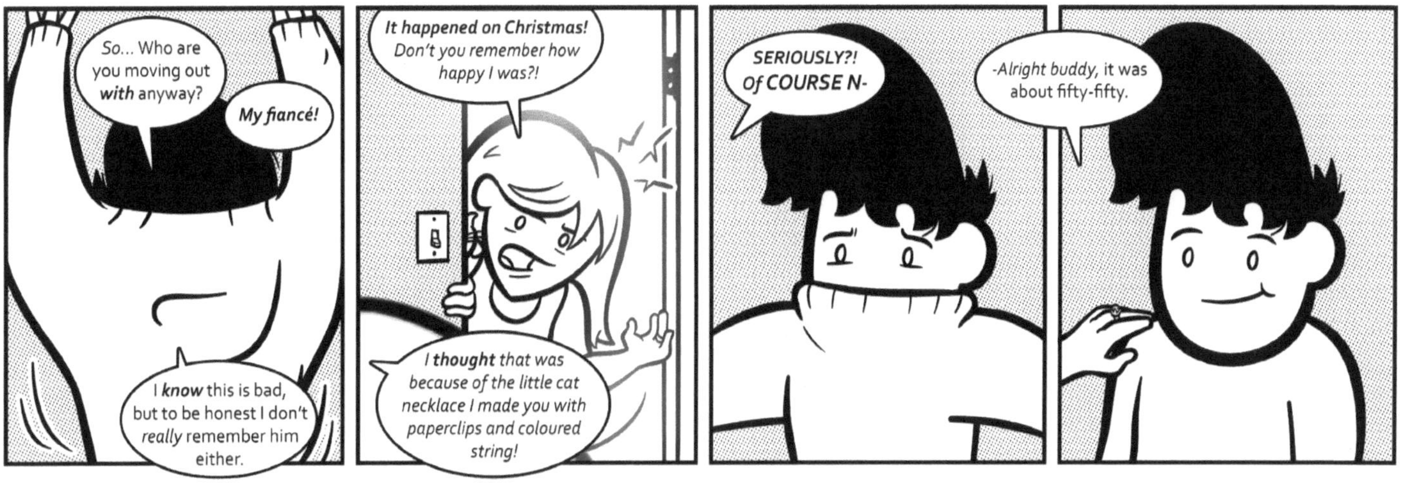
So... Who are you moving out **with** anyway?
My fiancé!
I ***know*** this is bad, but to be honest I don't *really* remember him either.
It happened on Christmas! *Don't you remember how happy I was?!*
*I **thought** that was because of the little cat necklace I made you with paperclips and coloured string!*
SERIOUSLY?! Of COURSE N-
-Alright buddy, it was about fifty-fifty.

"For All Your Storage Needs"

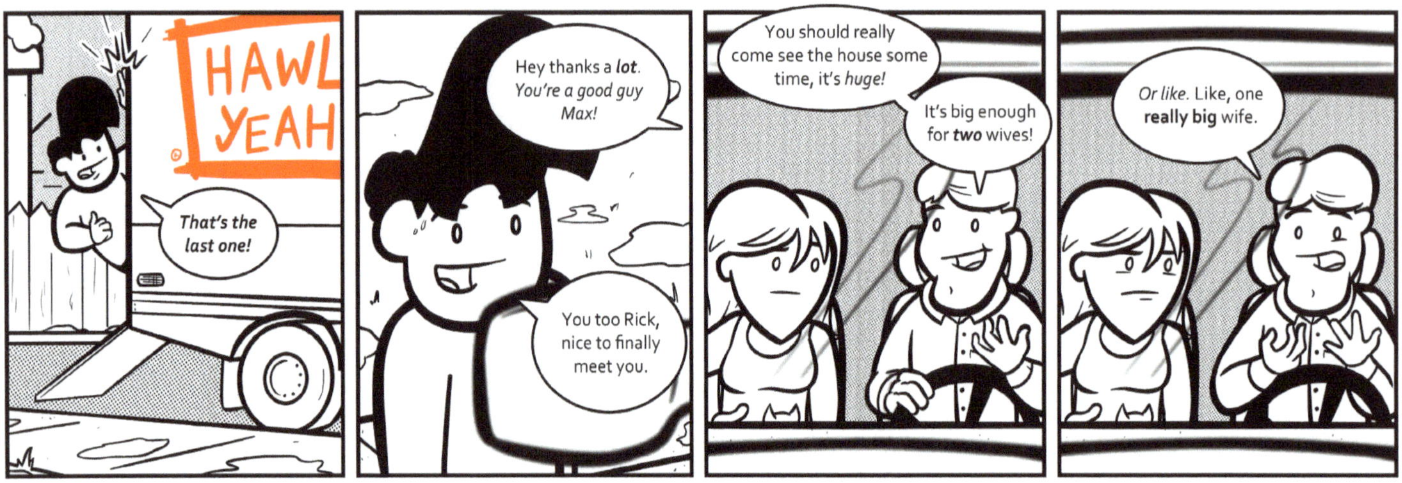

HAWL YEAH
That's the last one!
Hey thanks a ***lot***. *You're a good guy Max!*
You too Rick, nice to finally meet you.
You should really come see the house some time, it's *huge!*
It's big enough for ***two*** wives!
Or like. Like, one **really big** wife.

"Just A Little Farewell Tongue"

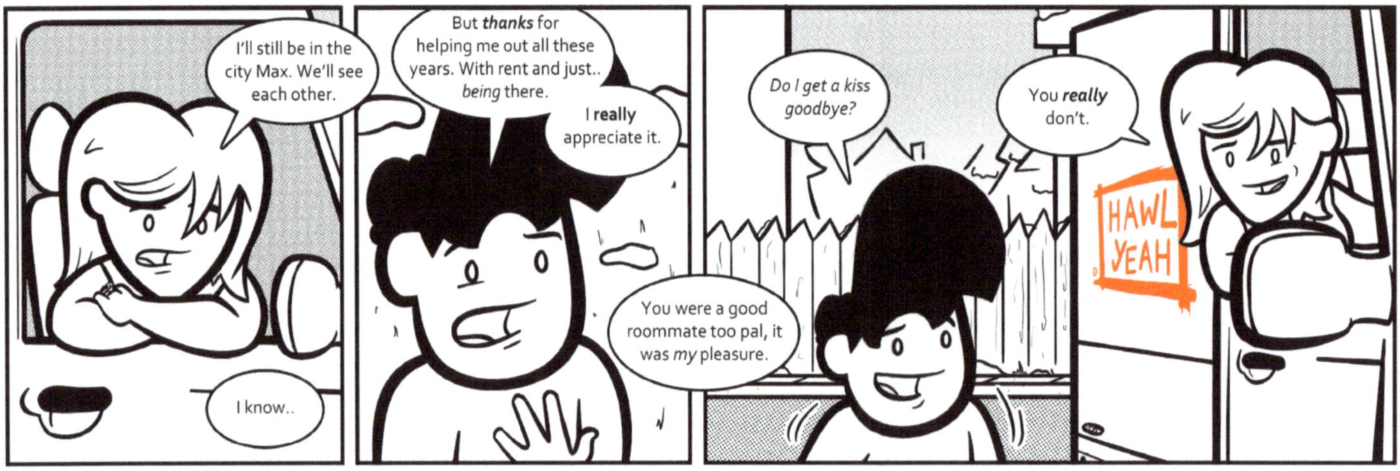

I'll still be in the city Max. We'll see each other.
I know..
But ***thanks*** for helping me out all these years. With rent and just.. *being* there.
I **really** appreciate it.
You were a good roommate too pal, it was *my* pleasure.
Do I get a kiss goodbye?
You ***really*** don't.
HAWL YEAH

"Cavernous"

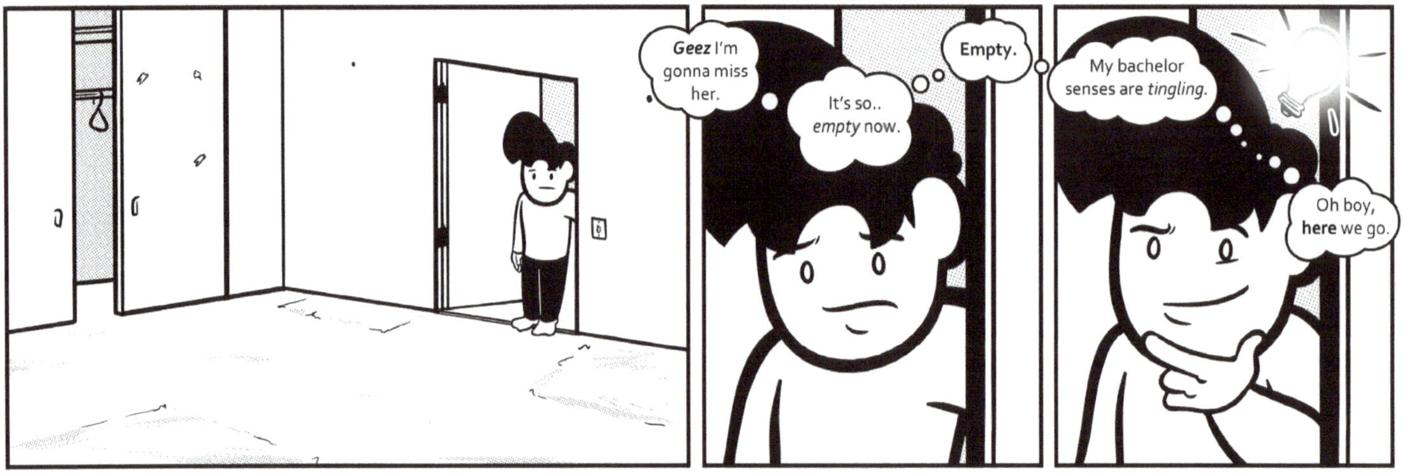

Geez I'm gonna miss her.
It's so.. *empty* now.
Empty.
My bachelor senses are *tingling.*
Oh boy, **here** we go.

"Small Victories In Quick Succession"

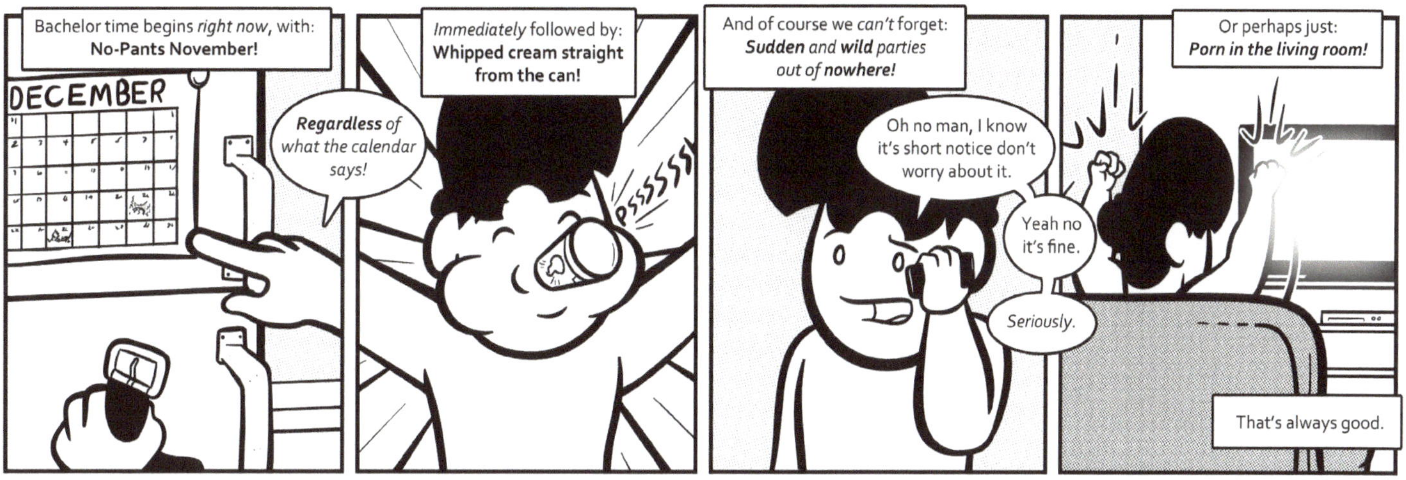

Bachelor time begins *right now*, with: **No-Pants November!**
DECEMBER
***Regardless** of what the calendar says!*
Immediately followed by: **Whipped cream straight from the can!**
PSSSSSS
And of course we *can't* forget: ***Sudden** and **wild** parties out of **nowhere!***
Oh no man, I know it's short notice don't worry about it.
Yeah no it's fine.
Seriously.
Or perhaps just: ***Porn in the living room!***
That's always good.

"Short Lived But Lived Hard"

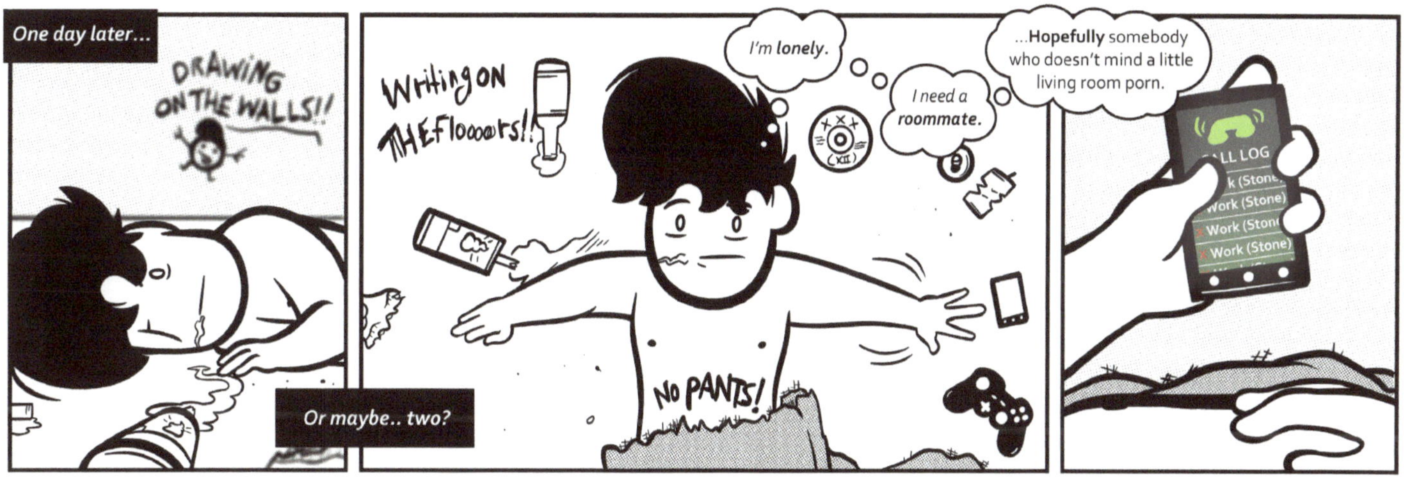

One day later...
DRAWING ON THE WALLS!!
Or maybe.. two?
Writing ON THE Flooors!!
*I'm **lonely**.*
*I need a **roommate**.*
...**Hopefully** somebody who doesn't mind a little living room porn.
NO PANTS!
Work (Stone)
Work (Stone)

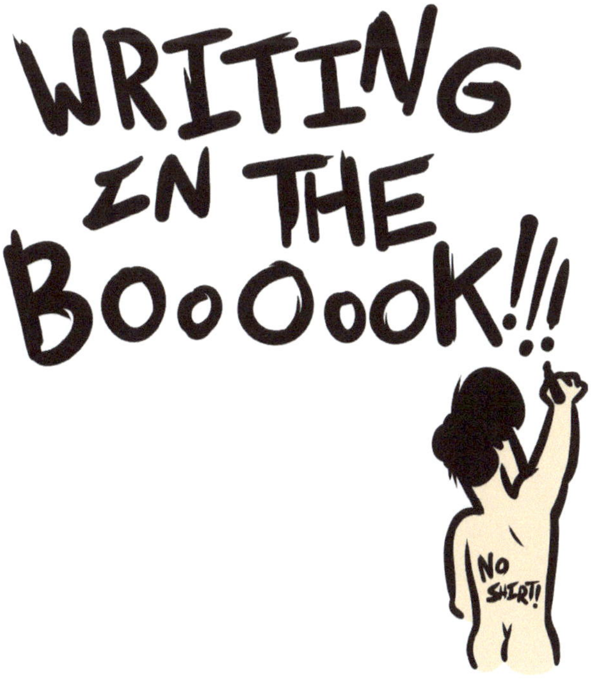

WRITING IN THE BOoOooK!!!
NO SHIRT!

THE NIGHT BEFORE THE NIGHT BEFORE CHRISTMAS

"Upon On The Rooftop"

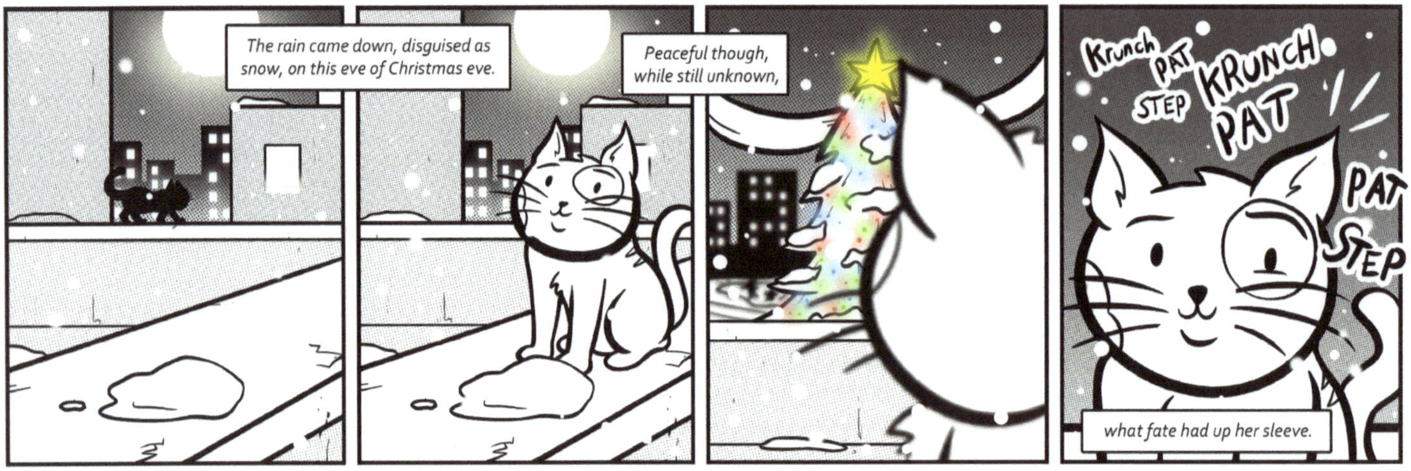
The rain came down, disguised as snow, on this eve of Christmas eve.
Peaceful though, while still unknown,
Krunch
PAT
STEP
KRUNCH
PAT
PAT
STEP
what fate had up her sleeve.

"Down In The Streets"

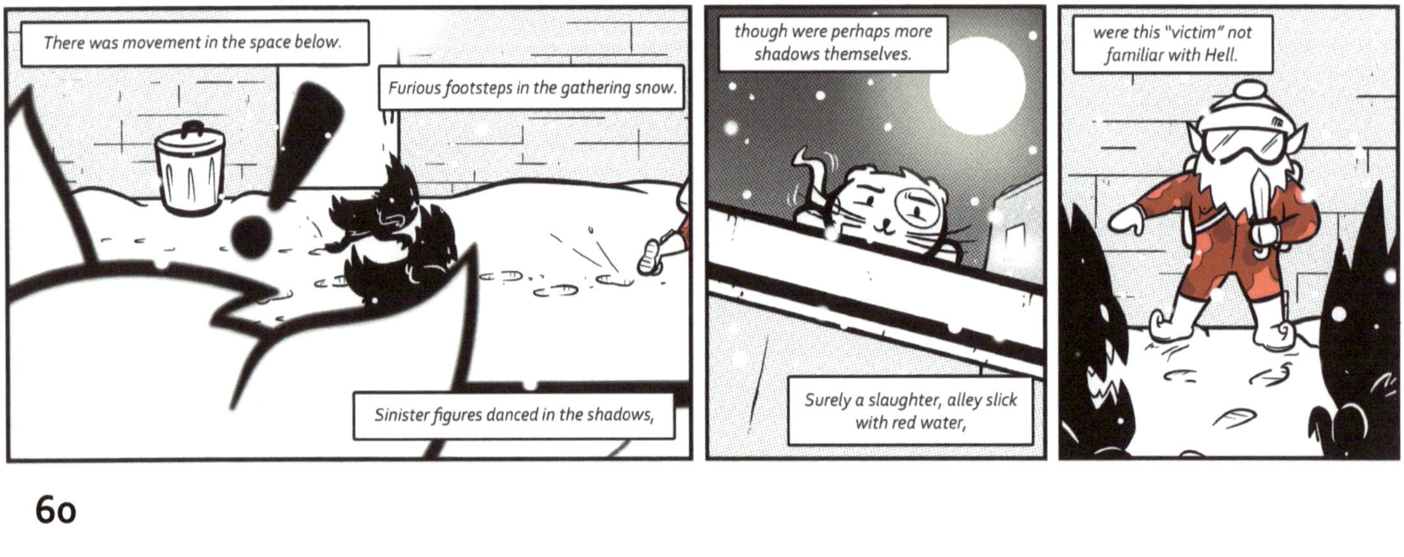
There was movement in the space below.
Furious footsteps in the gathering snow.
Sinister figures danced in the shadows,
though were perhaps more shadows themselves.
Surely a slaughter, alley slick with red water,
were this "victim" not familiar with Hell.

"Death Comes Swiftly"

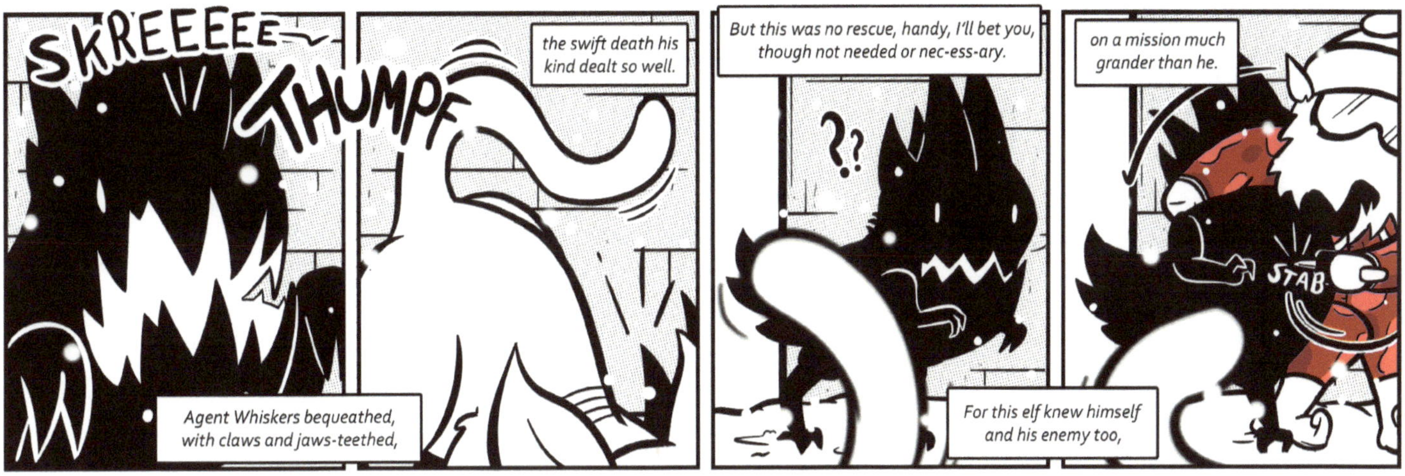

SKREEEEE
Agent Whiskers bequeathed, with claws and jaws-teethed,
THUMPF
the swift death his kind dealt so well.
But this was no rescue, handy, I'll bet you, though not needed or nec-ess-ary.
??
For this elf knew himself and his enemy too,
on a mission much grander than he.
STAB

"When The Devil Competes"

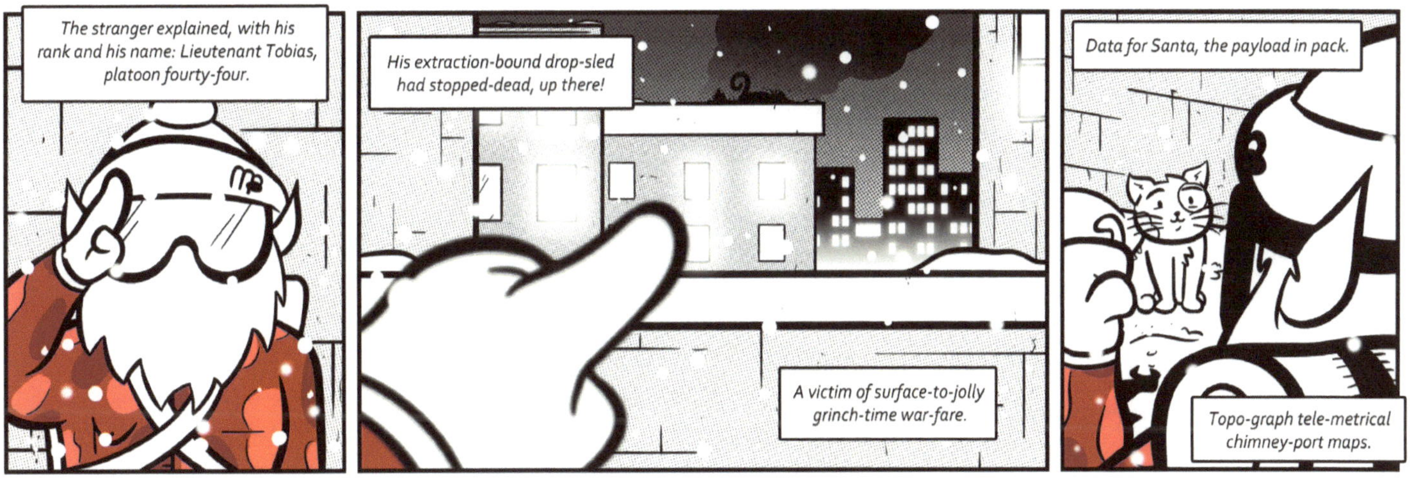

The stranger explained, with his rank and his name: Lieutenant Tobias, platoon fourty-four.
His extraction-bound drop-sled had stopped-dead, up there!
A victim of surface-to-jolly grinch-time war-fare.
Data for Santa, the payload in pack.
Topo-graph tele-metrical chimney-port maps.

"Fear Not For Angels"

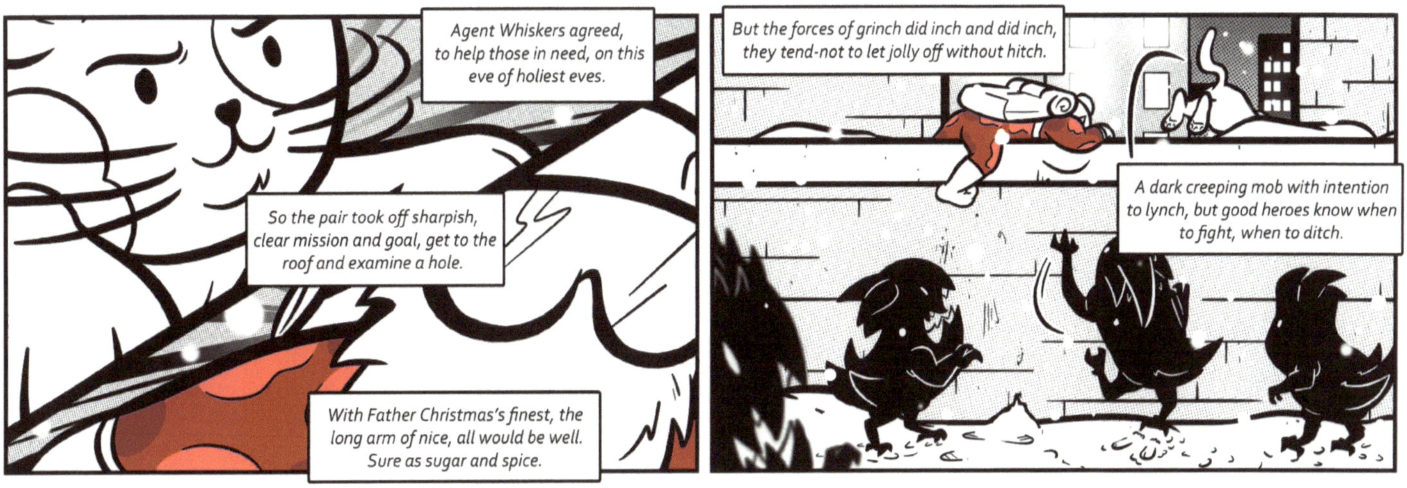

Agent Whiskers agreed, to help those in need, on this eve of holiest eves.
So the pair took off sharpish, clear mission and goal, get to the roof and examine a hole.
With Father Christmas's finest, the long arm of nice, all would be well. Sure as sugar and spice.
But the forces of grinch did inch and did inch, they tend-not to let jolly off without hitch.
A dark creeping mob with intention to lynch, but good heroes know when to fight, when to ditch.

"They Know Where They Tread"

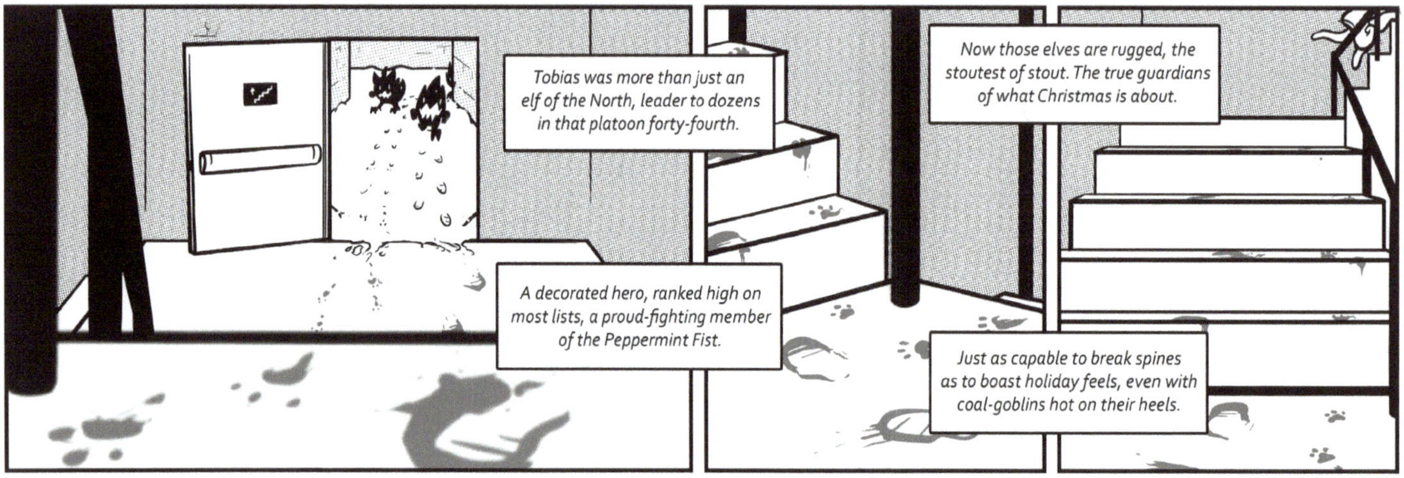
Tobias was more than just an elf of the North, leader to dozens in that platoon forty-fourth.
A decorated hero, ranked high on most lists, a proud-fighting member of the Peppermint Fist.
Now those elves are rugged, the stoutest of stout. The true guardians of what Christmas is about.
Just as capable to break spines as to boast holiday feels, even with coal-goblins hot on their heels.

"The Burdens Of Men"

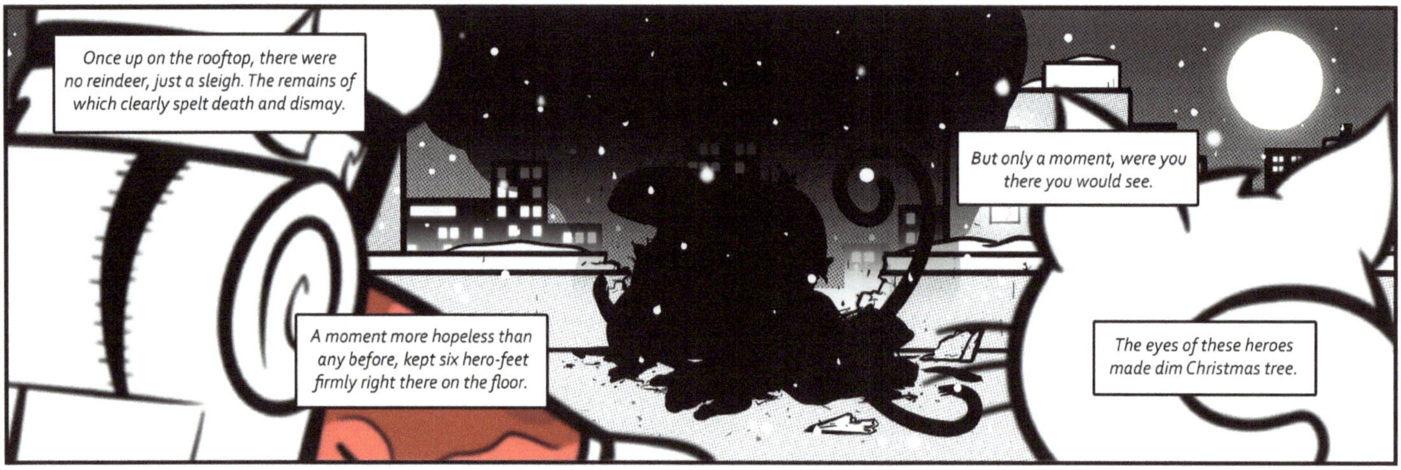
Once up on the rooftop, there were no reindeer, just a sleigh. The remains of which clearly spelt death and dismay.
A moment more hopeless than any before, kept six hero-feet firmly right there on the floor.
But only a moment, were you there you would see.
The eyes of these heroes made dim Christmas tree.

"Make Jealous The Dead"

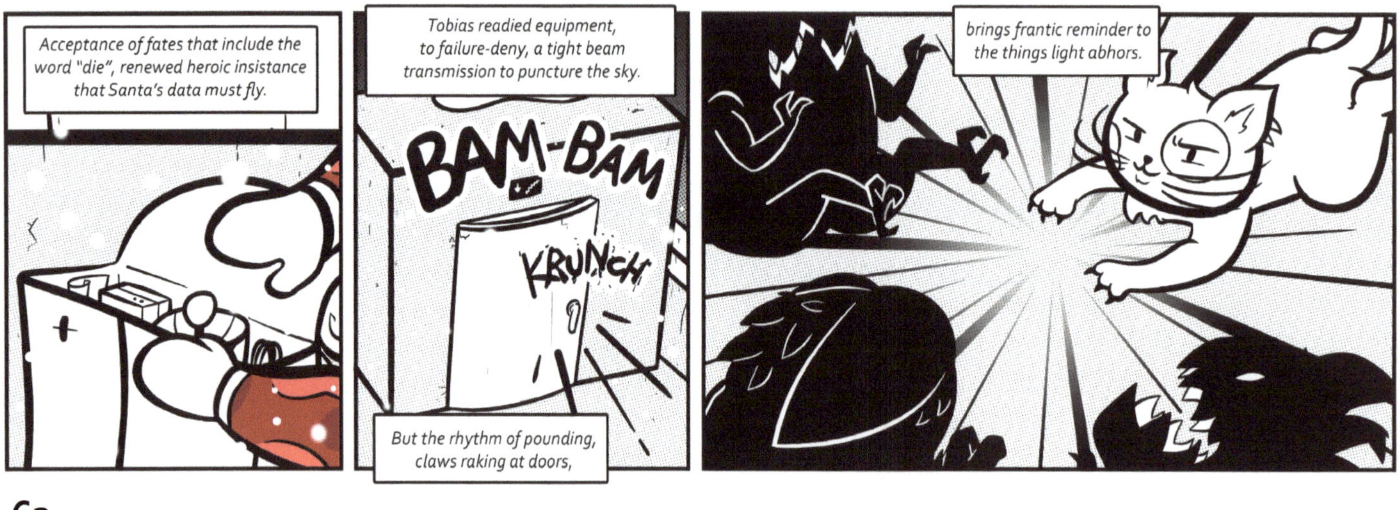
Acceptance of fates that include the word "die", renewed heroic insistance that Santa's data must fly.
Tobias readied equipment, to failure-deny, a tight beam transmission to puncture the sky.
BAM-BAM
KRUNCH
But the rhythm of pounding, claws raking at doors,
brings frantic reminder to the things light abhors.

"Have Need For The Divine"

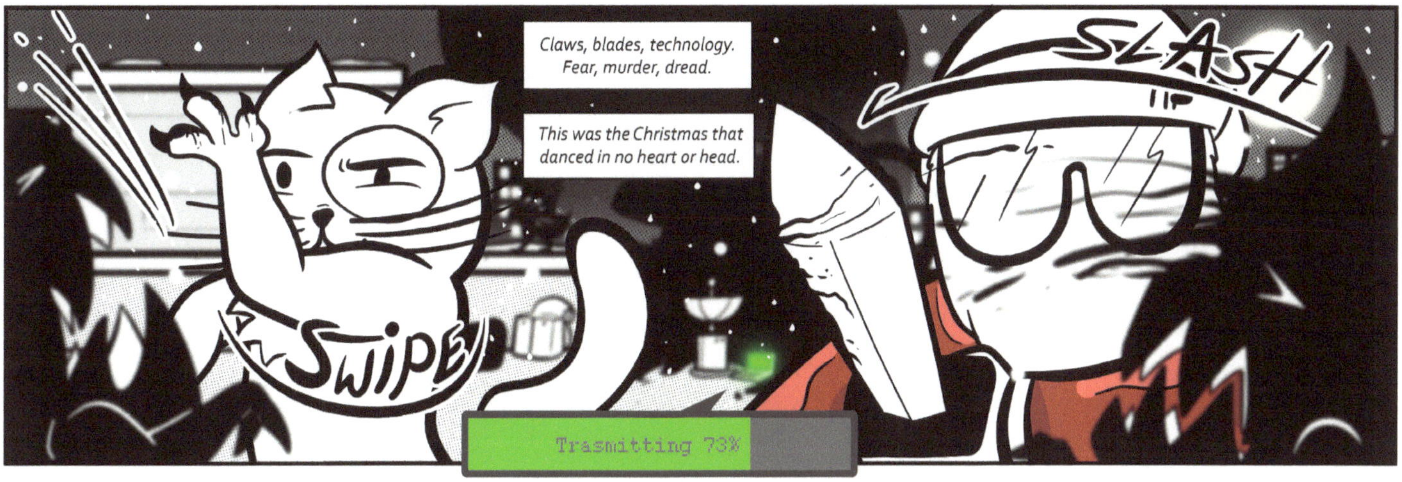
Claws, blades, technology.
Fear, murder, dread.
This was the Christmas that
danced in no heart or head.
SWIPE
SLASH
Trasmitting 73%

"Even Those Resting Grow Weary Of Time"

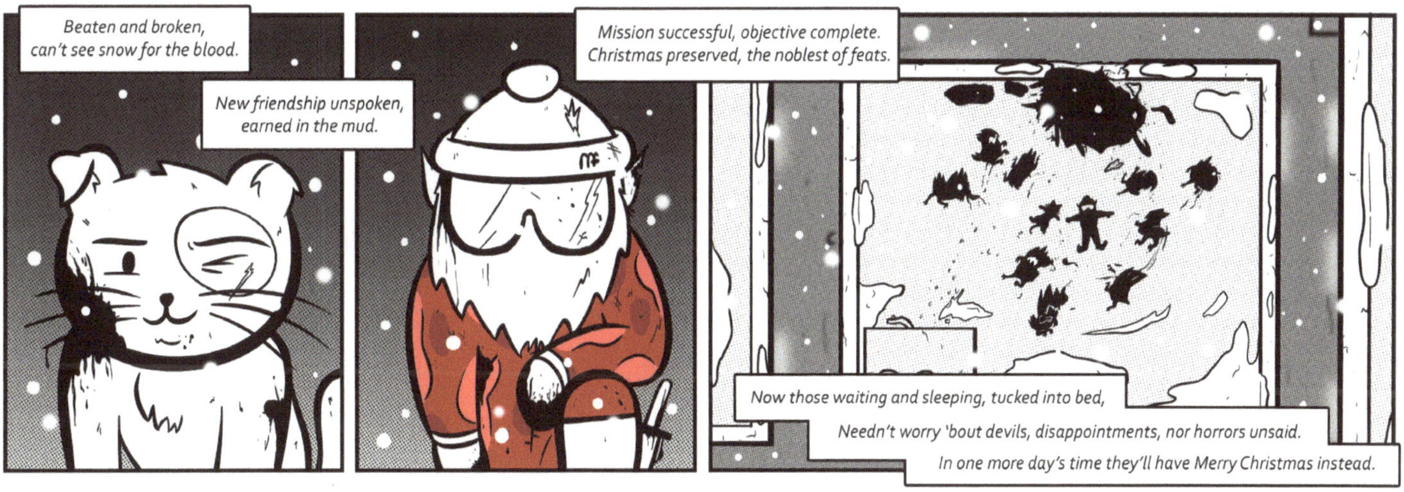
Beaten and broken,
can't see snow for the blood.
New friendship unspoken,
earned in the mud.
Mission successful, objective complete.
Christmas preserved, the noblest of feats.
Now those waiting and sleeping, tucked into bed,
Needn't worry 'bout devils, disappointments, nor horrors unsaid.
In one more day's time they'll have Merry Christmas instead.

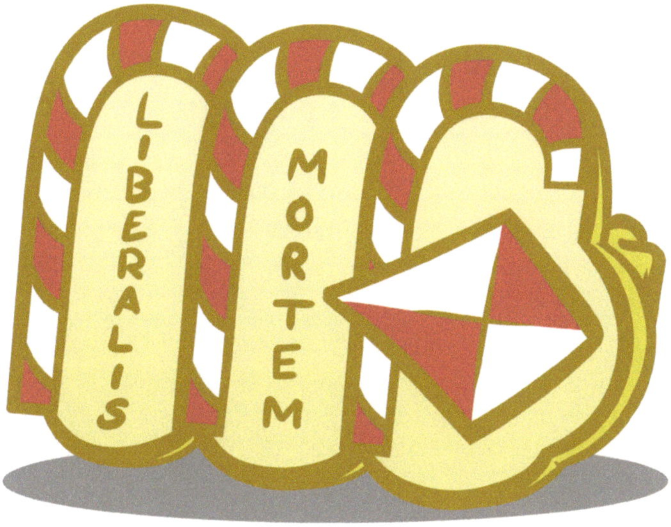
LIBERALIS
MORTEM

SUNDAY STRIPS

Think like syndication comic strips. These comics were large format and always in full colour! They are most certainly considered canon, but they were not at all involved with the story that played out during the week. These Sunday strips were just a chance to explore some character interactions and tell jokes that didn't fit into four panels. They jumped around in time and setting, were self-contained and obviously, they used to update on Sundays.

These strips began near to the beginning of *The Aversion Bureau*'s run and continued up until nearly the point where the first book came out. These strips contain some of my favourite jokes in the whole series and because they ran almost as long as the weekday comic, you'll get to watch the art go from *crap-to-capable* all over again!

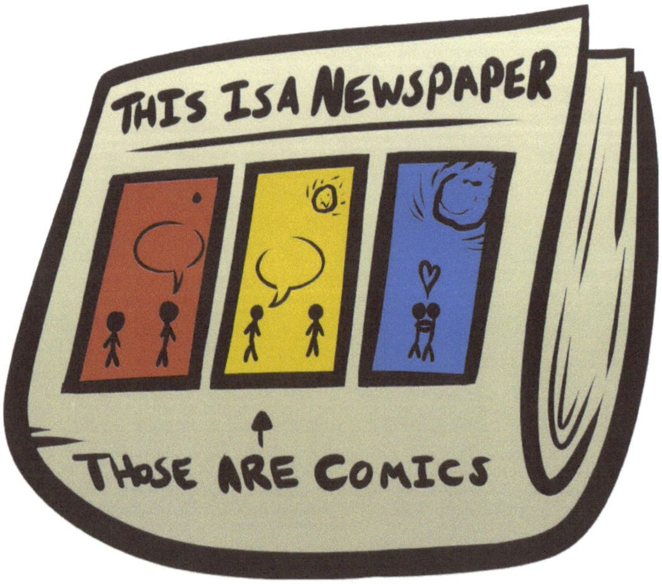
THIS IS A NEWSPAPER
THOSE ARE COMICS

Pictured: Comics that are not at all like Sunday strips.

"Man Talk"

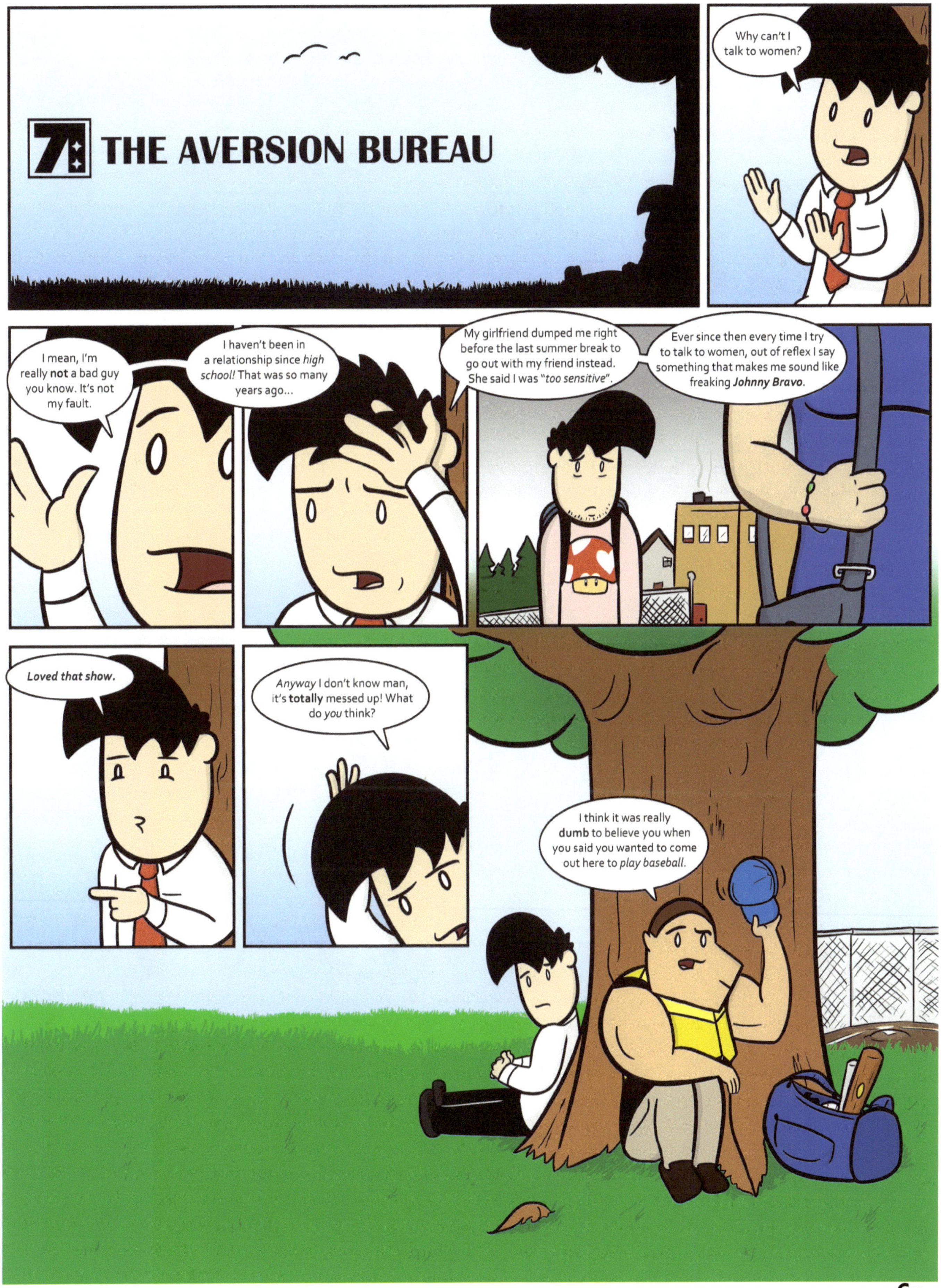
THE AVERSION BUREAU
Why can't I talk to women?
I mean, I'm really **not** a bad guy you know. It's not my fault.
I haven't been in a relationship since *high school!* That was so many years ago...
My girlfriend dumped me right before the last summer break to go out with my friend instead. She said I was "*too sensitive*".
Ever since then every time I try to talk to women, out of reflex I say something that makes me sound like freaking ***Johnny Bravo***.
Loved that show.
Anyway I don't know man, it's **totally** messed up! What do *you* think?
I think it was really **dumb** to believe you when you said you wanted to come out here to *play baseball*.

"Screamed The Dust Speck"

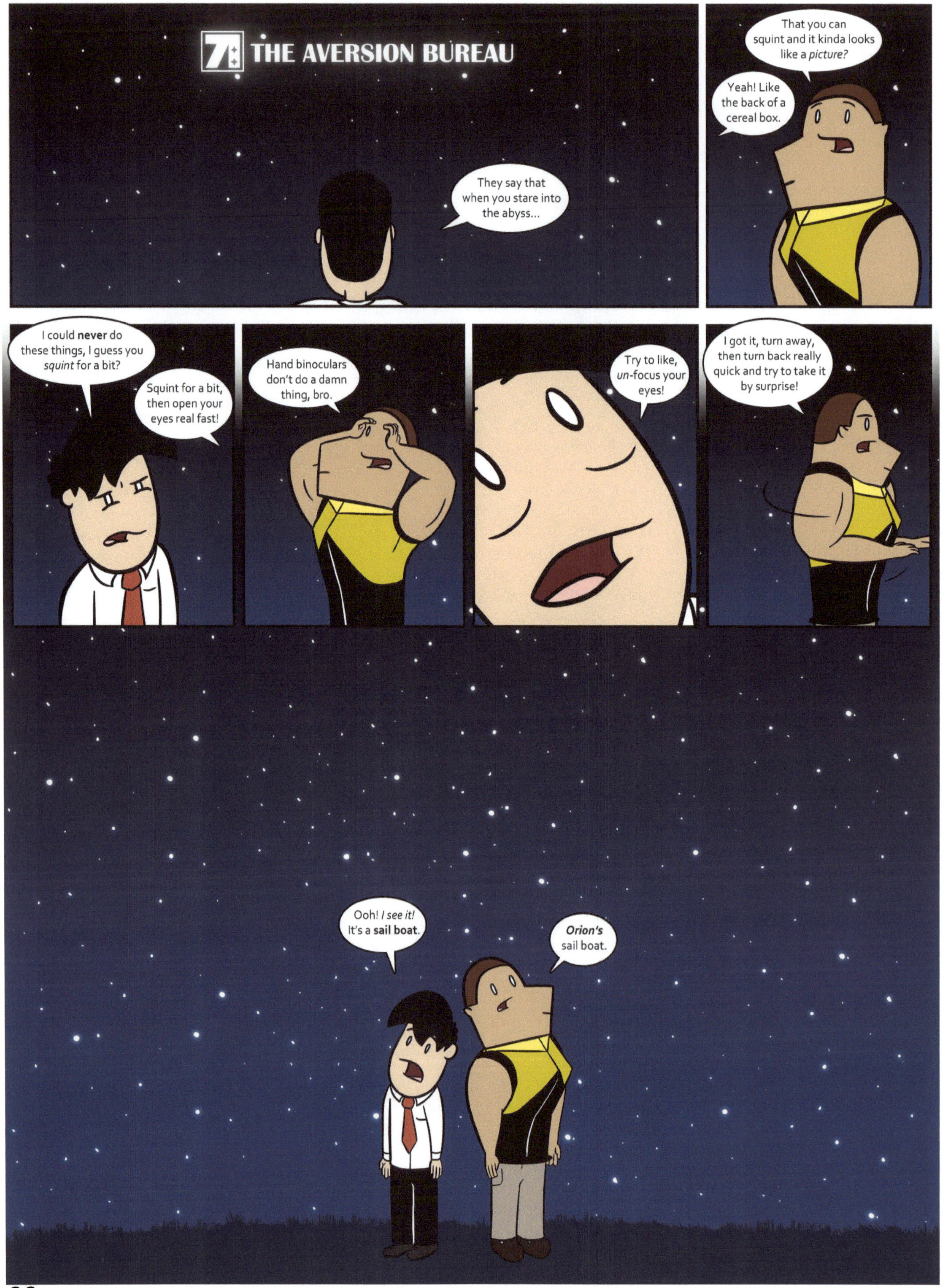
THE AVERSION BUREAU
They say that when you stare into the abyss...
That you can squint and it kinda looks like a *picture?*
Yeah! Like the back of a cereal box.
I could **never** do these things, I guess you *squint* for a bit?
Squint for a bit, then open your eyes real fast!
Hand binoculars don't do a damn thing, bro.
Try to like, *un*-focus your eyes!
I got it, turn away, then turn back really quick and try to take it by surprise!
Ooh! *I see it!* It's a **sail boat**.
Orion's sail boat.

"The Hard Way"

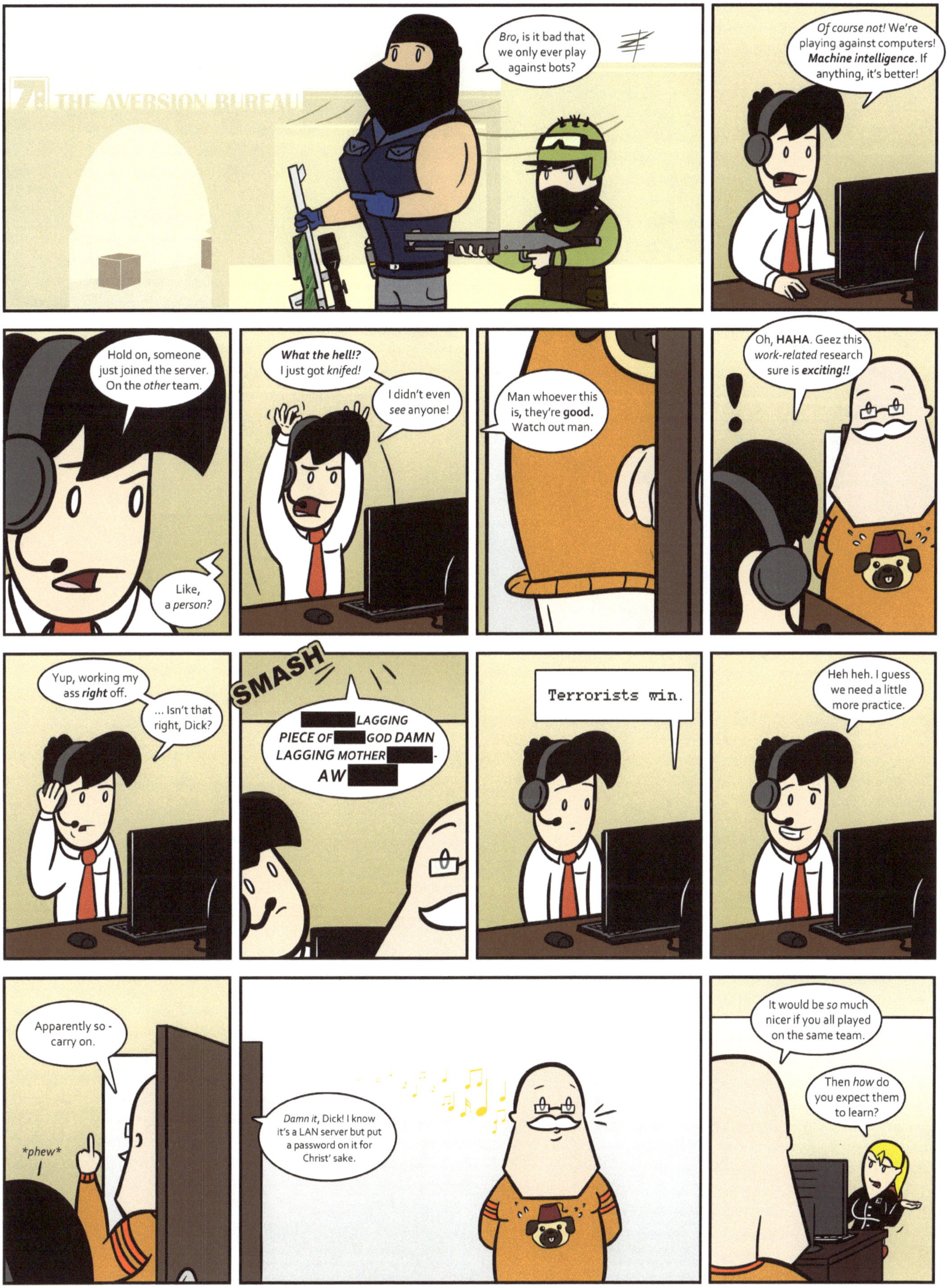

THE AVERSION BUREAU
Bro, is it bad that we only ever play against bots?
Of course not! We're playing against computers! ***Machine intelligence***. If anything, it's better!
Hold on, someone just joined the server. On the *other* team.
Like, a *person?*
What the hell!? I just got *knifed!*
I didn't even *see* anyone!
Man whoever this is, they're **good.** Watch out man.
!
Oh, **HAHA**. Geez this *work-related* research sure is ***exciting!!***
Yup, working my ass ***right*** off.
... Isn't that right, Dick?
SMASH
[redacted] *LAGGING PIECE OF* [redacted] *GOD DAMN LAGGING MOTHER* [redacted] *- AW* [redacted]
Terrorists win.
Heh heh. I guess we need a little more practice.
Apparently so - carry on.
phew
Damn it, Dick! I know it's a LAN server but put a password on it for Christ' sake.
It would be *so* much nicer if you all played on the same team.
Then *how* do you expect them to learn?

"Wet Work"

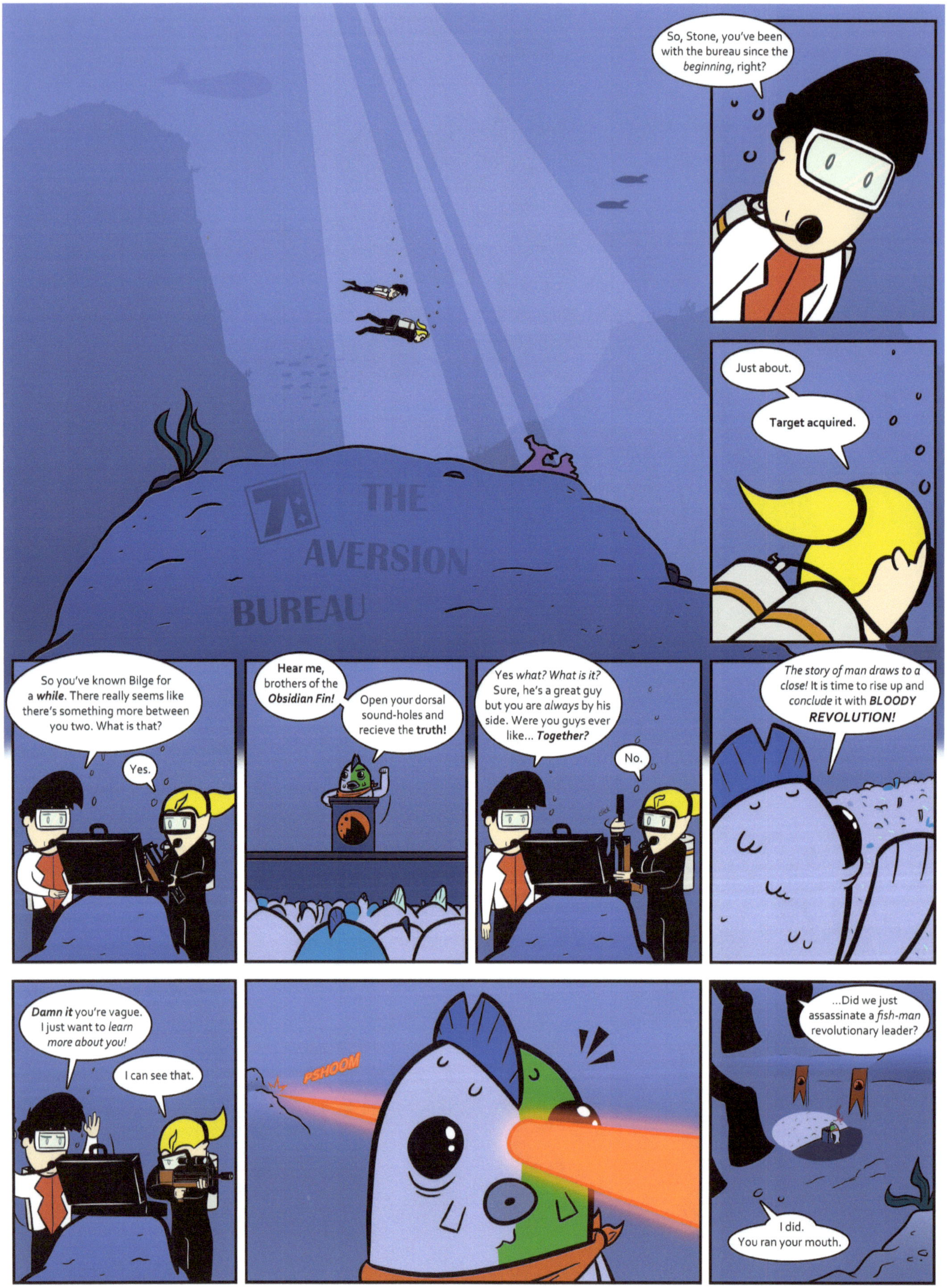

So, Stone, you've been with the bureau since the *beginning*, right?
THE AVERSION BUREAU
Just about.
Target acquired.
So you've known Bilge for a ***while***. There really seems like there's something more between you two. What is that?
Yes.
Hear me, brothers of the ***Obsidian Fin!***
Open your dorsal sound-holes and recieve the **truth!**
Yes *what? What is it?* Sure, he's a great guy but you are *always* by his side. Were you guys ever like... ***Together?***
No.
The story of man draws to a close! It is time to rise up and *conclude* it with ***BLOODY REVOLUTION!***
Damn it you're vague. I just want to *learn more about you!*
I can see that.
PSHOOM
...Did we just assassinate a *fish-man* revolutionary leader?
I did. You ran your mouth.

"The Times They Are A-Changin'"

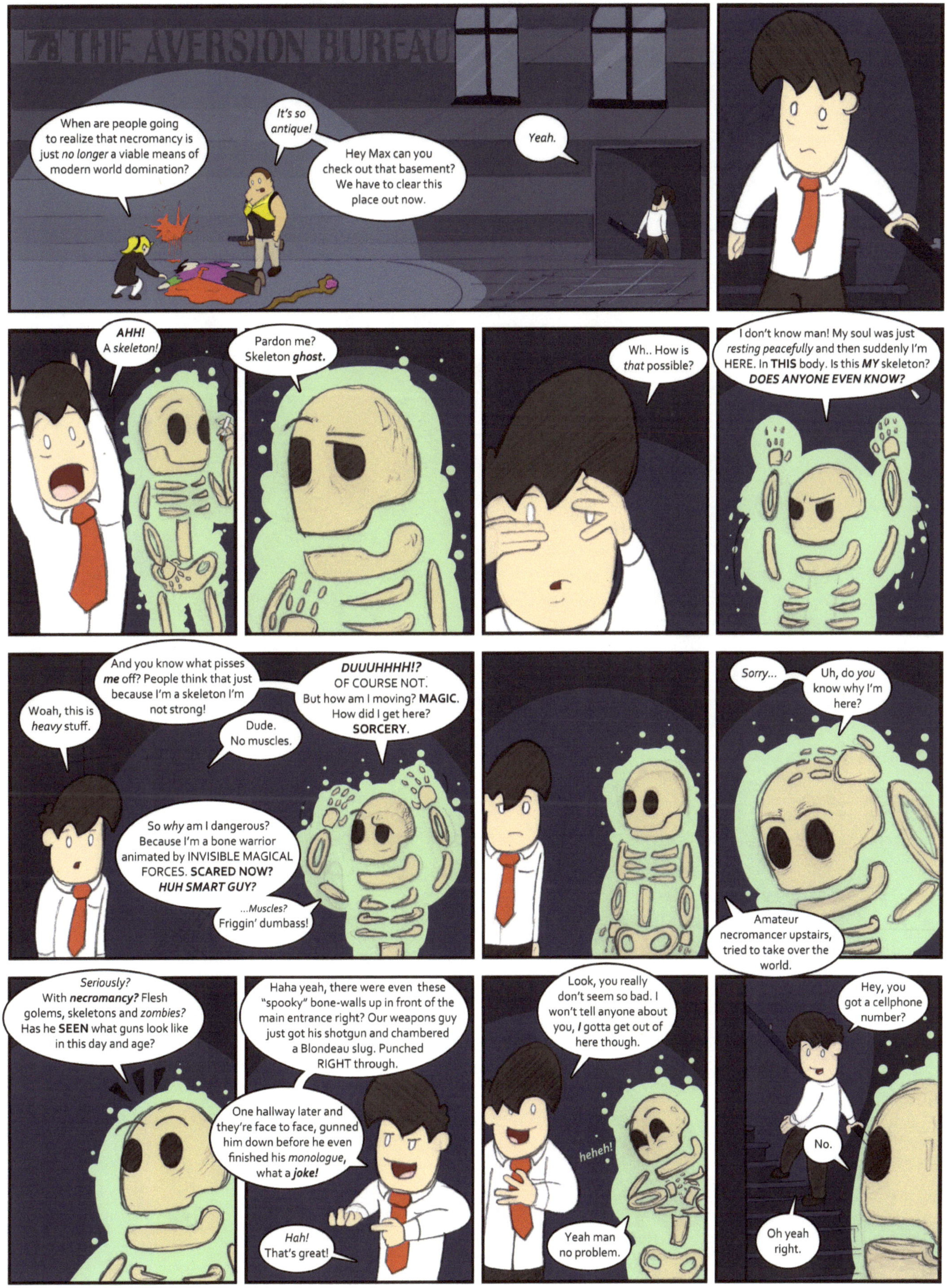
THE AVERSION BUREAU
When are people going to realize that necromancy is just *no longer* a viable means of modern world domination?
It's so antique!
Hey Max can you check out that basement? We have to clear this place out now.
Yeah.
AHH! *A skeleton!*
Pardon me? Skeleton ***ghost.***
Wh.. How is *that* possible?
I don't know man! My soul was just *resting peacefully* and then suddenly I'm HERE. In **THIS** body. Is this ***MY*** skeleton? ***DOES ANYONE EVEN KNOW?***
Woah, this is *heavy* stuff.
And you know what pisses ***me*** off? People think that just because I'm a skeleton I'm not strong!
Dude. No muscles.
DUUUHHHH!? OF COURSE NOT. But how am I moving? **MAGIC.** How did I get here? **SORCERY.**
So *why* am I dangerous? Because I'm a bone warrior animated by INVISIBLE MAGICAL FORCES. **SCARED NOW? *HUH SMART GUY?***
...Muscles? Friggin' dumbass!
Sorry...
Uh, do *you* know why I'm here?
Amateur necromancer upstairs, tried to take over the world.
Seriously? With ***necromancy?*** Flesh golems, skeletons and *zombies?* Has he **SEEN** what guns look like in this day and age?
Haha yeah, there were even these "spooky" bone-walls up in front of the main entrance right? Our weapons guy just got his shotgun and chambered a Blondeau slug. Punched RIGHT through.
One hallway later and they're face to face, gunned him down before he even finished his *monologue*, what a ***joke!***
Hah! That's great!
Look, you really don't seem so bad. I won't tell anyone about you, ***I*** gotta get out of here though.
heheh!
Yeah man no problem.
Hey, you got a cellphone number?
No.
Oh yeah right.

"Sweeter Than Sugar"

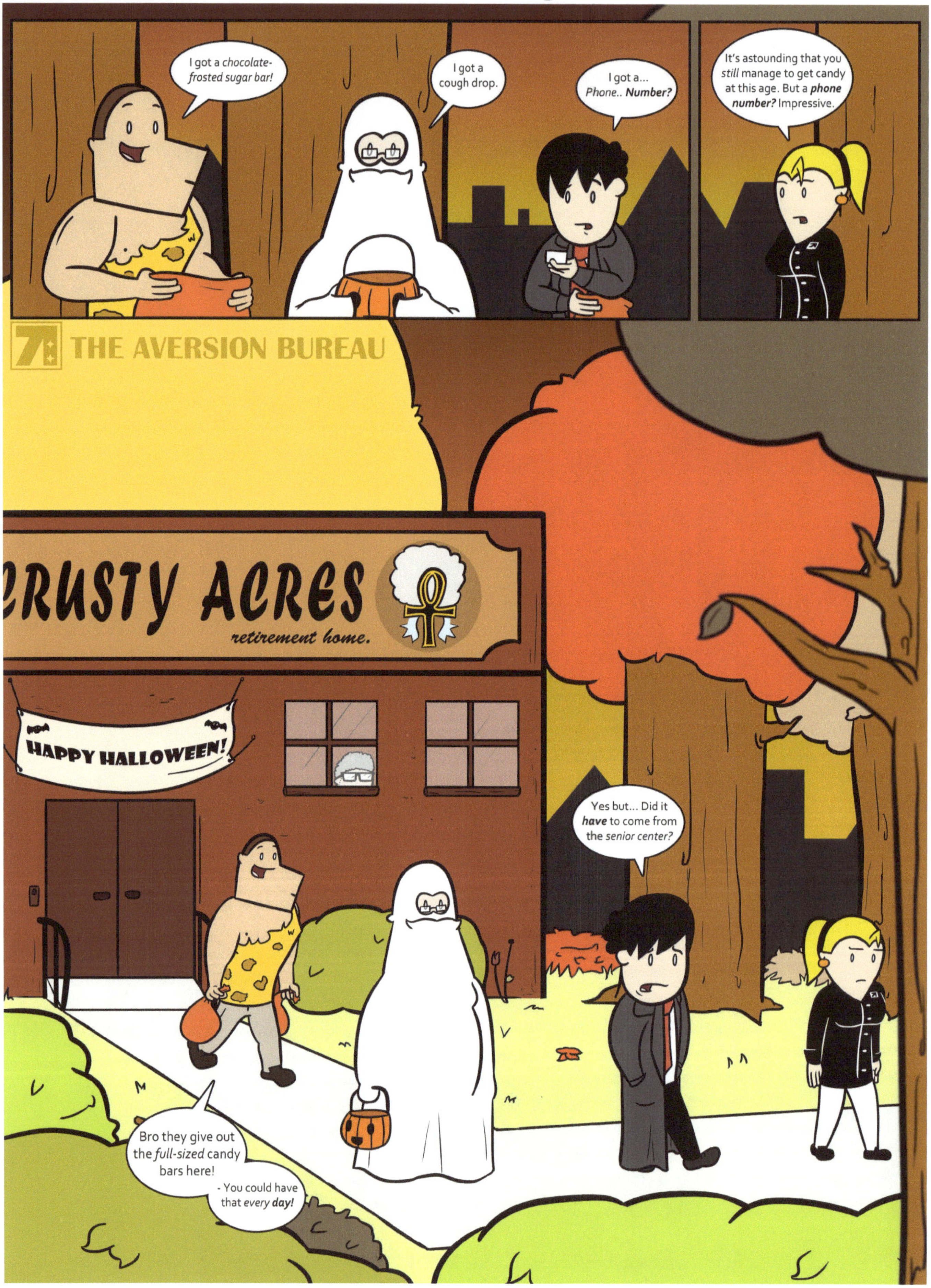

I got a *chocolate-frosted sugar bar!*
I got a cough drop.
I got a... *Phone.. **Number?***
It's astounding that you *still* manage to get candy at this age. But a ***phone number?*** Impressive.
THE AVERSION BUREAU
CRUSTY ACRES
retirement home.
HAPPY HALLOWEEN!
Yes but... Did it ***have*** to come from the *senior center?*
Bro they give out the *full-sized* candy bars here!
- You could have that *every **day!***

"With A Teaspoon I Dug His Grave"

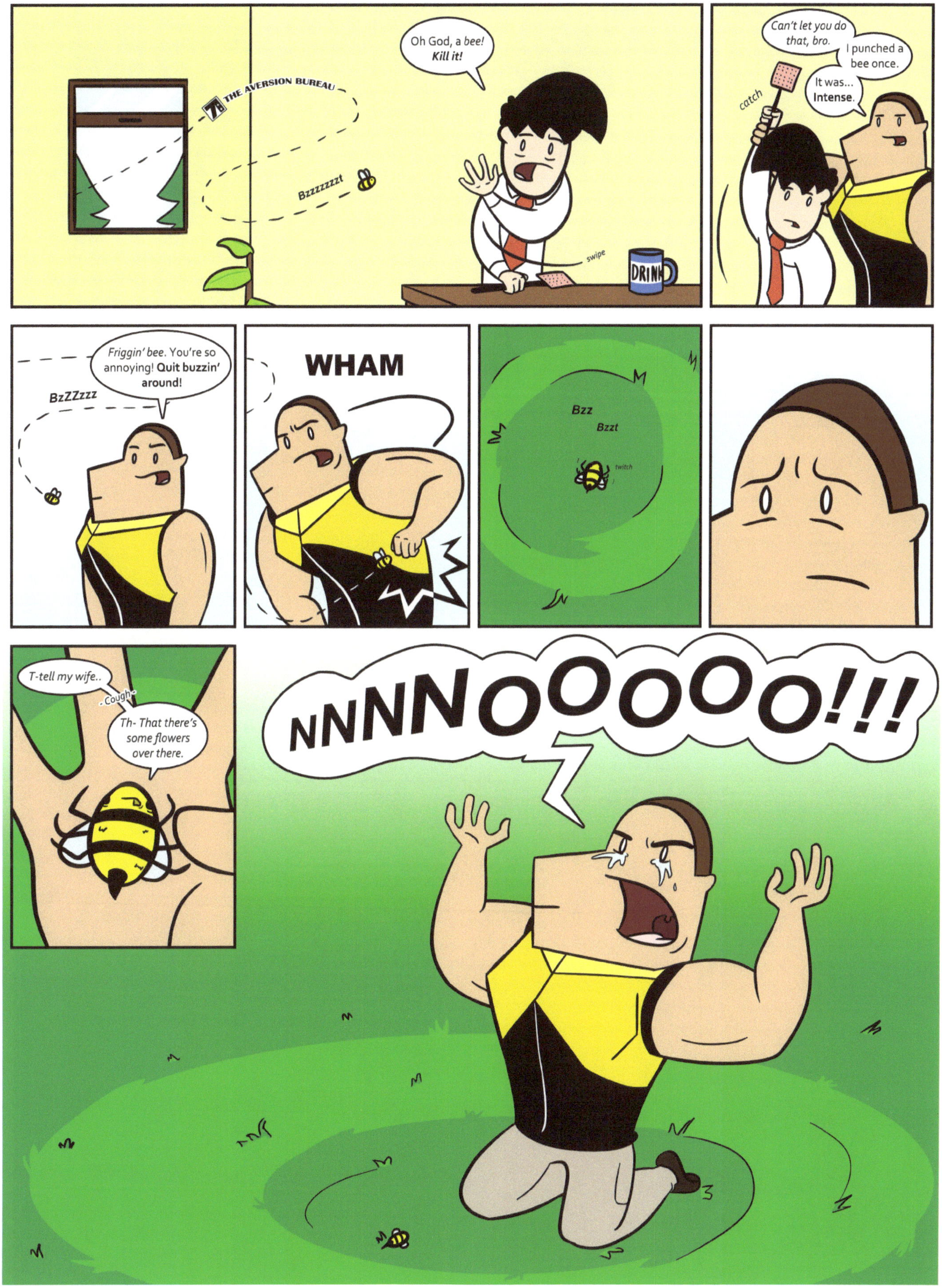
THE AVERSION BUREAU
Bzzzzzzzt
Oh God, a bee! Kill it!
swipe
DRINK
Can't let you do that, bro.
I punched a bee once.
It was... Intense.
catch
Friggin' bee. You're so annoying! Quit buzzin' around!
BzZZzzz
WHAM
Bzz
Bzzt
twitch
T-tell my wife..
-Cough-
Th- That there's some flowers over there.
NNNNOOOOOO!!!

"Scourge Of The Drive-In"

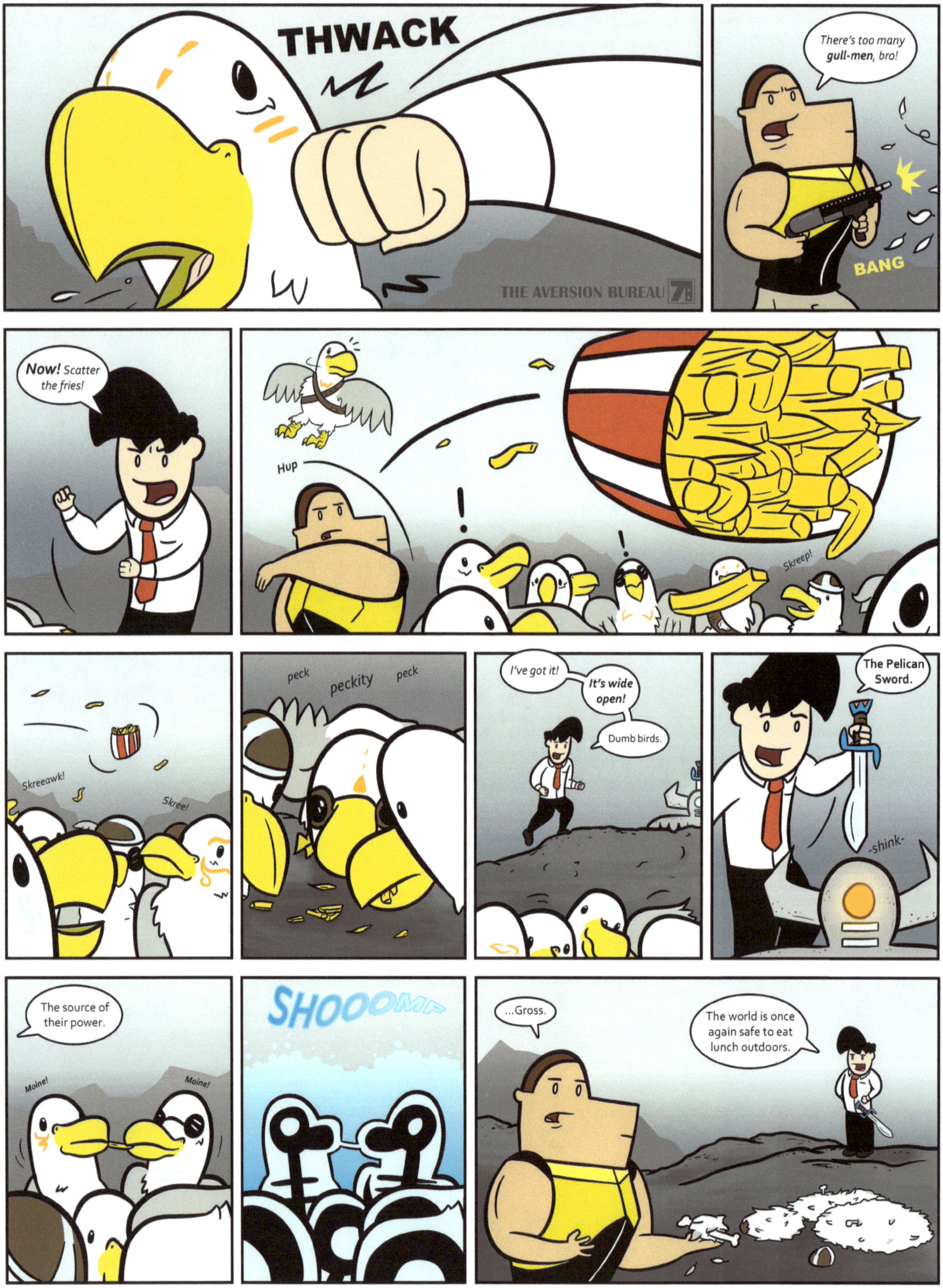
THWACK
THE AVERSION BUREAU
There's too many gull-men, bro!
BANG
Now! Scatter the fries!
Hup
!
!
Skreep!
Skreeawk!
Skree!
peck
peckity
peck
I've got it!
It's wide open!
Dumb birds.
The Pelican Sword.
-shink-
The source of their power.
Moine!
Moine!
SHOOOMF
...Gross.
The world is once again safe to eat lunch outdoors.

"Street Justice"

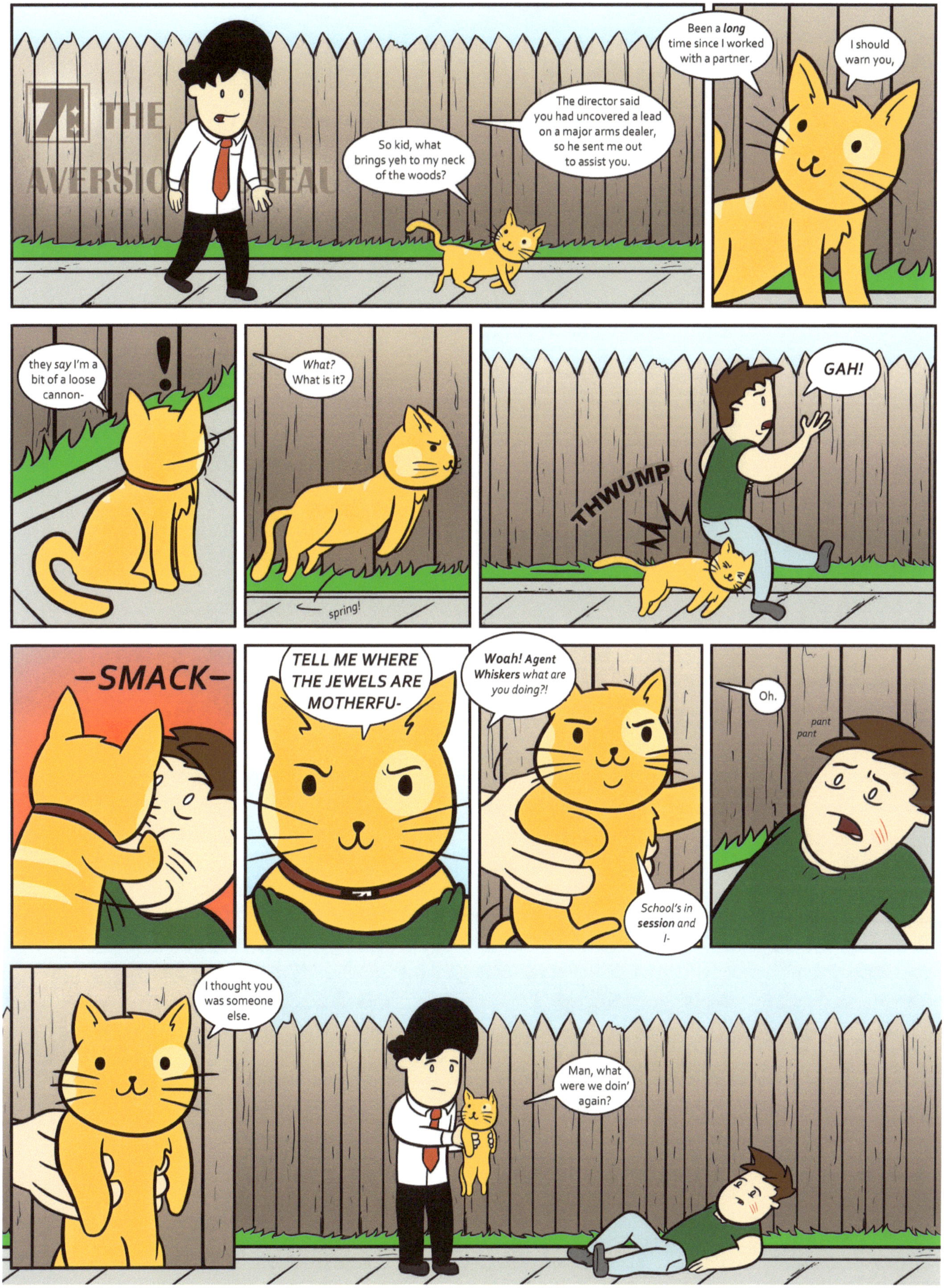

So kid, what brings yeh to my neck of the woods?
The director said you had uncovered a lead on a major arms dealer, so he sent me out to assist you.
Been a *long* time since I worked with a partner.
I should warn you,
they *say* I'm a bit of a loose cannon-
!
What? What is it?
spring!
THWUMP
GAH!
-SMACK-
TELL ME WHERE THE JEWELS ARE MOTHERFU-
Woah! Agent Whiskers what are you doing?!
School's in ***session*** *and I-*
Oh.
pant pant
I thought you was someone else.
Man, what were we doin' again?

"Tricks Of The Trade"

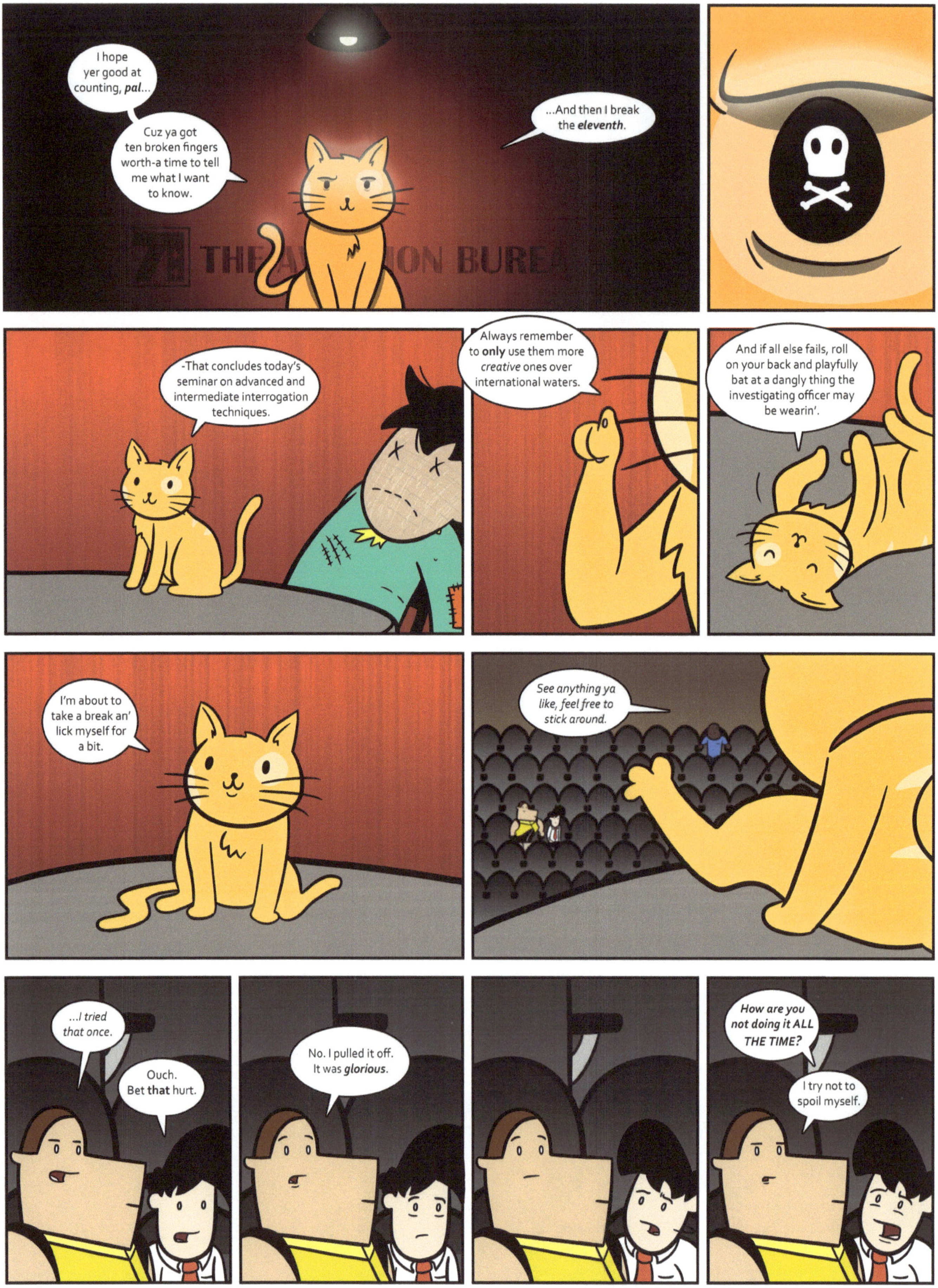
I hope yer good at counting, *pal*...
Cuz ya got ten broken fingers worth-a time to tell me what I want to know.
...And then I break the *eleventh*.
-That concludes today's seminar on advanced and intermediate interrogation techniques.
Always remember to **only** use them more *creative* ones over international waters.
And if all else fails, roll on your back and playfully bat at a dangly thing the investigating officer may be wearin'.
I'm about to take a break an' lick myself for a bit.
See anything ya like, feel free to stick around.
...I tried that once.
Ouch. Bet **that** hurt.
No. I pulled it off. It was ***glorious***.
How are you not doing it ALL THE TIME?
I try not to spoil myself.

"Let's Go Exploring"

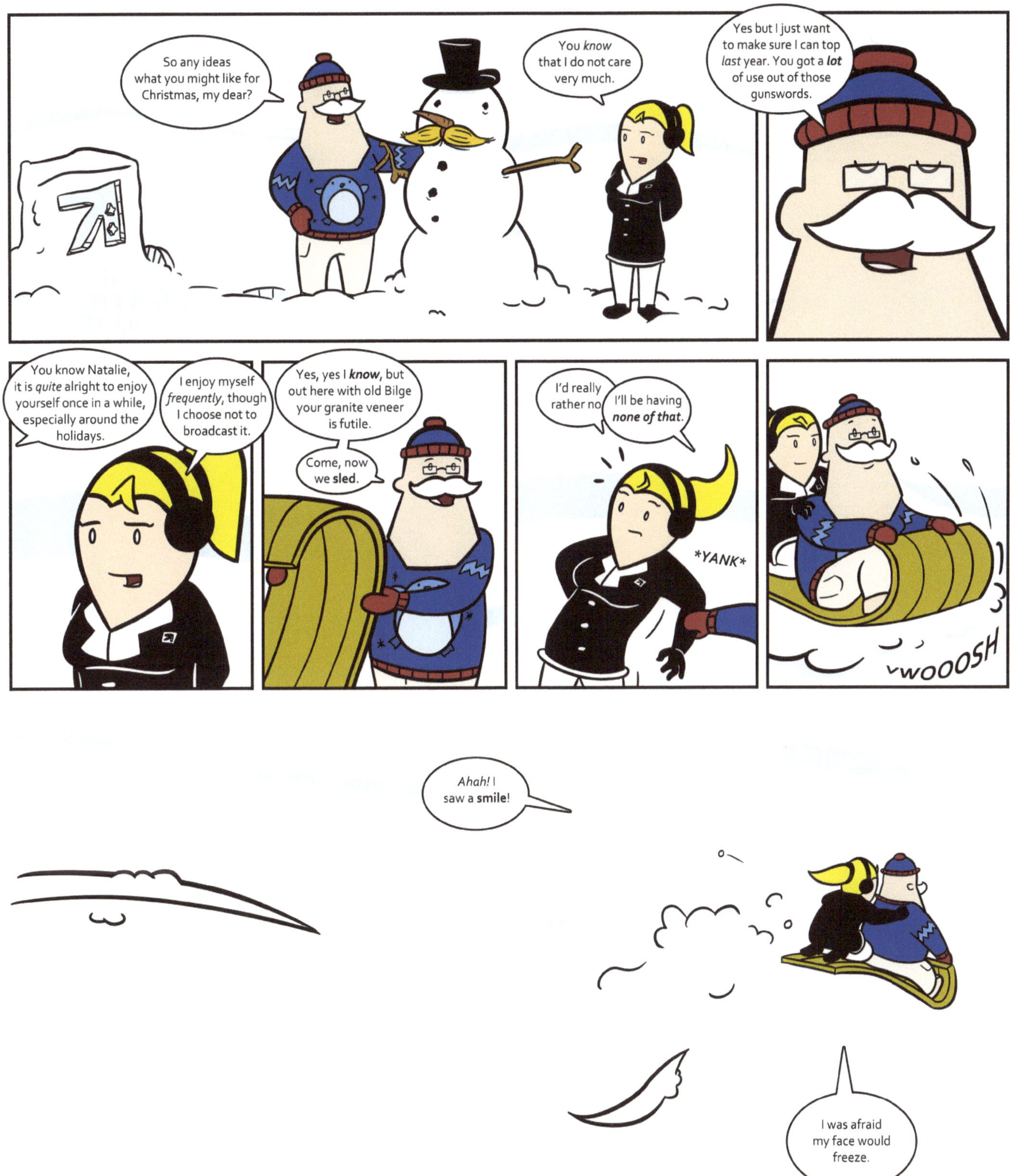

So any ideas what you might like for Christmas, my dear?
You *know* that I do not care very much.
Yes but I just want to make sure I can top *last* year. You got a ***lot*** of use out of those gunswords.
You know Natalie, it is *quite* alright to enjoy yourself once in a while, especially around the holidays.
I enjoy myself *frequently*, though I choose not to broadcast it.
Yes, yes I ***know***, but out here with old Bilge your granite veneer is futile.
Come, now we **sled**.
I'd really rather no
I'll be having ***none of that***.
YANK
WOOOSH
Ahah! I saw a **smile**!
I was afraid my face would freeze.

"Season's Greetings"

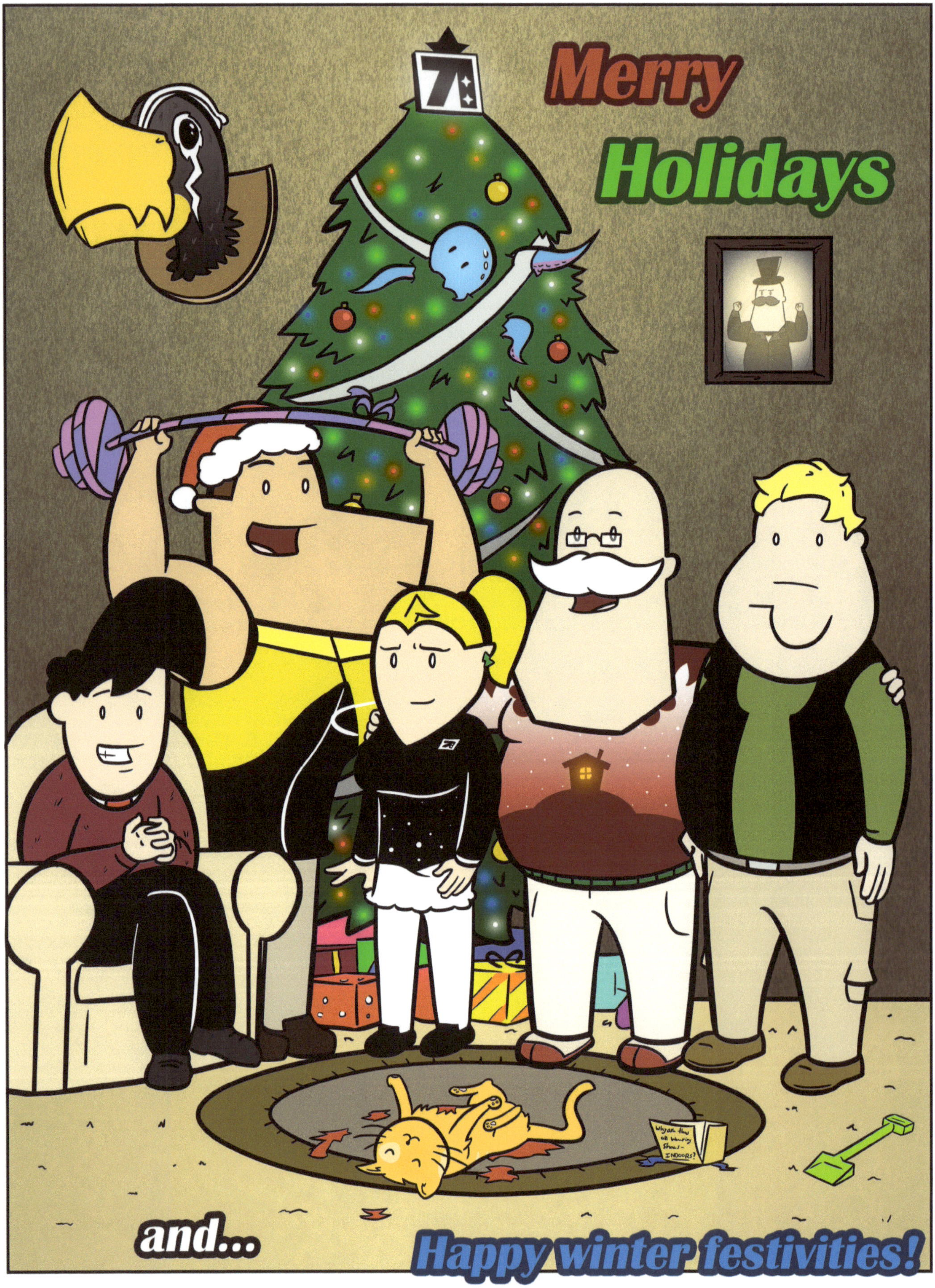
Merry
Holidays
Why are they all wearing shoes - INDOORS?
and...
Happy winter festivities!

"The Morning After"

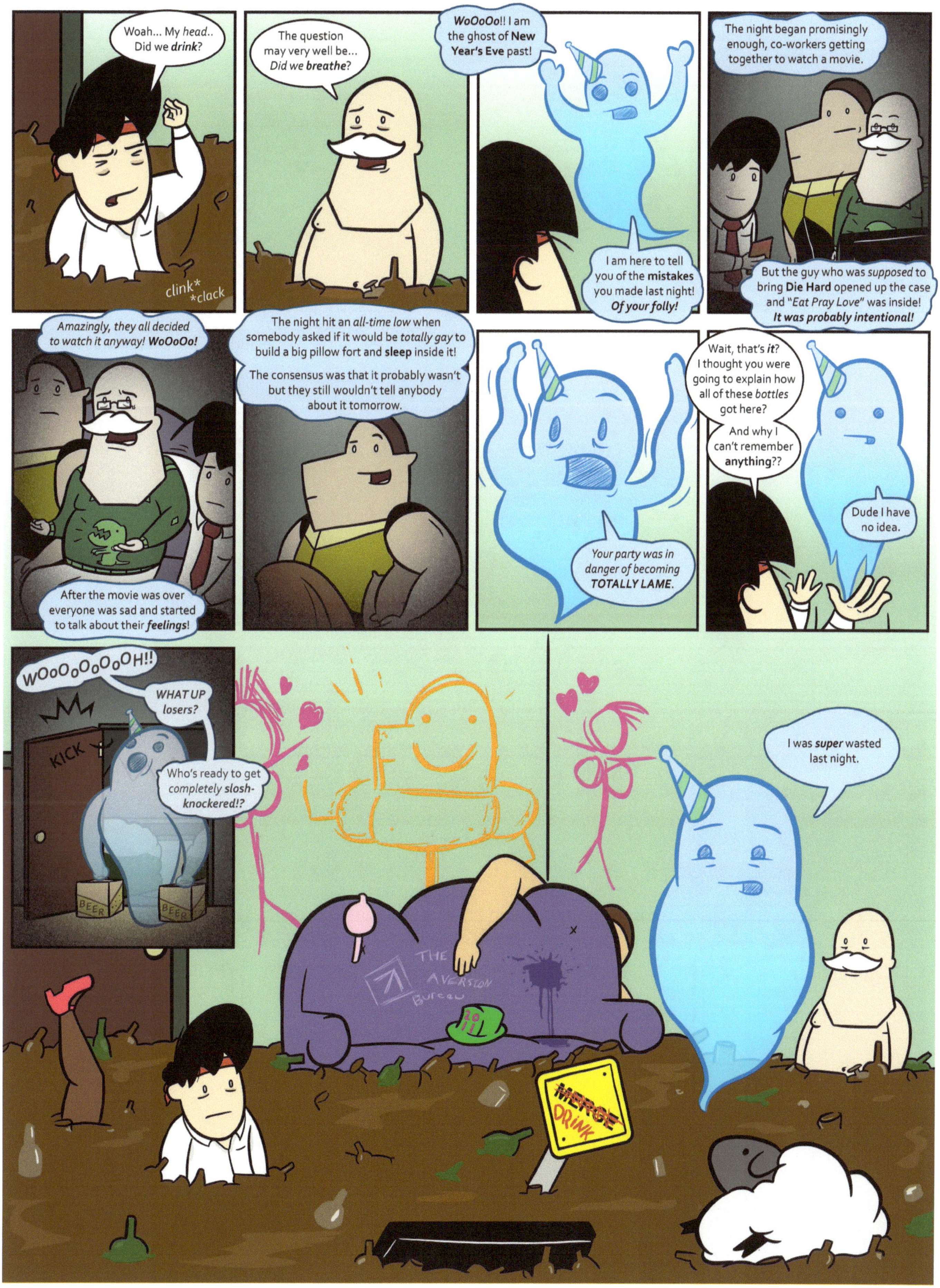
Woah... My *head*.. Did we **drink**?
clink* *clack
The question may very well be... *Did we* **breathe**?
WoOoOo!! I am the ghost of **New Year's Eve** past!
I am here to tell you of the **mistakes** you made last night! ***Of your folly!***
The night began promisingly enough, co-workers getting together to watch a movie.
But the guy who was *supposed* to bring **Die Hard** opened up the case and *"Eat Pray Love"* was inside! ***It was probably intentional!***
Amazingly, they all decided to watch it anyway! ***WoOoOo!***
After the movie was over everyone was sad and started to talk about their ***feelings***!
The night hit an *all-time low* when somebody asked if it would be *totally gay* to build a big pillow fort and **sleep** inside it!
The consensus was that it probably wasn't but they still wouldn't tell anybody about it tomorrow.
Your party was in danger of becoming ***TOTALLY LAME.***
Wait, that's ***it***? I thought you were going to explain how all of these *bottles* got here?
And why I can't remember **anything**??
Dude I have no idea.
WOOOOOOOOOH!!
WHAT UP losers?
KICK
Who's ready to get completely ***slosh-knockered!?***
BEER
BEER
THE AVERSION Bureau
MERGE
DRINK
I was ***super*** wasted last night.

"Oh How It Would Be"

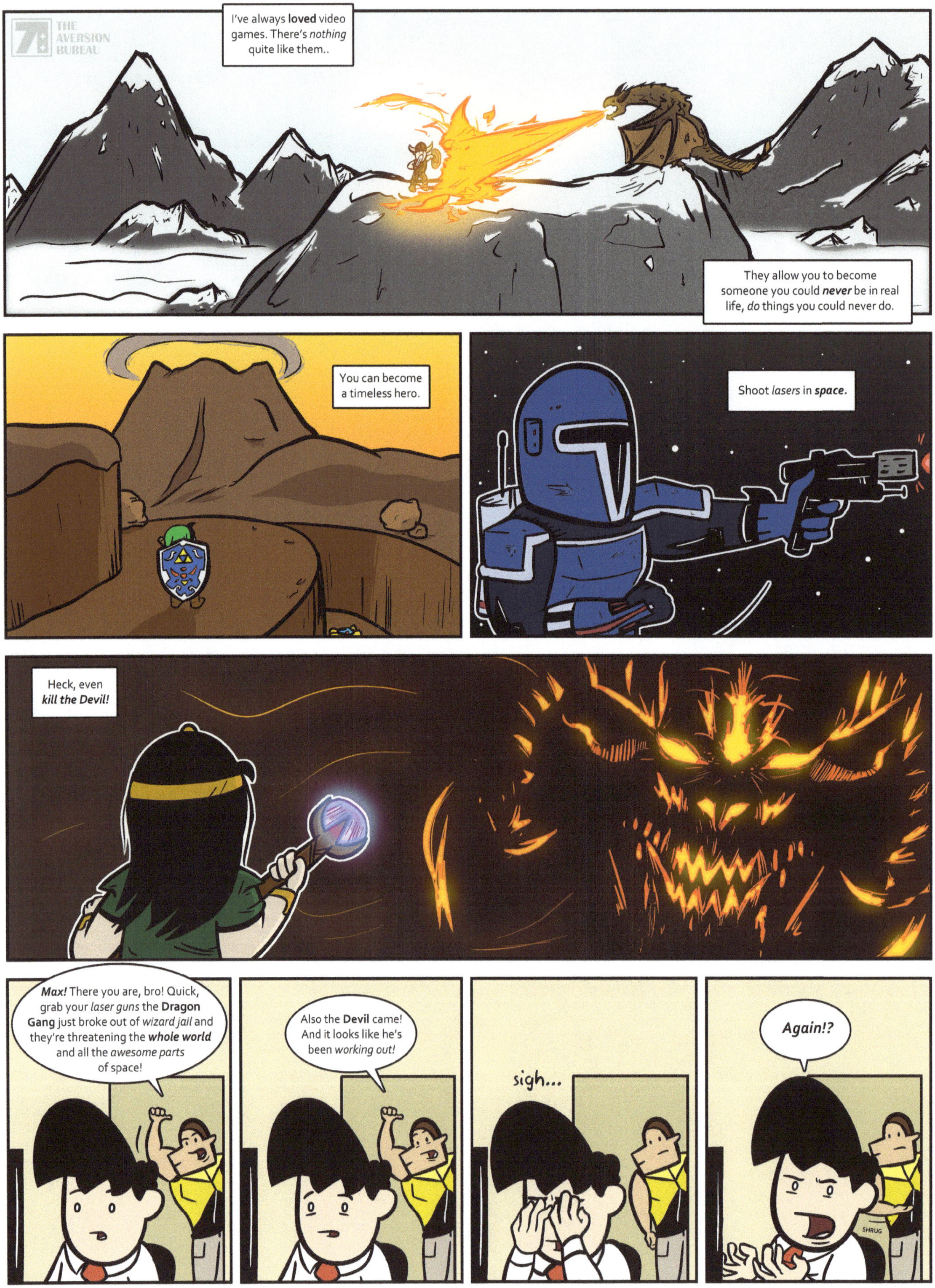
I've always **loved** video games. There's *nothing* quite like them..
They allow you to become someone you could ***never*** be in real life, *do* things you could never do.
You can become a timeless hero.
Shoot *lasers* in ***space.***
Heck, even ***kill the Devil!***
Max! There you are, bro! Quick, grab your *laser guns* the **Dragon Gang** just broke out of *wizard jail* and they're threatening the ***whole world*** and all the *awesome parts* of space!
Also the **Devil** came! And it looks like he's been *working out!*
sigh...
Again!?
SHRUG

"Retirement Plan"

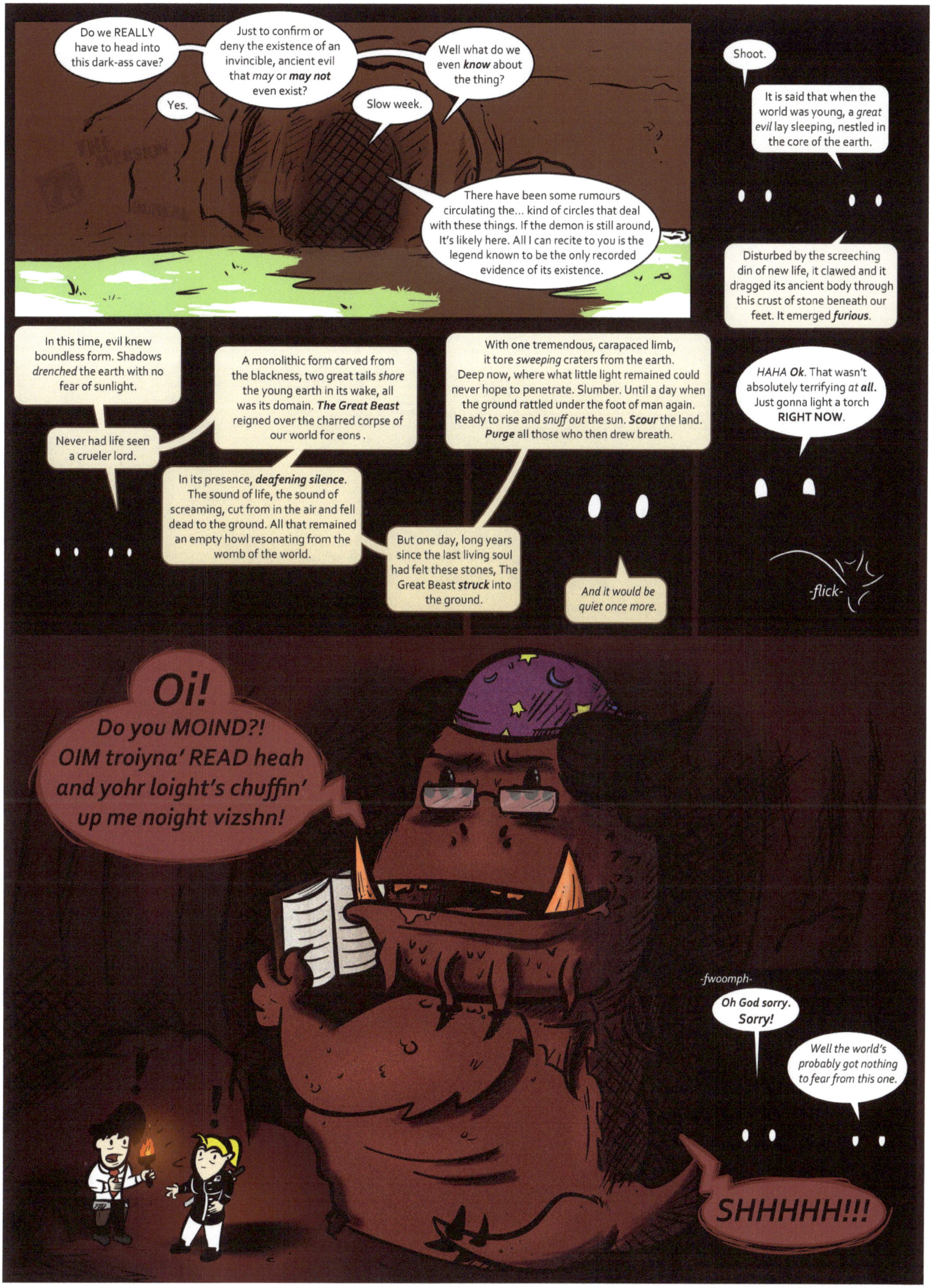

Do we REALLY have to head into this dark-ass cave?
Just to confirm or deny the existence of an invincible, ancient evil that *may* or ***may not*** even exist?
Yes.
Well what do we even ***know*** about the thing?
Slow week.
There have been some rumours circulating the... kind of circles that deal with these things. If the demon is still around, It's likely here. All I can recite to you is the legend known to be the only recorded evidence of its existence.
Shoot.
It is said that when the world was young, a *great evil* lay sleeping, nestled in the core of the earth.
Disturbed by the screeching din of new life, it clawed and it dragged its ancient body through this crust of stone beneath our feet. It emerged ***furious***.
In this time, evil knew boundless form. Shadows *drenched* the earth with no fear of sunlight.
Never had life seen a crueler lord.
A monolithic form carved from the blackness, two great tails *shore* the young earth in its wake, all was its domain. ***The Great Beast*** reigned over the charred corpse of our world for eons .
In its presence, ***deafening silence***. The sound of life, the sound of screaming, cut from in the air and fell dead to the ground. All that remained an empty howl resonating from the womb of the world.
With one tremendous, carapaced limb, it tore *sweeping* craters from the earth. Deep now, where what little light remained could never hope to penetrate. Slumber. Until a day when the ground rattled under the foot of man again. Ready to rise and *snuff out* the sun. ***Scour*** the land. ***Purge*** all those who then drew breath.
But one day, long years since the last living soul had felt these stones, The Great Beast ***struck*** into the ground.
And it would be quiet once more.
HAHA ***Ok***. That wasn't absolutely terrifying *at* ***all***. Just gonna light a torch **RIGHT NOW**.
-flick-
Oi!
Do you MOIND?! OIM troiyna' READ heah and yohr loight's chuffin' up me noight vizshn!
-fwoomph-
Oh God sorry. Sorry!
Well the world's probably got nothing to fear from this one.
SHHHHH!!!

Note from the author: I am aware this is an incorrect usage of the word 'chuff'. Time makes fools of us all.

"Setting The Bar Low"

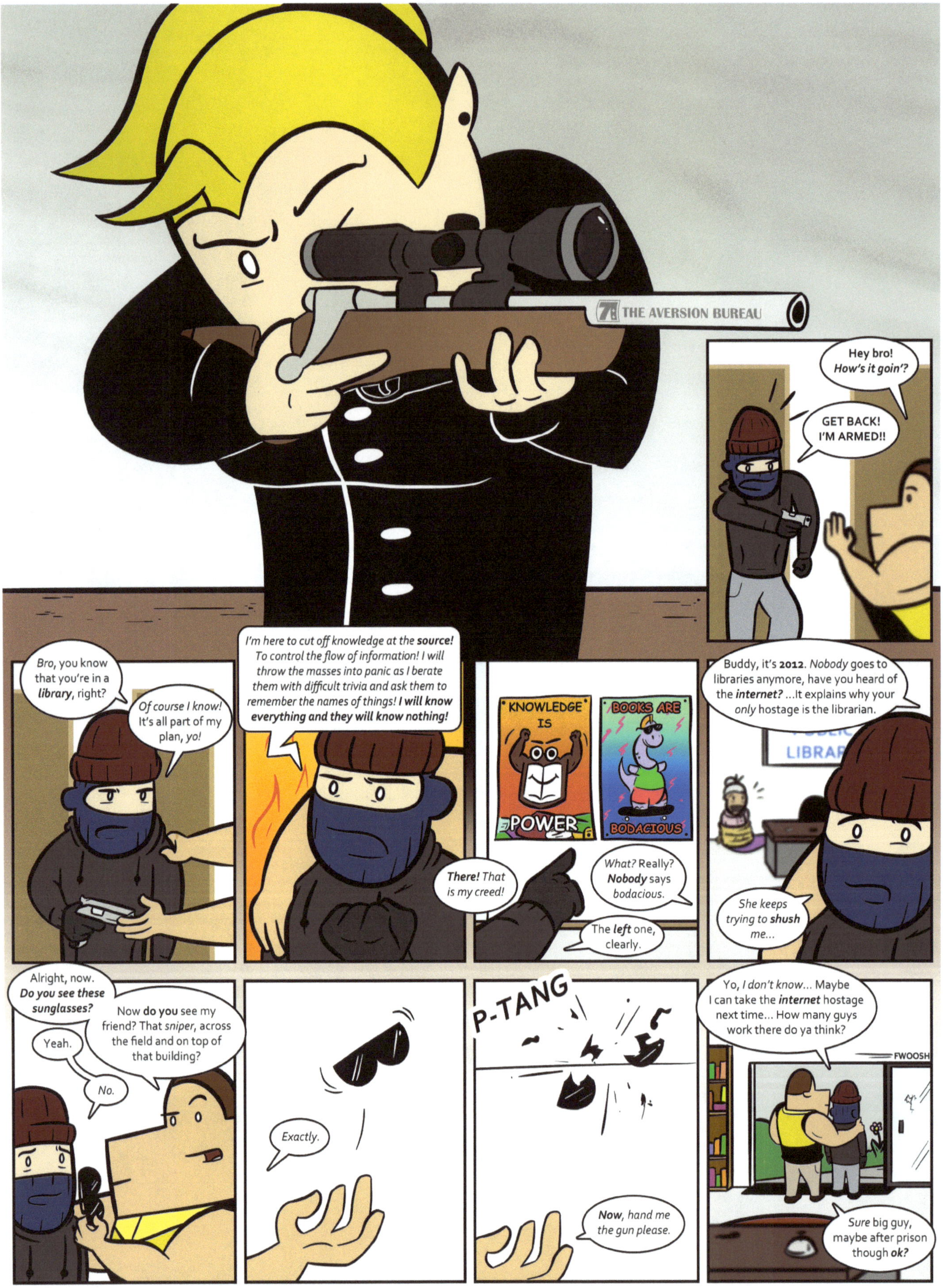
THE AVERSION BUREAU
Hey bro! How's it goin'?
GET BACK! I'M ARMED!!
Bro, you know that you're in a library, right?
Of course I know! It's all part of my plan, yo!
I'm here to cut off knowledge at the source! To control the flow of information! I will throw the masses into panic as I berate them with difficult trivia and ask them to remember the names of things! I will know everything and they will know nothing!
KNOWLEDGE IS POWER
BOOKS ARE BODACIOUS
There! That is my creed!
What? Really? Nobody says bodacious.
The left one, clearly.
Buddy, it's 2012. Nobody goes to libraries anymore, have you heard of the internet? ...It explains why your only hostage is the librarian.
She keeps trying to shush me...
Alright, now. Do you see these sunglasses?
Yeah.
Now do you see my friend? That sniper, across the field and on top of that building?
No.
Exactly.
P-TANG
Now, hand me the gun please.
Yo, I don't know... Maybe I can take the internet hostage next time... How many guys work there do ya think?
FWOOSH
Sure big guy, maybe after prison though ok?

"Magic Of The Mind"

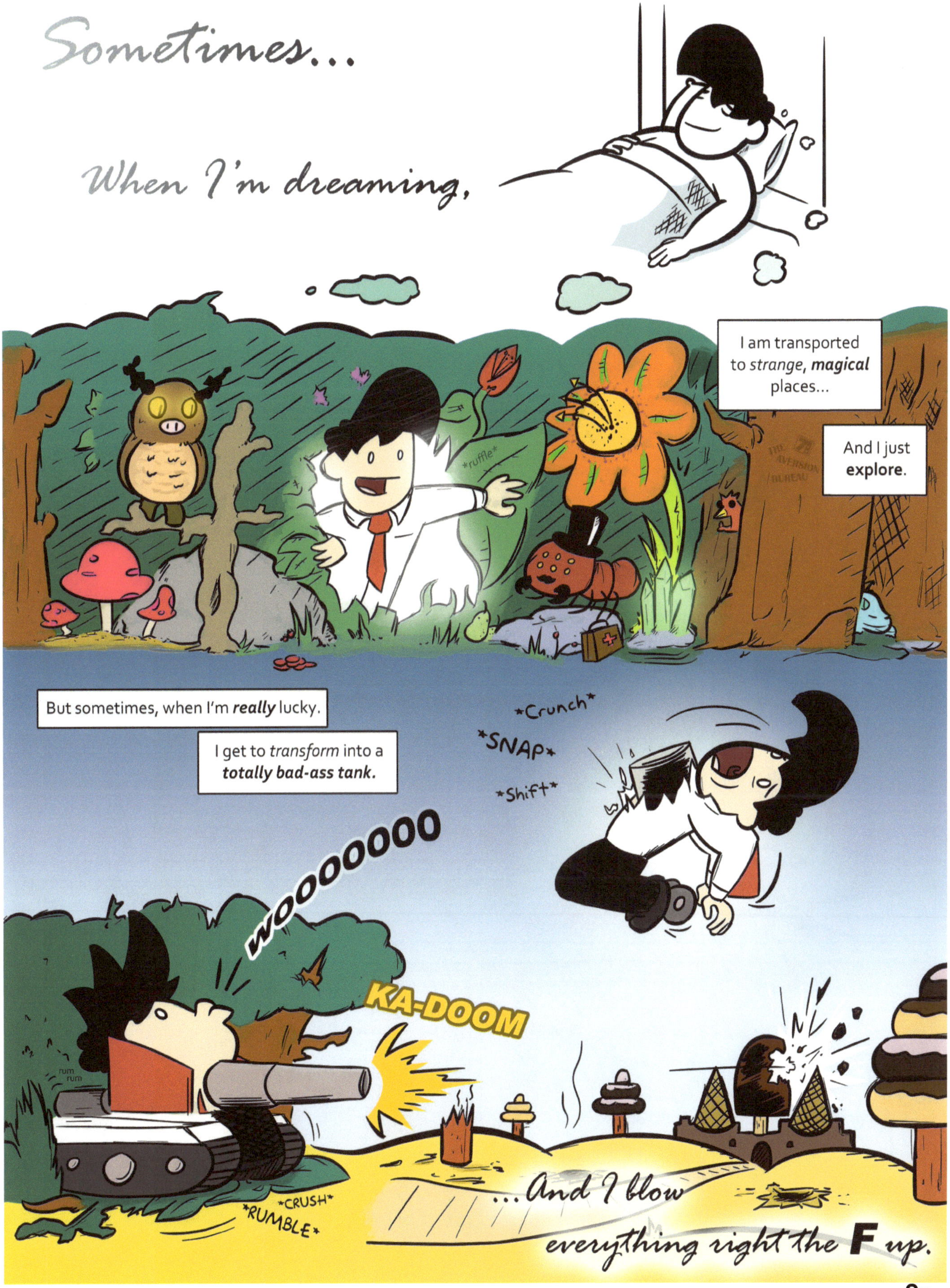

Sometimes...
When I'm dreaming,
I am transported to *strange*, ***magical*** places...
And I just **explore**.
ruffle
But sometimes, when I'm ***really*** lucky.
I get to *transform* into a ***totally bad-ass tank.***
Crunch
SNAP
Shift
WOOOOOOO
KA-DOOM
rum rum
CRUSH
RUMBLE
...And I blow everything right the F up.

"Let Your Heart Sing"

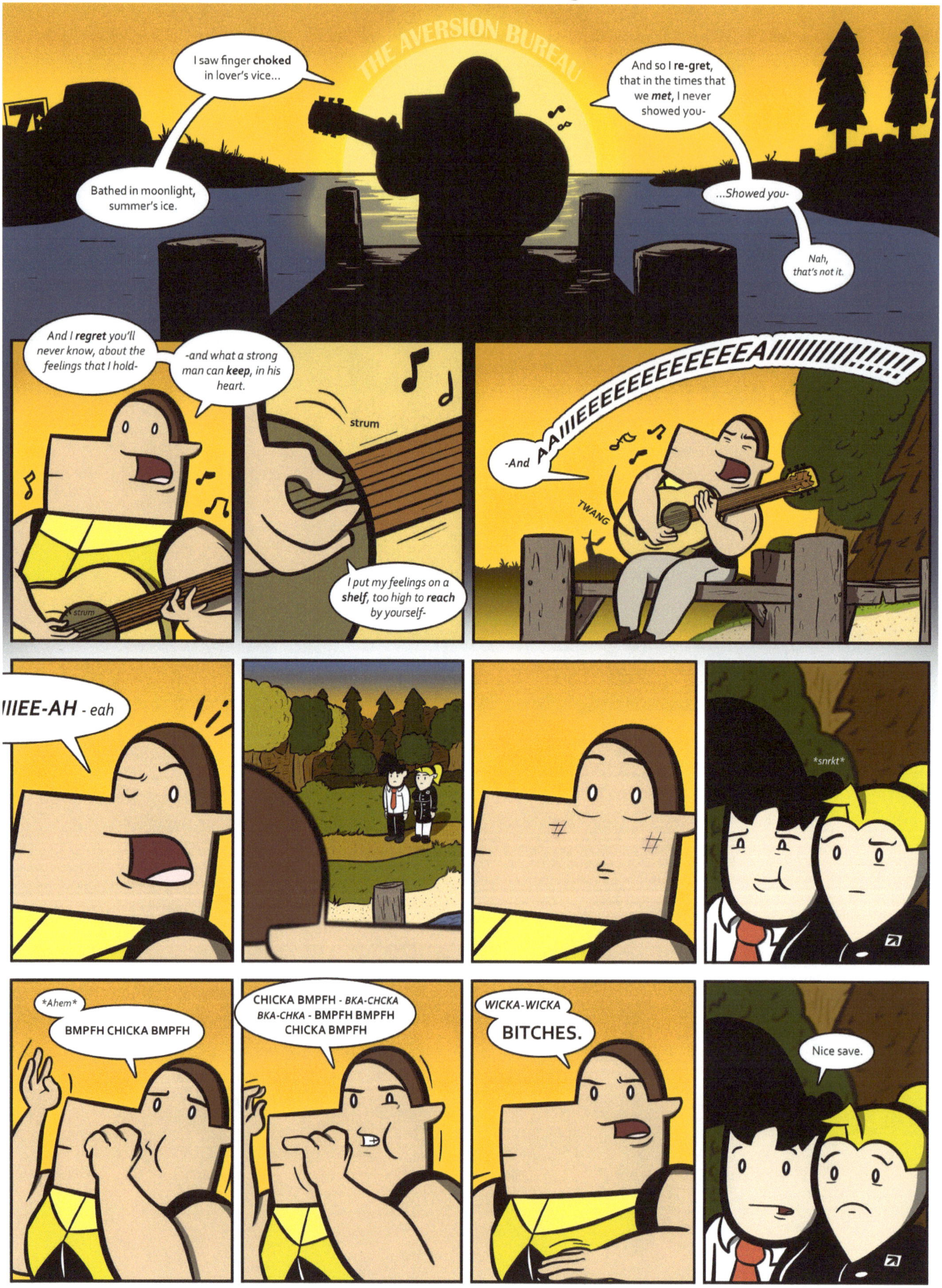
THE AVERSION BUREAU
I saw finger **choked** in lover's vice...
Bathed in moonlight, summer's ice.
And so I **re-gret**, that in the times that we **met**, I never showed you-
...Showed you-
Nah, that's not it.
*And I **regret** you'll never know, about the feelings that I hold-*
*-and what a strong man can **keep**, in his heart.*
strum
strum
*I put my feelings on a **shelf**, too high to **reach** by yourself-*
-And AAIIIEEEEEEEEEEEEEA!!!!!!!!!!!!!!
TWANG
IIEE-AH - *eah*
snrkt
Ahem
BMPFH CHICKA BMPFH
CHICKA BMPFH - *BKA-CHCKA BKA-CHKA* - BMPFH BMPFH CHICKA BMPFH
WICKA-WICKA
BITCHES.
Nice save.

"Last Stand"

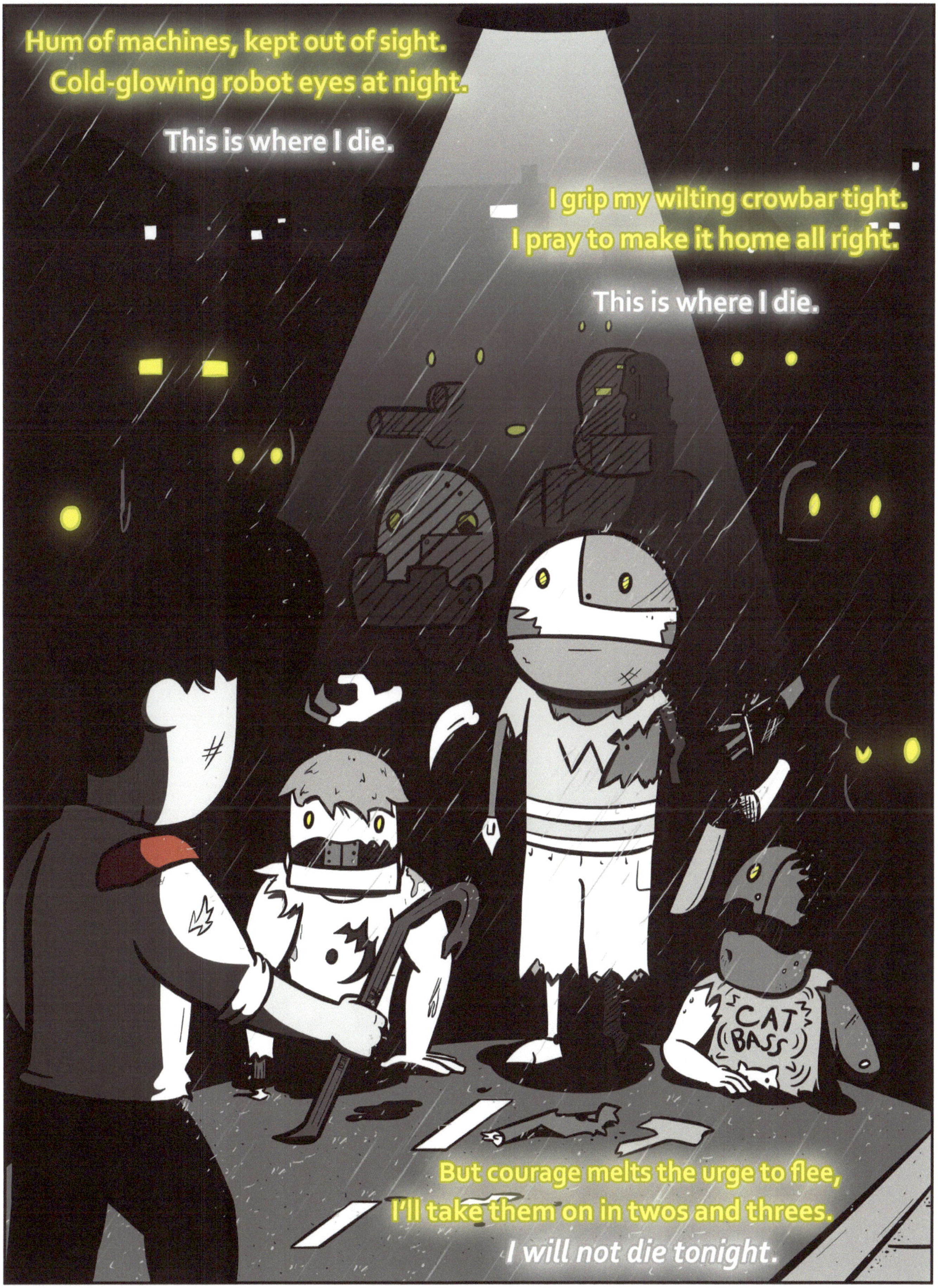
Hum of machines, kept out of sight.
Cold-glowing robot eyes at night.
This is where I die.
I grip my wilting crowbar tight.
I pray to make it home all right.
This is where I die.
CAT BASS
But courage melts the urge to flee,
I'll take them on in twos and threes.
I will not die tonight.

"And All The Other Places Too"

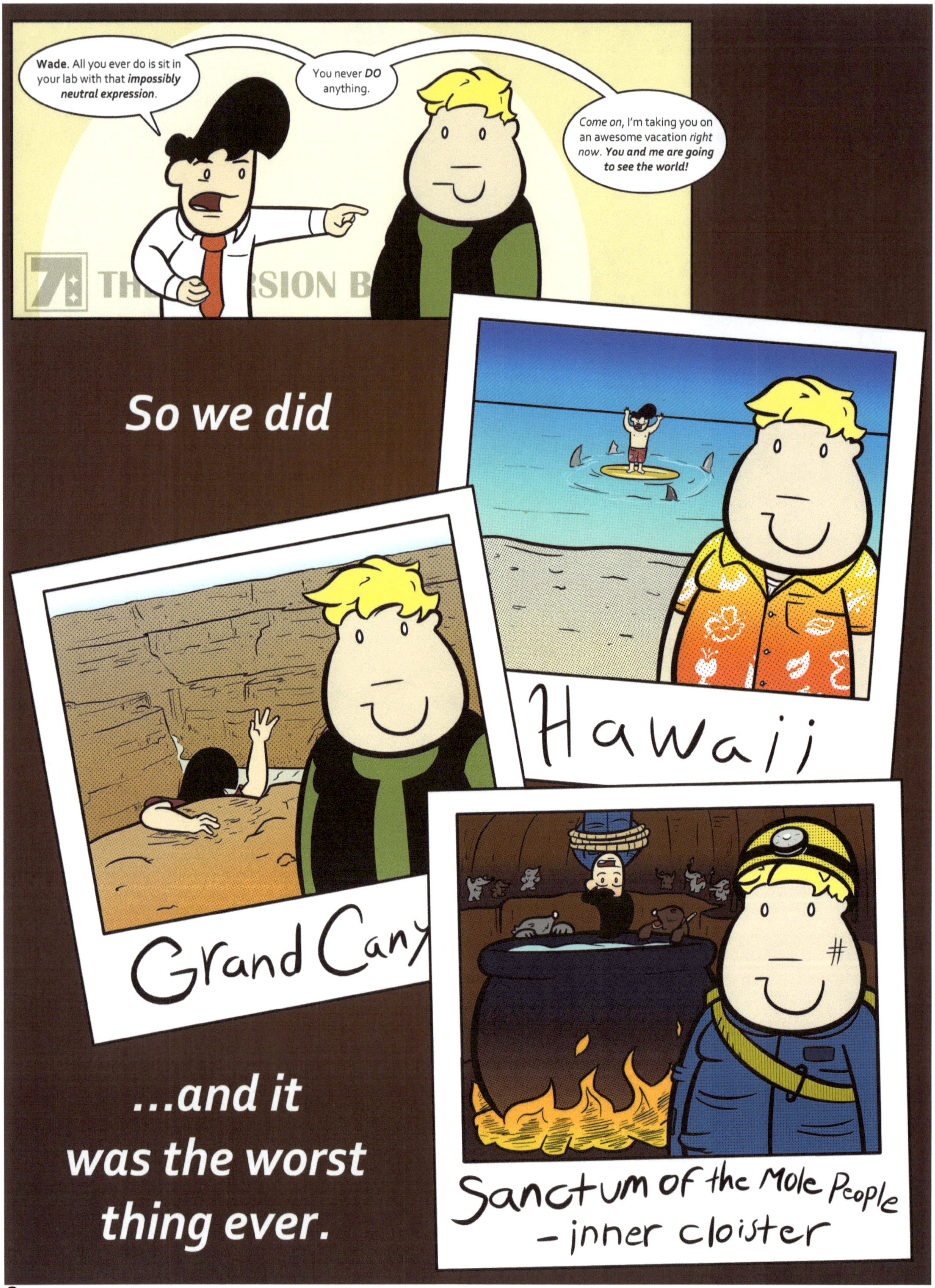

Wade. All you ever do is sit in your lab with that ***impossibly neutral expression***.
You never ***DO*** anything.
Come on, I'm taking you on an awesome vacation *right now*. ***You and me are going to see the world!***
So we did
Hawaii
Grand Cany
Sanctum of the Mole People - inner cloister
...and it was the worst thing ever.

"Max And Wade's Totally Bogus Trip"

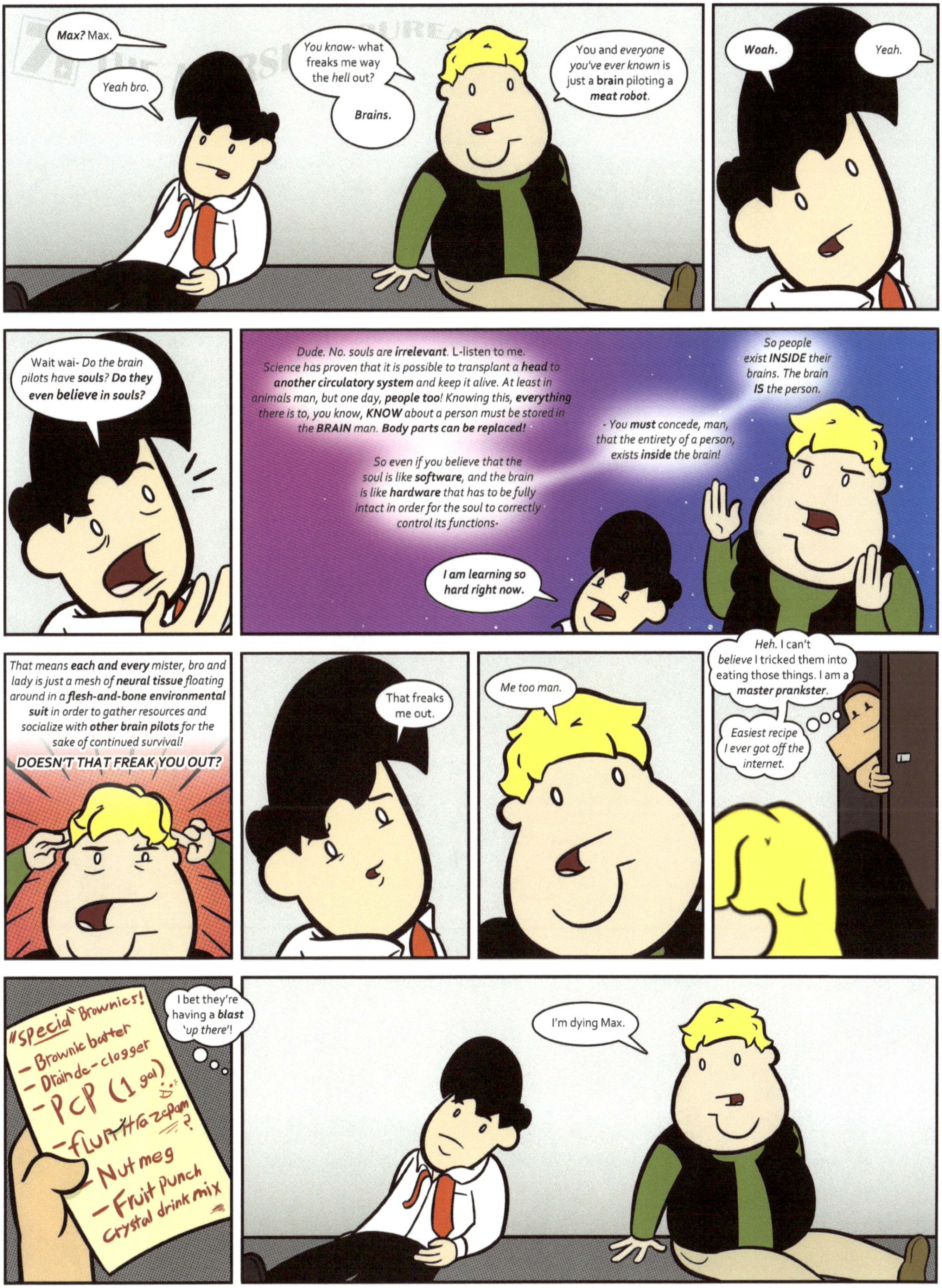

Max? Max.
Yeah bro.
You know- what freaks me way the *hell* out?
Brains.
You and everyone you've ever known is just a **brain** piloting a ***meat robot***.
Woah.
Yeah.
Wait wai- *Do the brain pilots have **souls**? **Do they even believe in souls?***
*Dude. No. souls are **irrelevant**. L-listen to me. Science has proven that it is possible to transplant a **head** to **another circulatory system** and keep it alive. At least in animals man, but one day, **people too**! Knowing this, **everything** there is to, you know, **KNOW** about a person must be stored in the **BRAIN** man. **Body parts can be replaced!***
*So even if you believe that the soul is like **software**, and the brain is like **hardware** that has to be fully intact in order for the soul to correctly control its functions-*
*- You **must** concede, man, that the entirety of a person, exists **inside** the brain!*
*So people exist **INSIDE** their brains. The brain **IS** the person.*
I am learning so hard right now.
*That means **each and every** mister, bro and lady is just a mesh of **neural tissue** floating around in a **flesh-and-bone environmental suit** in order to gather resources and socialize with **other brain pilots** for the sake of continued survival!*
DOESN'T THAT FREAK YOU OUT?
That freaks me out.
Me too man.
Heh. I can't *believe* I tricked them into eating those things. I am a ***master prankster***.
Easiest recipe I ever got off the internet.
"Special" Brownies!
- Brownie batter
- Drain de-clogger
- PCP (1 gal)
- flunitrazepam ?
- Nut meg
- Fruit punch crystal drink mix
I bet they're having a ***blast*** *'up there'*!
I'm dying Max.

"Alternative History"

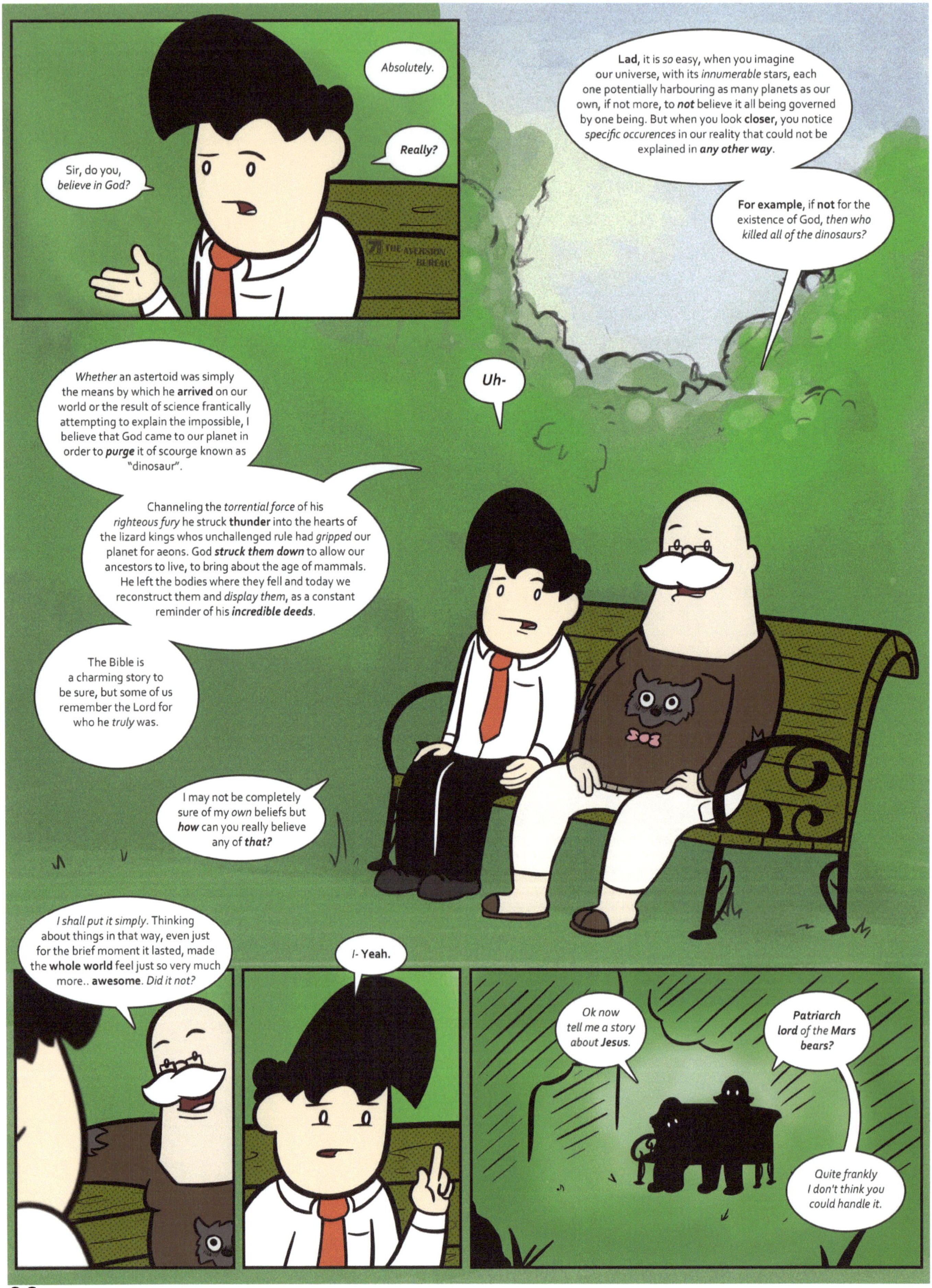

Sir, do you, believe in God?
Absolutely.
Really?
Lad, it is so easy, when you imagine our universe, with its innumerable stars, each one potentially harbouring as many planets as our own, if not more, to not believe it all being governed by one being. But when you look closer, you notice specific occurences in our reality that could not be explained in any other way.
For example, if not for the existence of God, then who killed all of the dinosaurs?
Uh-
Whether an astertoid was simply the means by which he arrived on our world or the result of science frantically attempting to explain the impossible, I believe that God came to our planet in order to purge it of scourge known as "dinosaur".
Channeling the torrential force of his righteous fury he struck thunder into the hearts of the lizard kings whos unchallenged rule had gripped our planet for aeons. God struck them down to allow our ancestors to live, to bring about the age of mammals. He left the bodies where they fell and today we reconstruct them and display them, as a constant reminder of his incredible deeds.
The Bible is a charming story to be sure, but some of us remember the Lord for who he truly was.
I may not be completely sure of my own beliefs but how can you really believe any of that?
I shall put it simply. Thinking about things in that way, even just for the brief moment it lasted, made the whole world feel just so very much more.. awesome. Did it not?
I- Yeah.
Ok now tell me a story about Jesus.
Patriarch lord of the Mars bears?
Quite frankly I don't think you could handle it.

"Ode To Battle"

There were four of us at the pub that night.
Right from the start I could tell they were looking to kick it off.

Taking up prime real-estate on the counter. Just ***waiting****.*
Sinister silouhettes glinting in the dim pub light.

Skinny-necked bastards*.*

The first one flips his lid and pours toward me-
I can't take them all on. Yet they are coming.

They are coming...

I take a shot from their leader, but it finds me staggered.
The second one is down, the floor is ***slick*** *with him.*

I have won*. I hold the final combatant aloft.*
He is gone. I lay him with his mates.

And as I take my well-earned rest I lay among them.
Who am I *to live while they are shattered?*

Who am I indeed.

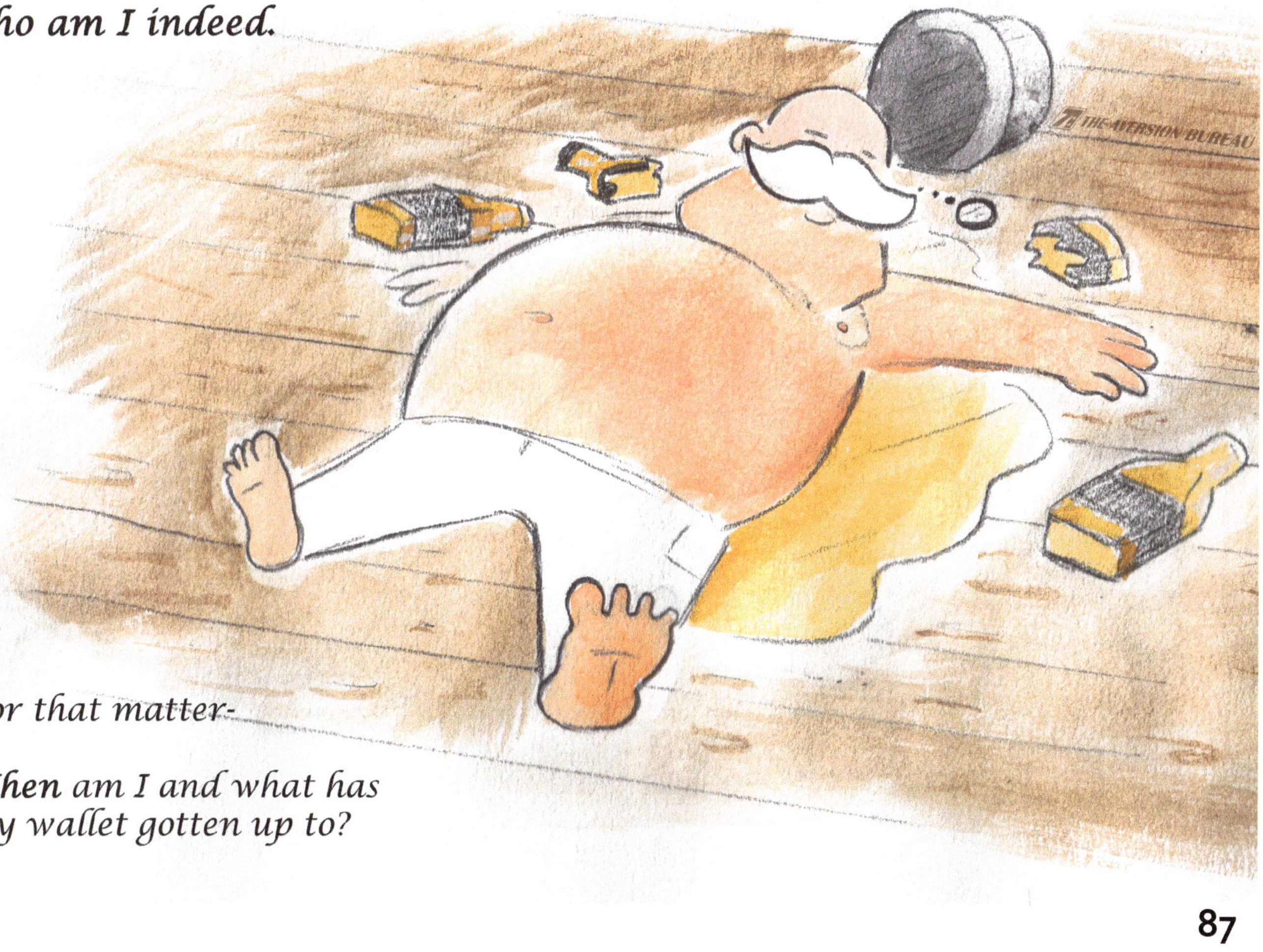
THE AVERSION BUREAU

For that matter-

When *am I and what has*
my wallet gotten up to?

"Skills That Pay Bills"

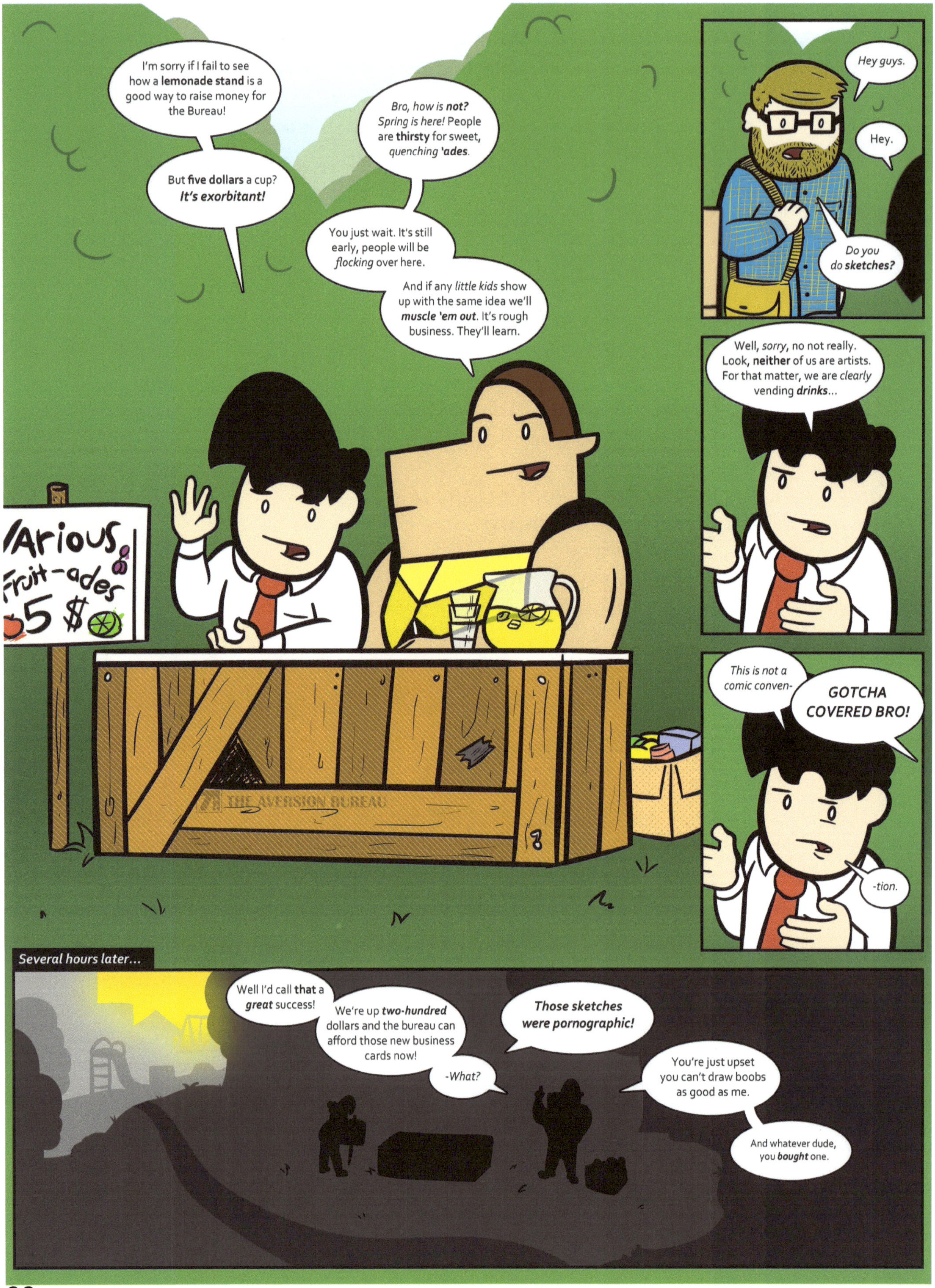

I'm sorry if I fail to see how a **lemonade stand** is a good way to raise money for the Bureau!
But **five dollars** a cup? ***It's exorbitant!***
Bro, how is ***not?*** *Spring is here!* People are **thirsty** for sweet, *quenching* ***'ades***.
You just wait. It's still early, people will be *flocking* over here.
And if any *little kids* show up with the same idea we'll ***muscle 'em out***. It's rough business. They'll learn.
Various Fruit-ades 5 $
THE AVERSION BUREAU
Hey guys.
Hey.
Do you do ***sketches?***
Well, *sorry*, no not really. Look, **neither** of us are artists. For that matter, we are *clearly* vending ***drinks***...
This is not a comic conven-
GOTCHA COVERED BRO!
-tion.
Several hours later...
Well I'd call **that** a ***great*** success!
We're up ***two-hundred*** dollars and the bureau can afford those new business cards now!
-What?
Those sketches were pornographic!
You're just upset you can't draw boobs as good as me.
And whatever dude, you ***bought*** one.

"Idle Hands Are The Bro's Playthings"

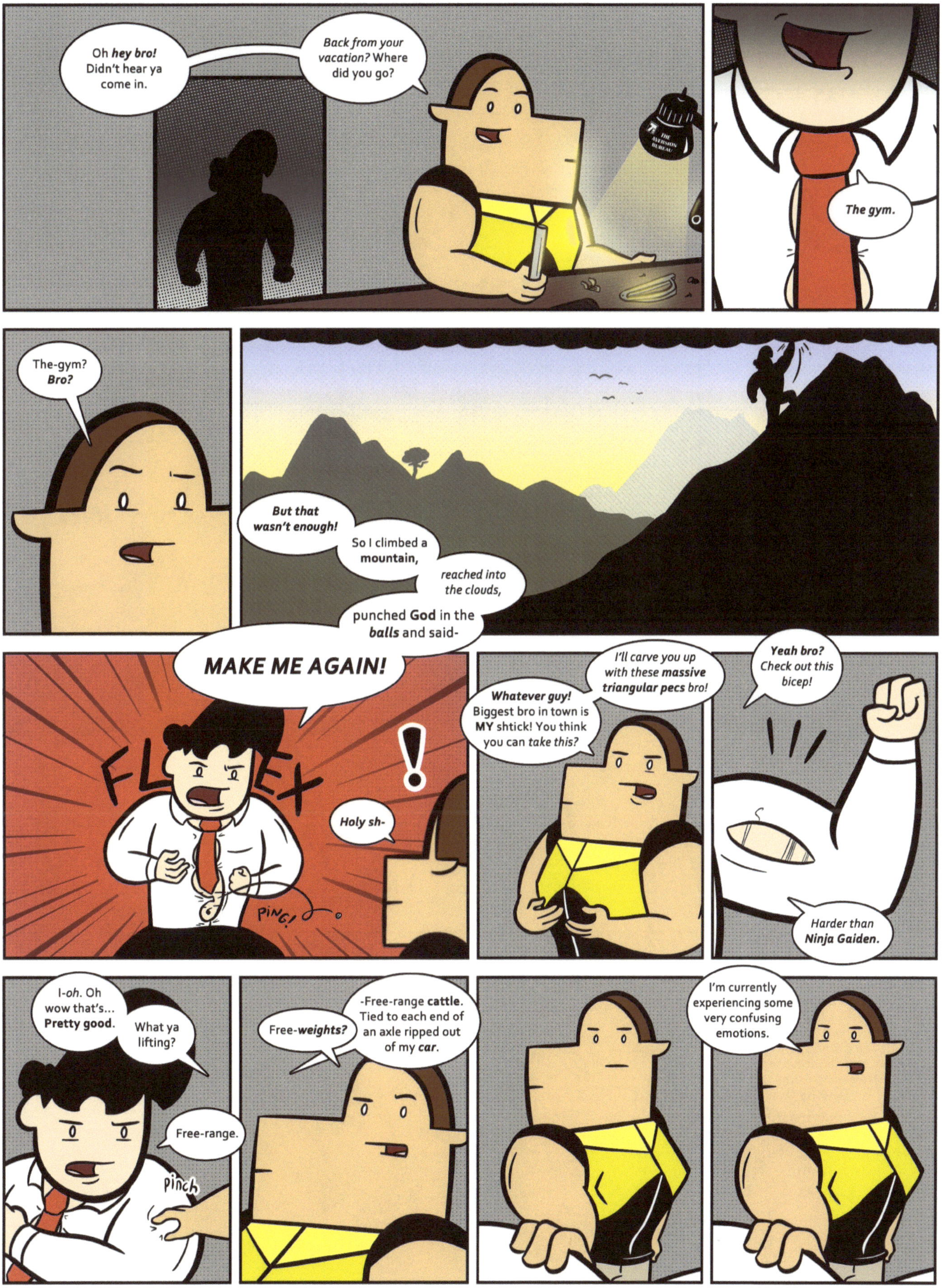
Oh hey bro! Didn't hear ya come in.
Back from your vacation? Where did you go?
THE AVERSION BUREAU
The gym.
The-gym? Bro?
But that wasn't enough!
So I climbed a mountain,
reached into the clouds,
punched God in the balls and said-
MAKE ME AGAIN!
FLEX
Holy sh-
PING!
I'll carve you up with these massive triangular pecs bro!
Whatever guy! Biggest bro in town is MY shtick! You think you can take this?
Yeah bro? Check out this bicep!
Harder than Ninja Gaiden.
I-oh. Oh wow that's... Pretty good.
What ya lifting?
Free-range.
pinch
Free-weights?
-Free-range cattle. Tied to each end of an axle ripped out of my car.
I'm currently experiencing some very confusing emotions.

"All Grown Up"

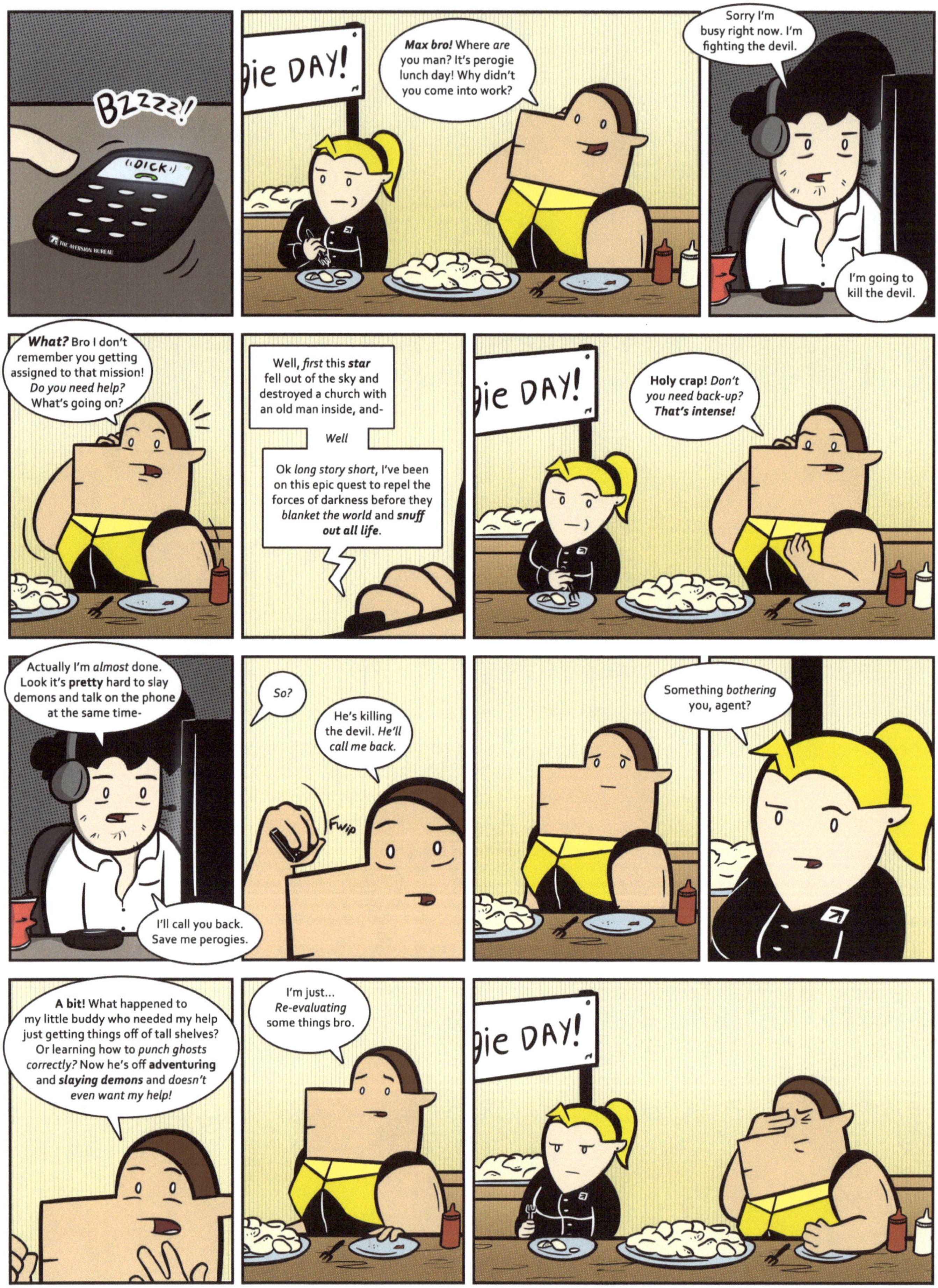
Bzzzz!
DICK
THE AVERSION BUREAU
gie DAY!
Max bro! Where *are* you man? It's perogie lunch day! Why didn't you come into work?
Sorry I'm busy right now. I'm fighting the devil.
I'm going to kill the devil.
What? Bro I don't remember you getting assigned to that mission! *Do you need help?* What's going on?
Well, *first* this ***star*** fell out of the sky and destroyed a church with an old man inside, and-
Well
Ok *long story short*, I've been on this epic quest to repel the forces of darkness before they *blanket the world* and ***snuff out all life***.
gie DAY!
Holy crap! *Don't you need back-up?* ***That's intense!***
Actually I'm *almost* done. Look it's **pretty** hard to slay demons and talk on the phone at the same time-
I'll call you back. Save me perogies.
So?
He's killing the devil. *He'll call me back.*
Fwip
Something *bothering* you, agent?
A bit! What happened to my little buddy who needed my help just getting things off of tall shelves? Or learning how to *punch ghosts correctly?* Now he's off **adventuring** and ***slaying demons*** and *doesn't even want my help!*
I'm just... *Re-evaluating* some things bro.
gie DAY!

"It Is Deafening"

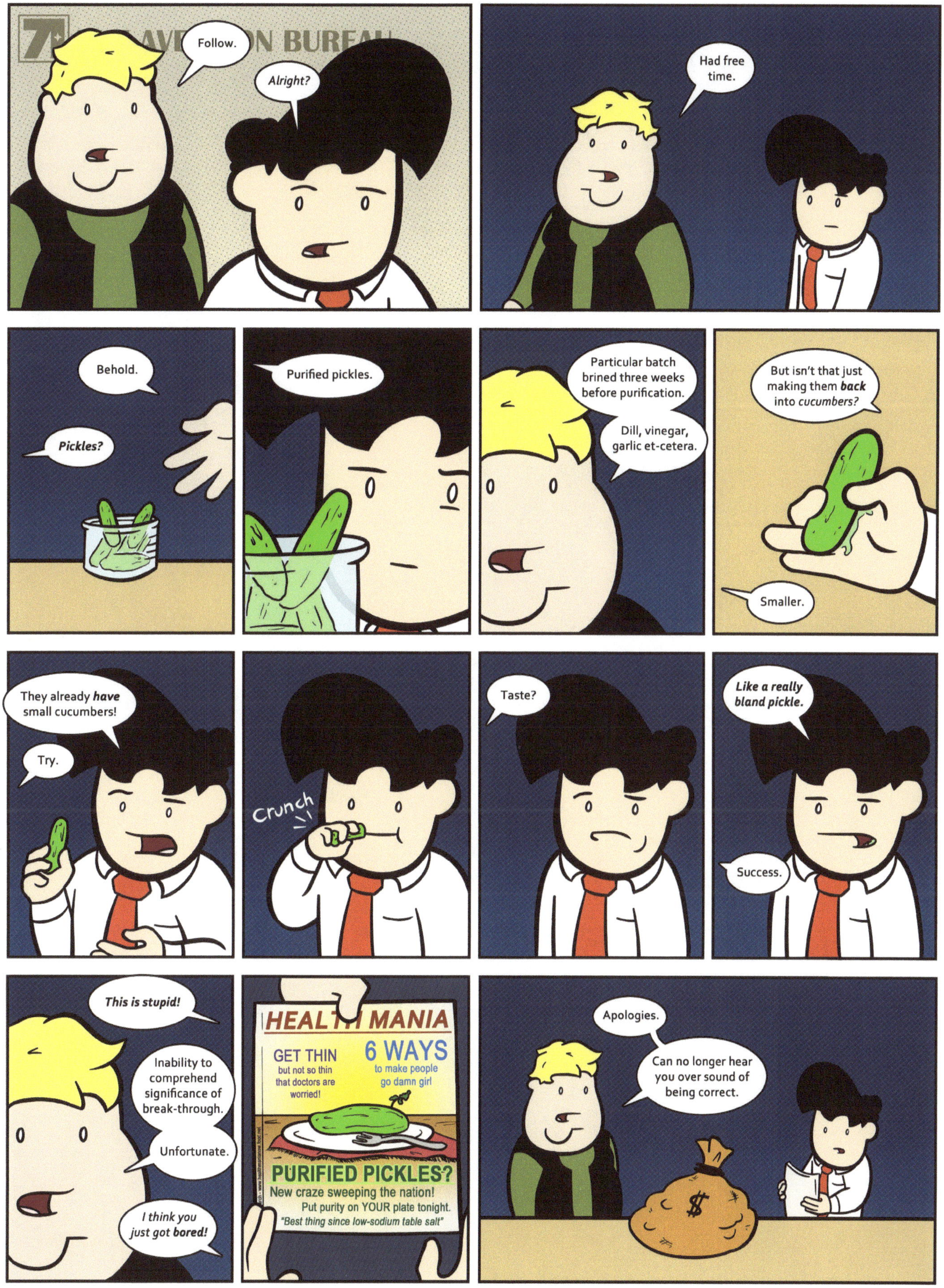
Follow.
Alright?
Had free time.
Behold.
Pickles?
Purified pickles.
Particular batch brined three weeks before purification.
Dill, vinegar, garlic et-cetera.
But isn't that just making them *back* into *cucumbers?*
Smaller.
They already *have* small cucumbers!
Try.
Crunch
Taste?
Like a really bland pickle.
Success.
This is stupid!
Inability to comprehend significance of break-through.
Unfortunate.
I think you just got bored!
HEALTH MANIA
GET THIN
but not so thin that doctors are worried!
6 WAYS
to make people go damn girl
PURIFIED PICKLES?
New craze sweeping the nation!
Put purity on YOUR plate tonight.
"Best thing since low-sodium table salt"
Apologies.
Can no longer hear you over sound of being correct.

"Turn Your Head"

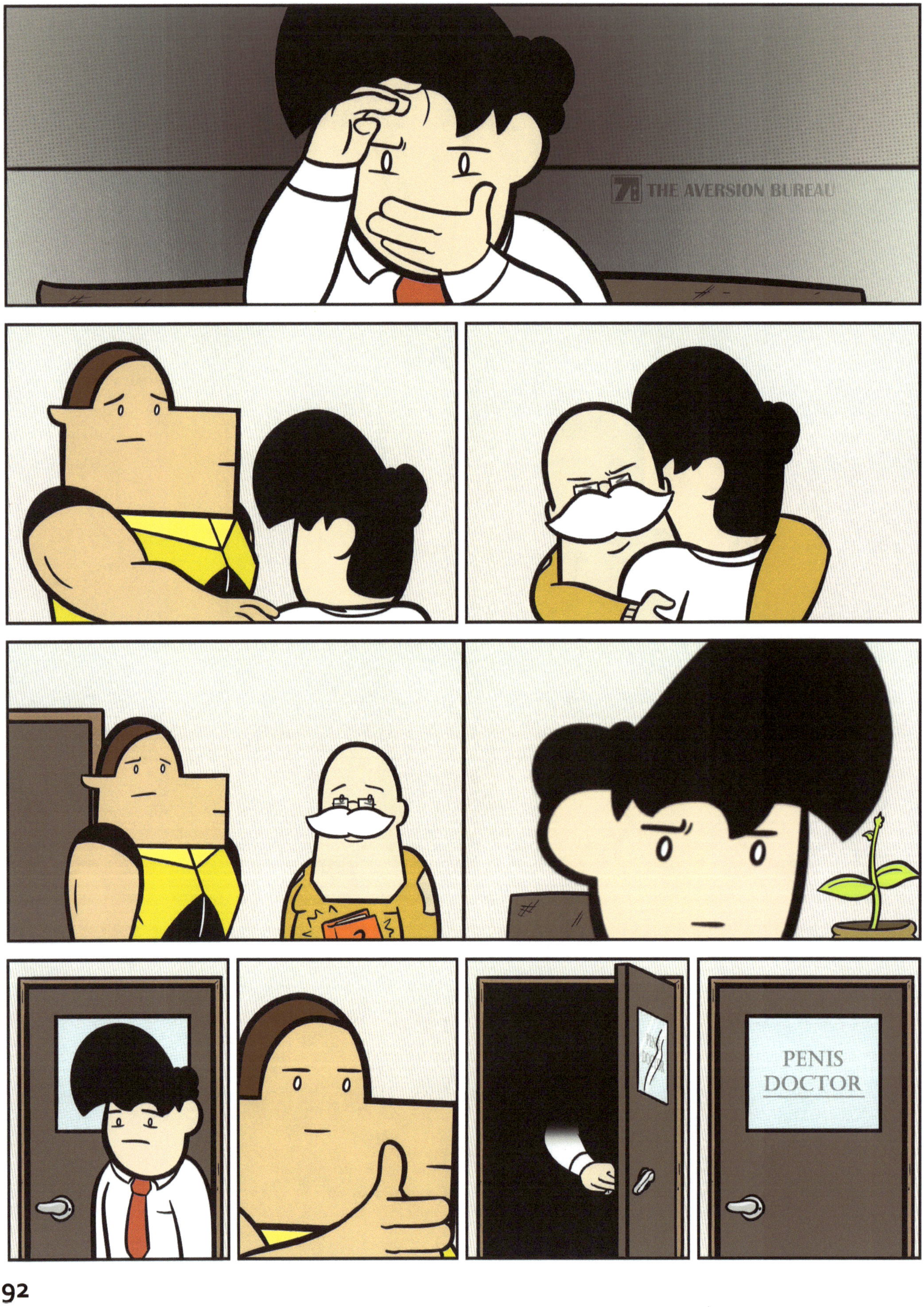
THE AVERSION BUREAU
PENIS
DOCTOR

"Showing Appreciation"

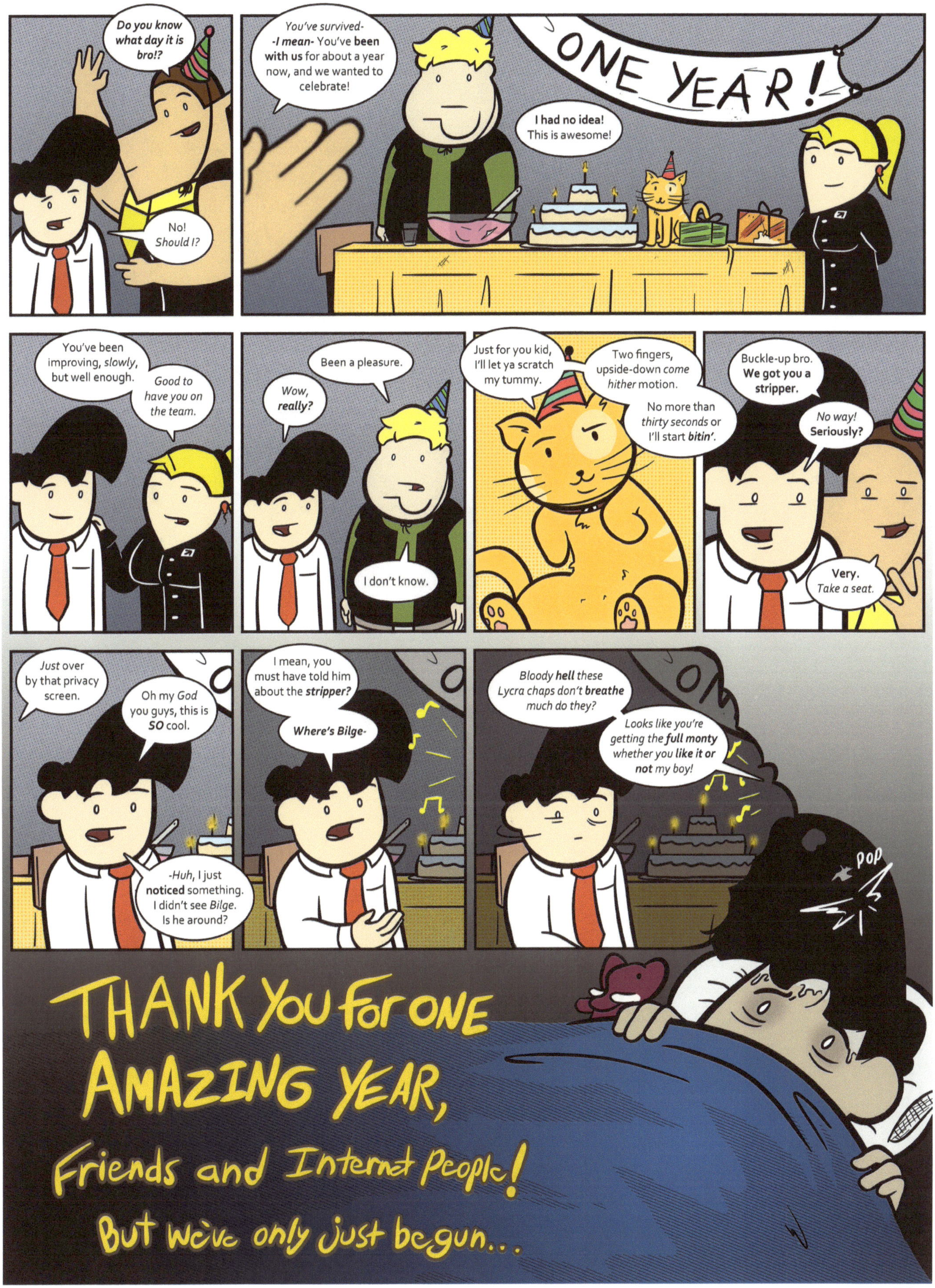

Do you know what day it is bro!?
No! *Should I?*
*You've survived- **-I mean-*** You've **been with us** for about a year now, and we wanted to celebrate!
ONE YEAR!
I had no idea! This is awesome!
You've been improving, *slowly*, but well enough.
Good to have you on the team.
*Wow, **really?***
Been a pleasure.
I don't know.
Just for you kid, I'll let ya scratch my tummy.
Two fingers, upside-down *come hither* motion.
No more than *thirty seconds* or I'll start ***bitin'***.
Buckle-up bro. **We got you a stripper.**
No way! **Seriously?**
Very. *Take a seat.*
Just over by that privacy screen.
Oh my *God* you guys, this is ***SO*** cool.
-Huh, I just **noticed** something. I didn't see *Bilge*. Is he around?
I mean, you must have told him about the ***stripper?***
Where's Bilge-
*Bloody **hell** these Lycra chaps don't **breathe** much do they?*
*Looks like you're getting the **full monty** whether you **like it** or **not** my boy!*
POP
THANK YOU for ONE AMAZING YEAR,
Friends and Internet People!
But we've only just begun...

"The Syllabic Imperative"

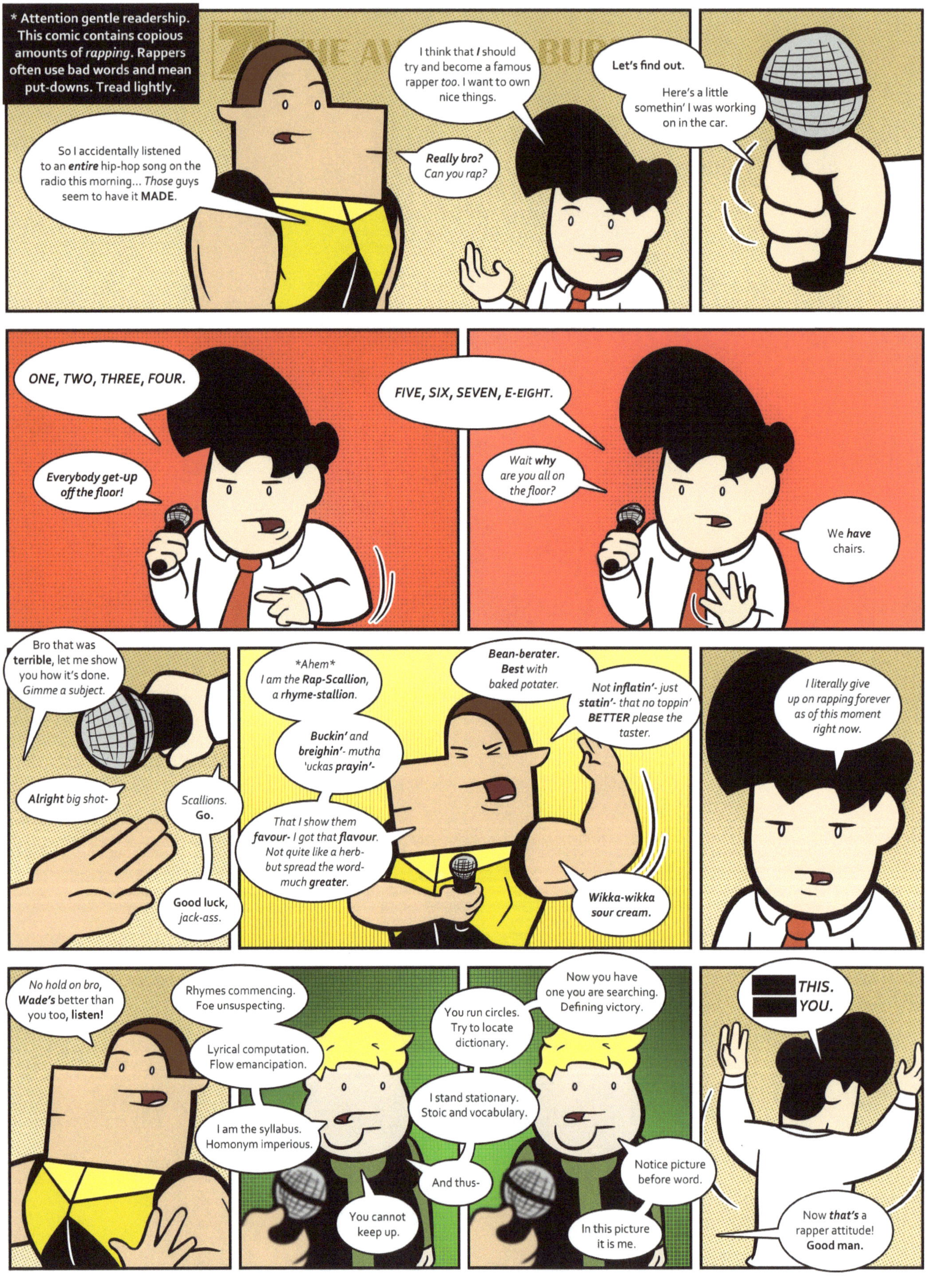
* Attention gentle readership. This comic contains copious amounts of rapping. Rappers often use bad words and mean put-downs. Tread lightly.
So I accidentally listened to an entire hip-hop song on the radio this morning... Those guys seem to have it MADE.
I think that I should try and become a famous rapper too. I want to own nice things.
Really bro? Can you rap?
Let's find out.
Here's a little somethin' I was working on in the car.
ONE, TWO, THREE, FOUR.
Everybody get-up off the floor!
FIVE, SIX, SEVEN, E-EIGHT.
Wait why are you all on the floor?
We have chairs.
Bro that was terrible, let me show you how it's done. Gimme a subject.
Alright big shot-
Scallions. Go.
Good luck, jack-ass.
Ahem I am the Rap-Scallion, a rhyme-stallion.
Buckin' and breighin'- mutha 'uckas prayin'-
That I show them favour- I got that flavour. Not quite like a herb- but spread the word- much greater.
Bean-berater. Best with baked potater.
Not inflatin'- just statin'- that no toppin' BETTER please the taster.
Wikka-wikka sour cream.
I literally give up on rapping forever as of this moment right now.
No hold on bro, Wade's better than you too, listen!
Rhymes commencing. Foe unsuspecting.
Lyrical computation. Flow emancipation.
I am the syllabus. Homonym imperious.
You cannot keep up.
You run circles. Try to locate dictionary.
Now you have one you are searching. Defining victory.
I stand stationary. Stoic and vocabulary.
And thus-
Notice picture before word.
In this picture it is me.
[redacted] THIS. [redacted] YOU.
Now that's a rapper attitude! Good man.

"The Syllabic Imperative Part 2"

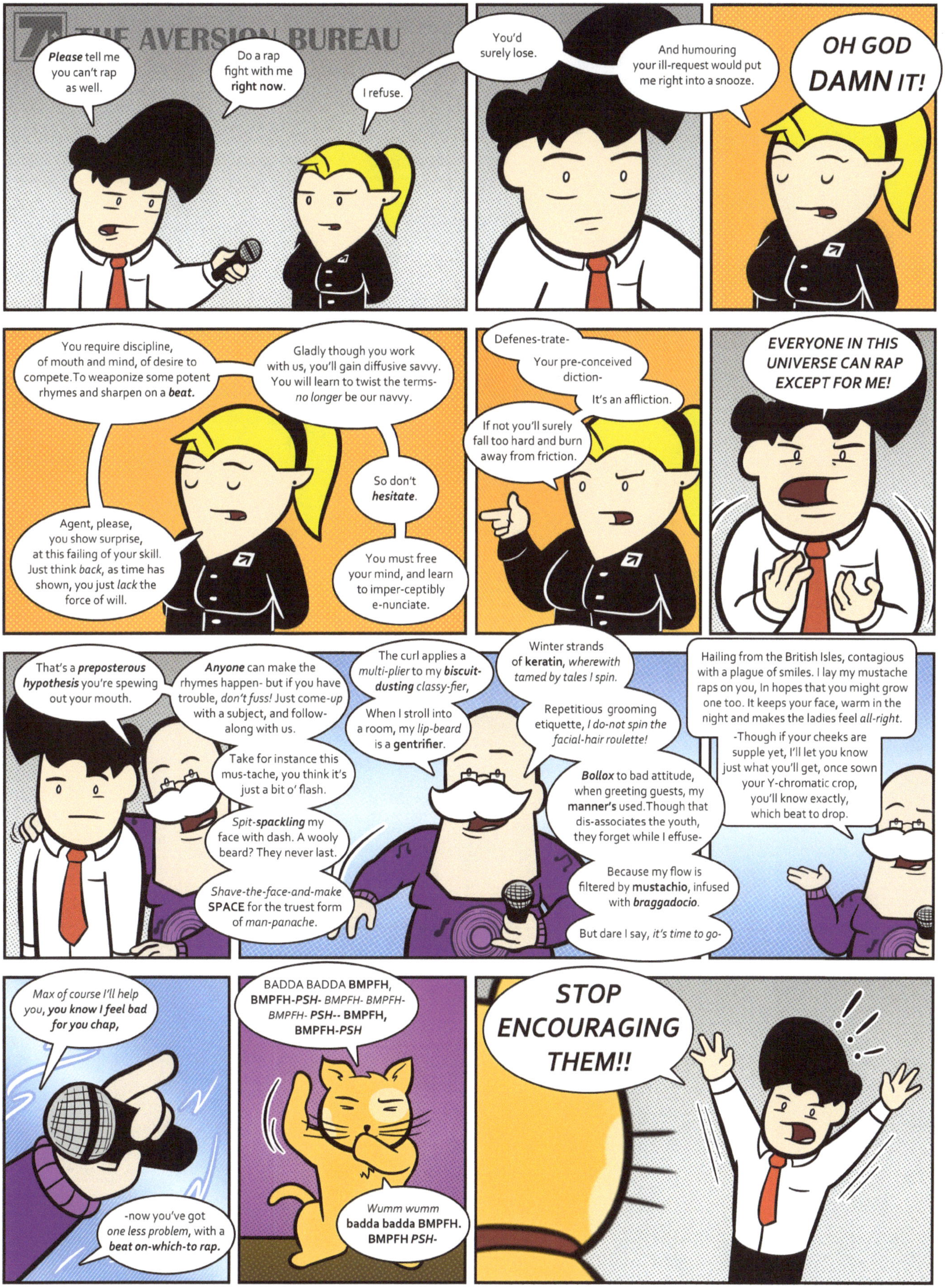

Please tell me you can't rap as well.
Do a rap fight with me **right now**.
I refuse.
You'd surely lose.
And humouring your ill-request would put me right into a snooze.
OH GOD **DAMN** IT!
You require discipline, of mouth and mind, of desire to compete. To weaponize some potent rhymes and sharpen on a ***beat.***
Gladly though you work with us, you'll gain diffusive savvy. You will learn to twist the terms- *no longer* be our navvy.
So don't ***hesitate***.
Agent, please, you show surprise, at this failing of your skill. Just think *back*, as time has shown, you just *lack* the force of will.
You must free your mind, and learn to imper-ceptibly e-nunciate.
Defenes-trate-
Your pre-conceived diction-
It's an affliction.
If not you'll surely fall too hard and burn away from friction.
EVERYONE IN THIS UNIVERSE CAN RAP EXCEPT FOR ME!
That's a ***preposterous hypothesis*** you're spewing out your mouth.
Anyone can make the rhymes happen- but if you have trouble, *don't fuss!* Just come-up with a subject, and follow-along with us.
Take for instance this mus-tache, you think it's just a bit o' flash.
*Spit-**spackling*** my face with dash. A wooly beard? They never last.
Shave-the-face-and-make **SPACE** for the truest form of *man-panache.*
The curl applies a *multi-plier* to my ***biscuit-dusting*** *classy-fier,*
When I stroll into a room, my *lip-beard* is a **gentrifier**.
Winter strands of **keratin**, *wherewith tamed by tales I spin.*
Repetitious grooming etiquette, *I do-not spin the facial-hair roulette!*
Bollox to bad attitude, when greeting guests, my **manner's** used. Though that dis-associates the youth, they forget while I effuse-
Because my flow is filtered by **mustachio**, infused with ***braggadocio***.
But dare I say, *it's time to go-*
Hailing from the British Isles, contagious with a plague of smiles. I lay my mustache raps on you, In hopes that you might grow one too. It keeps your face, warm in the night and makes the ladies feel *all-right*.
-Though if your cheeks are supple yet, I'll let you know just what you'll get, once sown your Y-chromatic crop, you'll know exactly, which beat to drop.
Max of course I'll help you, ***you know I feel bad for you chap,***
-now you've got *one less problem*, with a ***beat on-which-to rap.***
BADDA BADDA **BMPFH, BMPFH-*PSH-*** *BMPFH- BMPFH- BMPFH-* ***PSH--*** **BMPFH, BMPFH-*PSH***
Wumm wumm **badda badda BMPFH. BMPFH *PSH-***
STOP ENCOURAGING THEM!!

"The Thought That Counts"

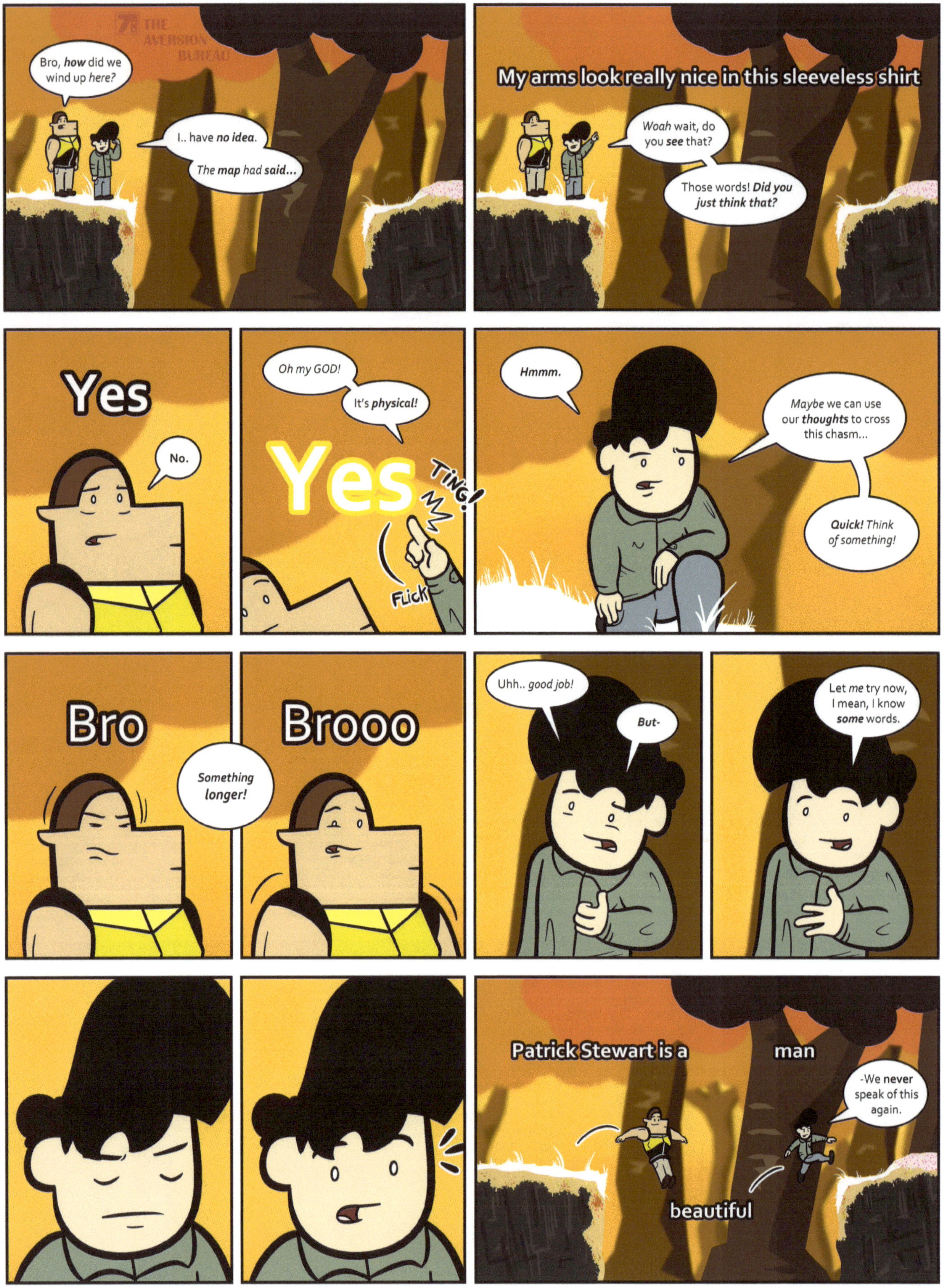

Bro, how did we wind up here?
I.. have no idea.
The map had said...
My arms look really nice in this sleeveless shirt
Woah wait, do you see that?
Those words! Did you just think that?
Yes
No.
Oh my GOD!
It's physical!
Yes
TING!
FLICK
Hmmm.
Maybe we can use our thoughts to cross this chasm...
Quick! Think of something!
Bro
Something longer!
Brooo
Uhh.. good job!
But-
Let me try now, I mean, I know some words.
Patrick Stewart is a
beautiful
man
-We never speak of this again.

"Teach A Fish To Man"

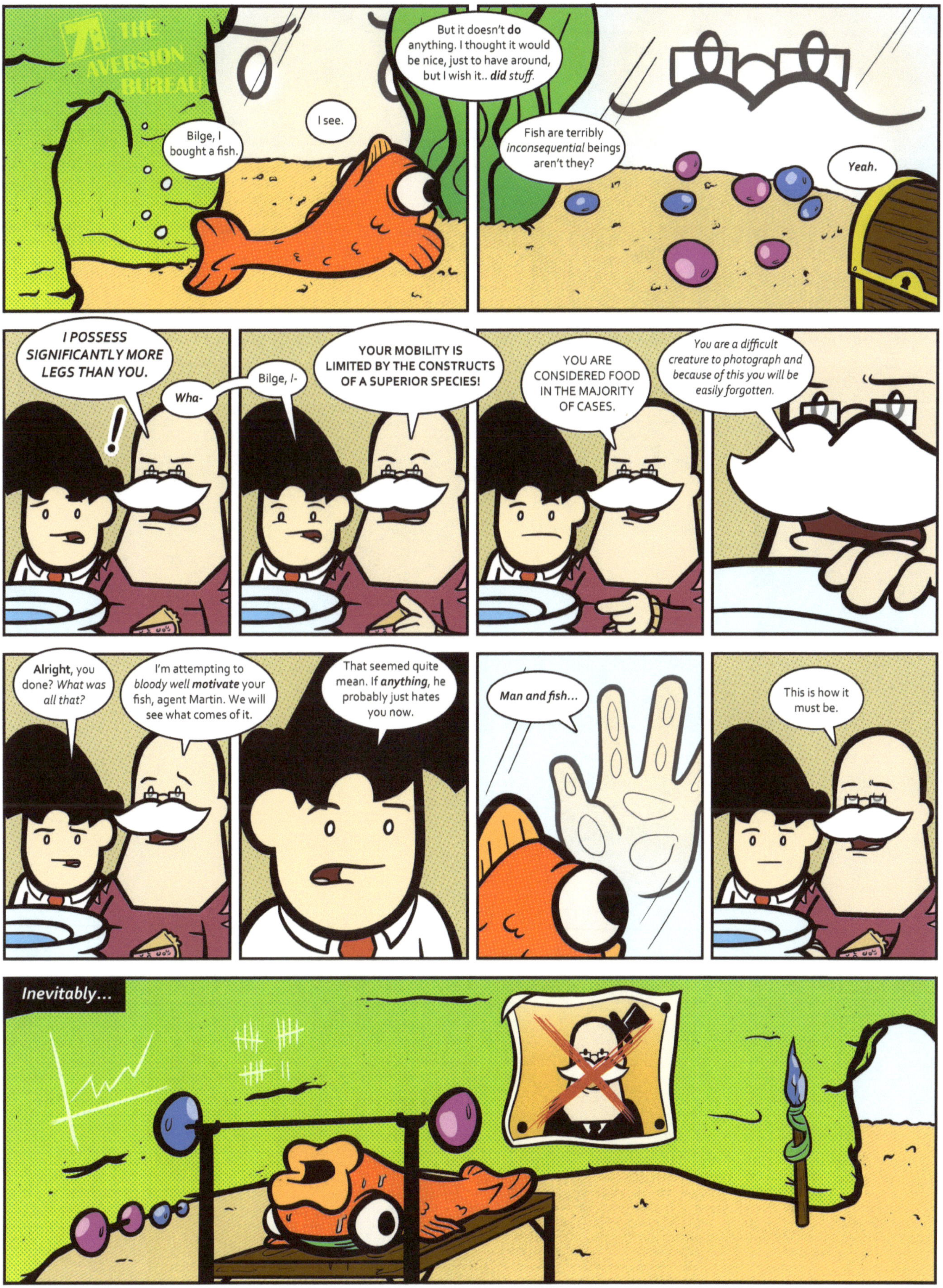
THE AVERSION BUREAU
Bilge, I bought a fish.
I see.
But it doesn't **do** anything. I thought it would be nice, just to have around, but I wish it.. ***did stuff.***
Fish are terribly *inconsequential* beings aren't they?
Yeah.
I POSSESS SIGNIFICANTLY MORE LEGS THAN YOU.
Wha-
Bilge, *I-*
YOUR MOBILITY IS LIMITED BY THE CONSTRUCTS OF A SUPERIOR SPECIES!
YOU ARE CONSIDERED FOOD IN THE MAJORITY OF CASES.
You are a difficult creature to photograph and because of this you will be easily forgotten.
Alright, you done? *What was all that?*
I'm attempting to *bloody well **motivate*** your fish, agent Martin. We will see what comes of it.
That seemed quite mean. If ***anything***, he probably just hates you now.
Man and fish...
This is how it must be.
Inevitably...

"All The Little Things"

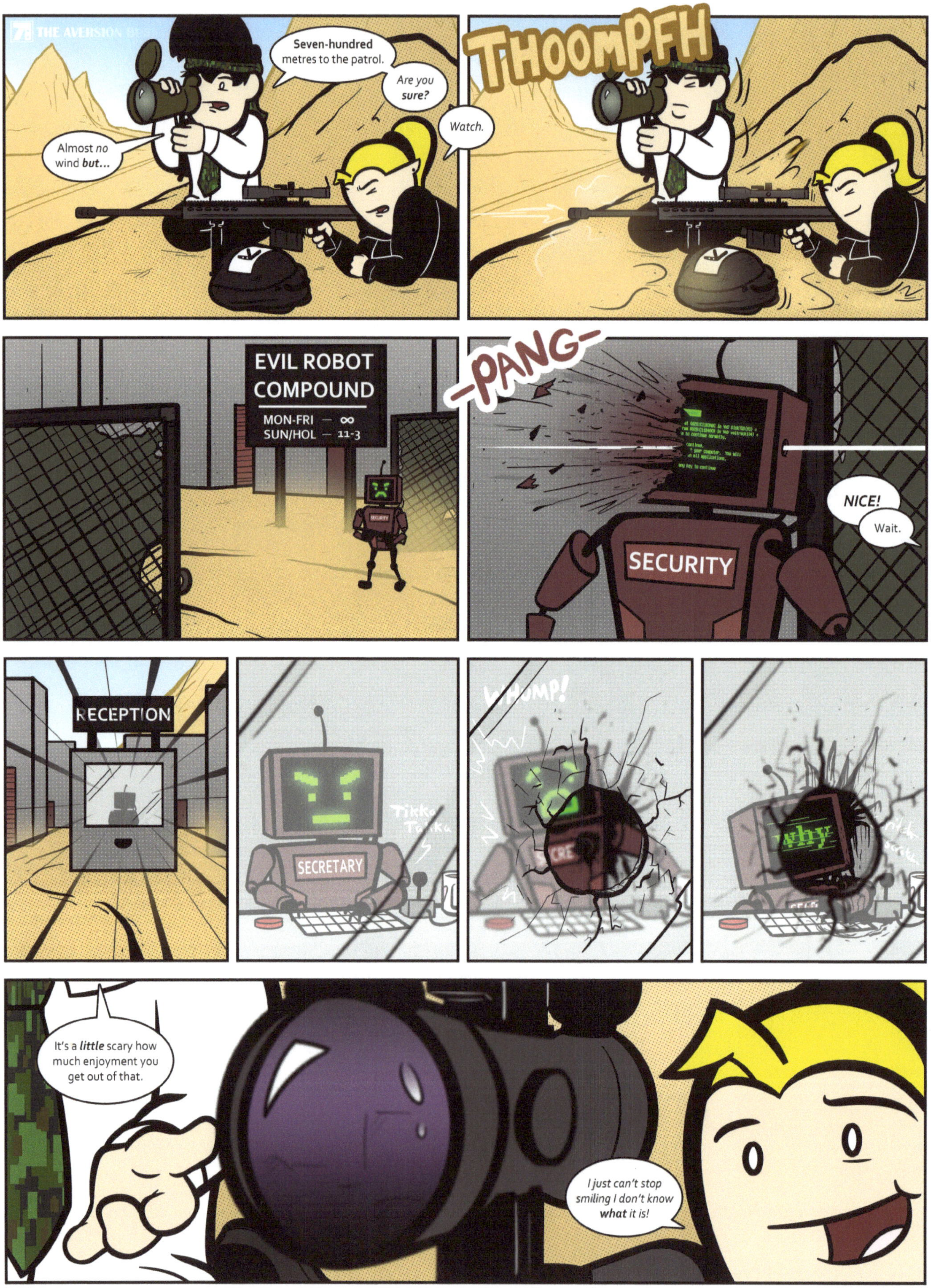

Seven-hundred metres to the patrol.
Are you *sure?*
Watch.
Almost *no* wind *but…*
THOOMPFH
EVIL ROBOT COMPOUND
MON-FRI — ∞
SUN/HOL — 11-3
SECURITY
-PANG-
SECURITY
NICE!
Wait.
RECEPTION
SECRETARY
why
It's a *little* scary how much enjoyment you get out of that.
I just can't stop smiling I don't know ***what*** *it is!*

"The Marching Song"

This. Is. The march-ing song.
We sing it as we march a-long.
For it. Is. The march-ing song.

      Bush and bramble un-der feet.
      We pack trail-mix, and jerk-ied meat.
      And sing. Our. March-ing sooong.

           This. Is. The march-ing song.
           We sing it as we march a-long.
           For we. Have. A march-ing song.

We move our feet to mouth-made beat.
We don't step-on worms, be-cause they're neat.
We march on-ward to right wrooongs.

           This still. Is. The march-ing song.
           To sing the whole-thing takes so long.
           But nevertheless it is our song.

And so bolstered now, we carry on.
Marching mountain-tops and neighbour's lawn.
We battle beasts and some-times hell-fire's spawwwn.
But never, with-out, our marching song.

           This. Was. The march-ing song.
           We're here al-ready, won't take so long.
           If you. Sing. The march-ing song.

THE CONTENTS OF A HIKING BAG PACKED BY MAX MARTIN

- **Nintendo DS** – Because nothing accentuates the majesty of nature like a tiny window to another realm entirely.

- **First Aid Kit** – For healing ouchies and saving lives, containing many invaluable individually-packaged alcohol pads for disinfecting wounds and cleaning the screen of your smart phone.

- **Bug Spray** – To kill or wound every living insect too fast or airborne to step on.

- **Bear Spray** – To mistake in an emergency for bug spray and obliterate overly-friendly butterflies in mid-flight.

- **Trail Mix** – A bag of assorted five-cent candies from the gas station. Official count given to the cashier stands at ± five.

- **Beef Jerky** – This came from a scary man at a roadside vendor so it may actually be horse.

- **A Rain Poncho** – Because it's fun to say. *Poncho*. Heh.

- ~~**A Gun** – To shoot bad guys.~~   *Damn it.*

- **Compass** – Whoops that's a watch.

- **A Single Condom** – Why?

- **Water** – (Sprite)

- **A Map** – Of Westeros.

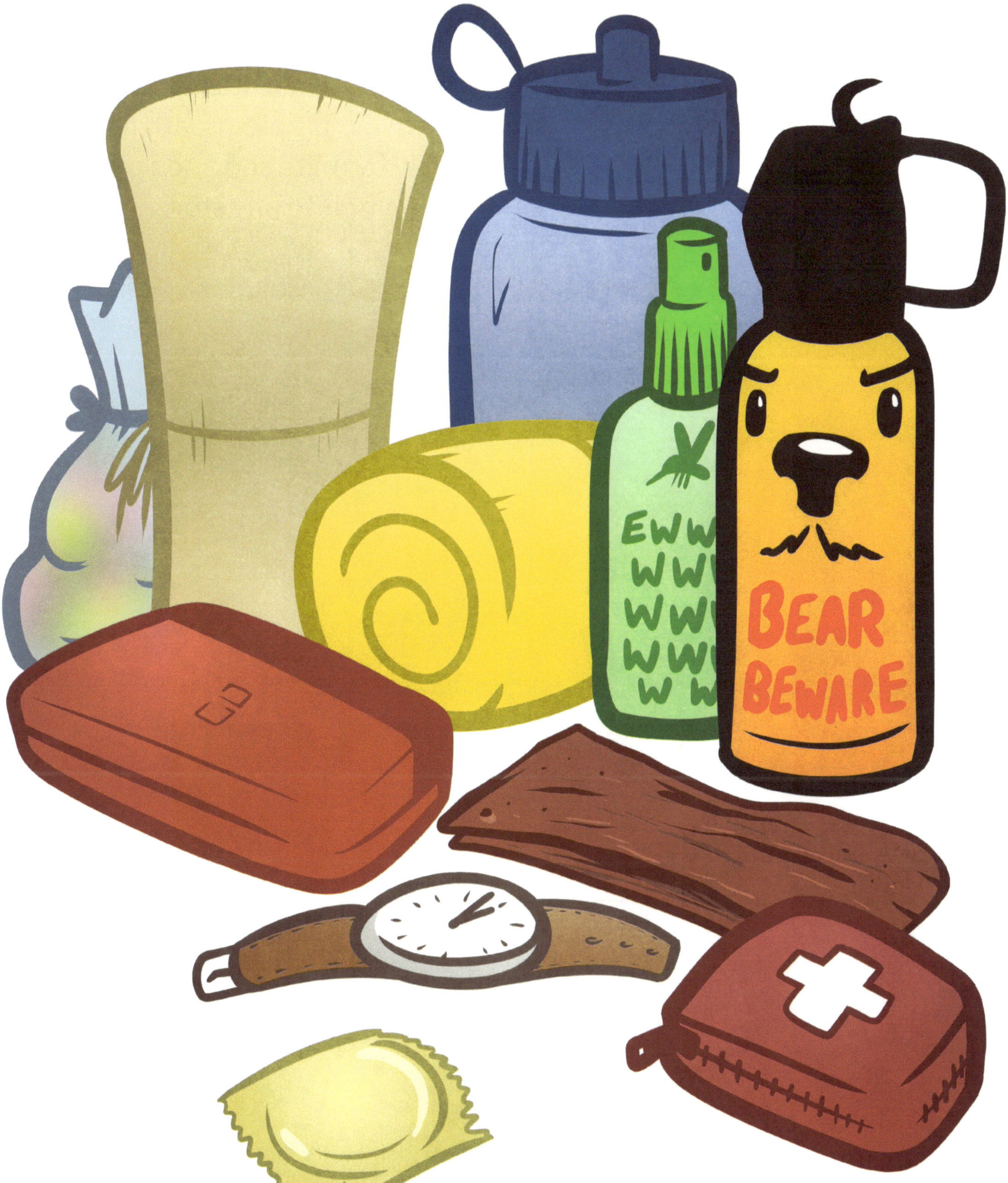
BEAR
BEWARE

ONE-OFFS

After *The Aversion Bureau* returned from a long hiatus taken to complete the first book, it returned with a multiple-month long run of non-story strips exploring new formats and a ton of jokes I had up my sleeve that didn't fit into any story.

Here they are now in all their non-sequitur glory.

"Imagination"

POK
fruit WATER
Heh heh.
Sluuurp!
Juice boxes make me feel like a bigass mosquito.

"The Suavest Man Alive"

puff
puff
-FLICK-
MMMMM
-Smooch-
SMOOCH
Your neck tastes shitty.

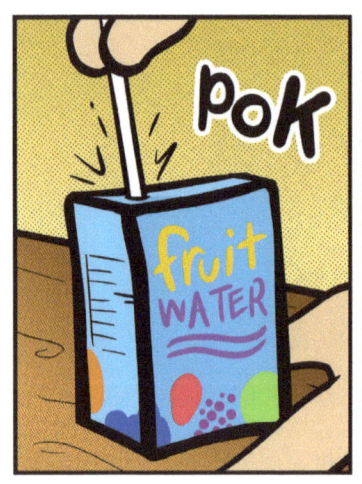

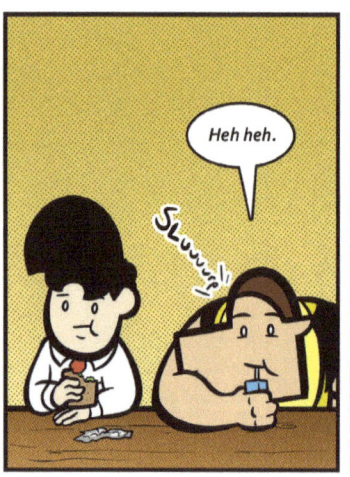

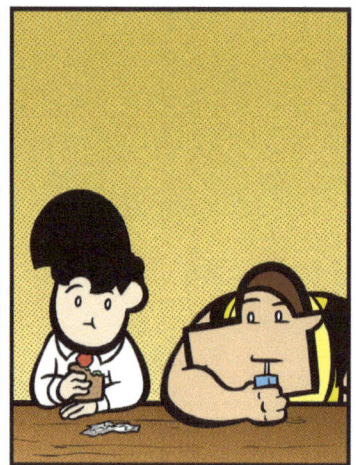

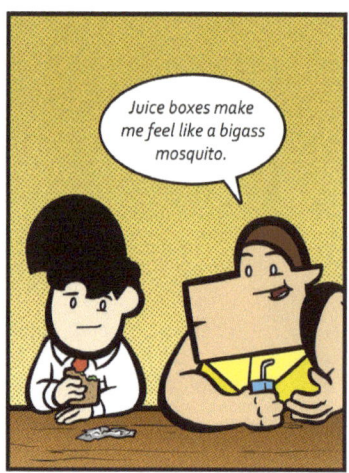

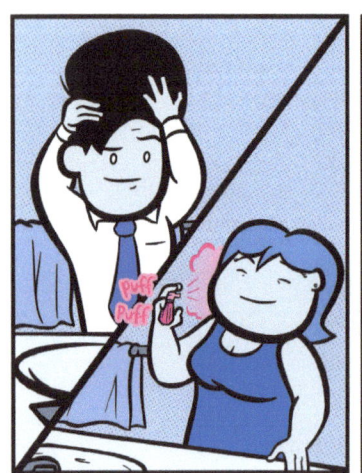

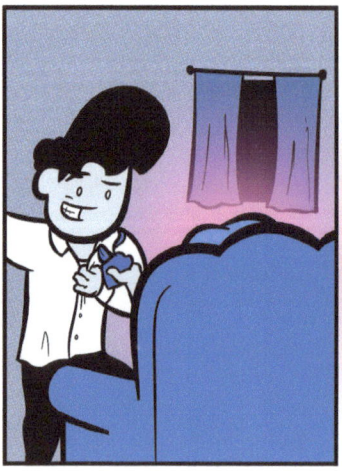

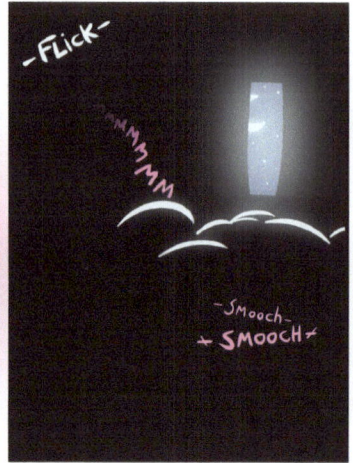

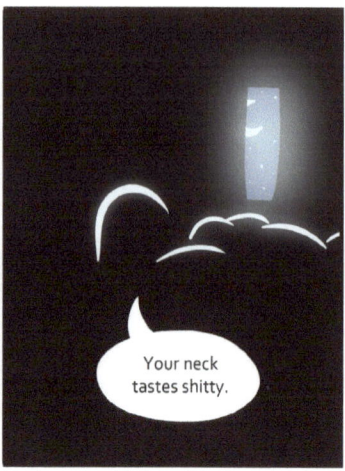

"Dishonoured"

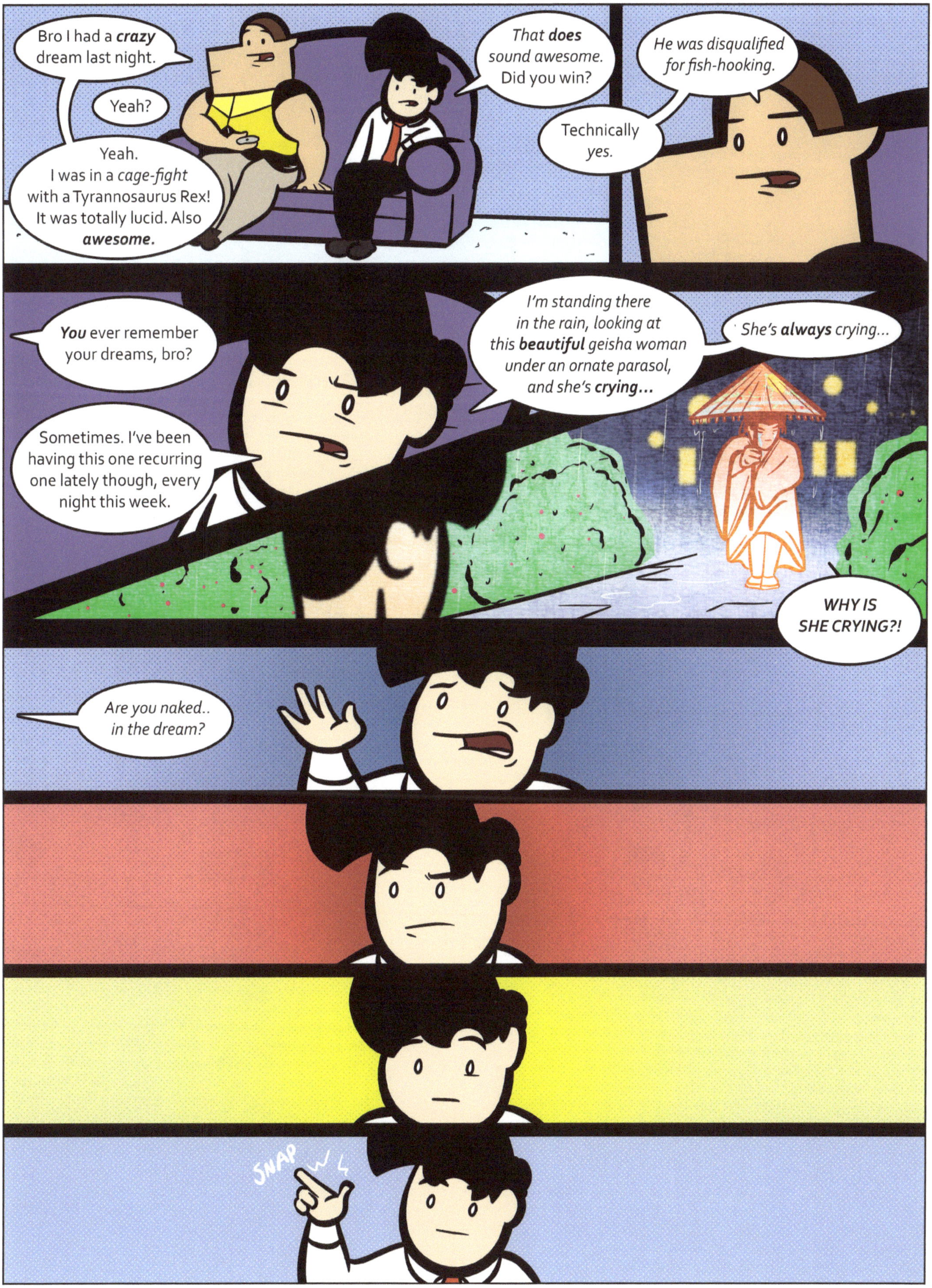

Bro I had a ***crazy*** dream last night.
Yeah?
Yeah. I was in a *cage-fight* with a Tyrannosaurus Rex! It was totally lucid. Also ***awesome.***
*That **does** sound awesome.* Did you win?
He was disqualified for fish-hooking.
Technically *yes.*
You ever remember your dreams, bro?
Sometimes. I've been having this one recurring one lately though, every night this week.
*I'm standing there in the rain, looking at this **beautiful** geisha woman under an ornate parasol, and she's **crying...***
*She's **always** crying...*
WHY IS SHE CRYING?!
Are you naked.. in the dream?
SNAP

"The Braided Snake Of Utility"

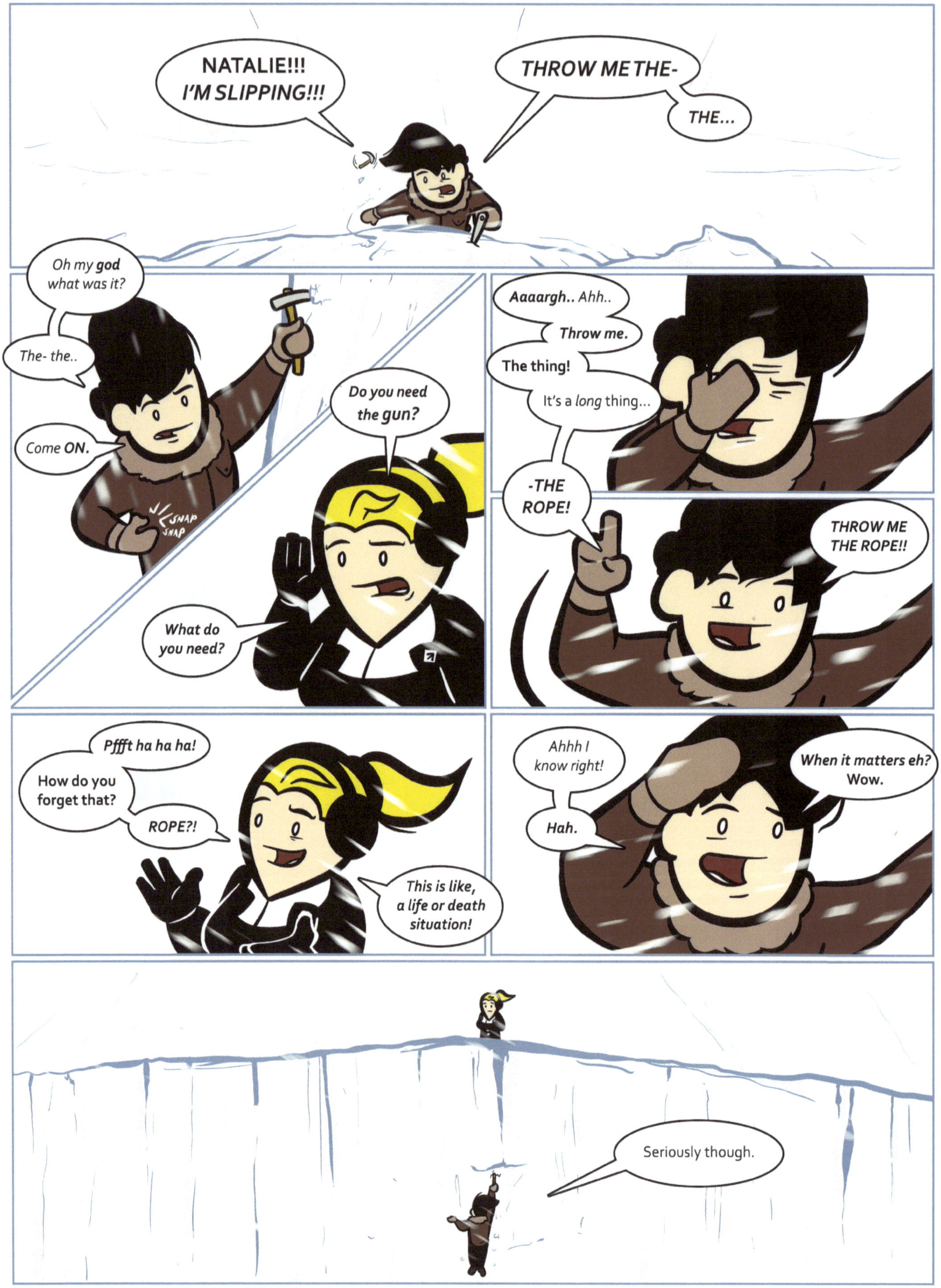

NATALIE!!! I'M SLIPPING!!!
THROW ME THE-
THE...
Oh my god what was it?
The- the..
Come ON.
SNAP SNAP
Do you need the gun?
What do you need?
Aaaargh.. Ahh..
Throw me.
The thing!
It's a long thing...
-THE ROPE!
THROW ME THE ROPE!!
Pffft ha ha ha!
How do you forget that?
ROPE?!
This is like, a life or death situation!
Ahhh I know right!
Hah.
When it matters eh? Wow.
Seriously though.

"Slow And Steady"

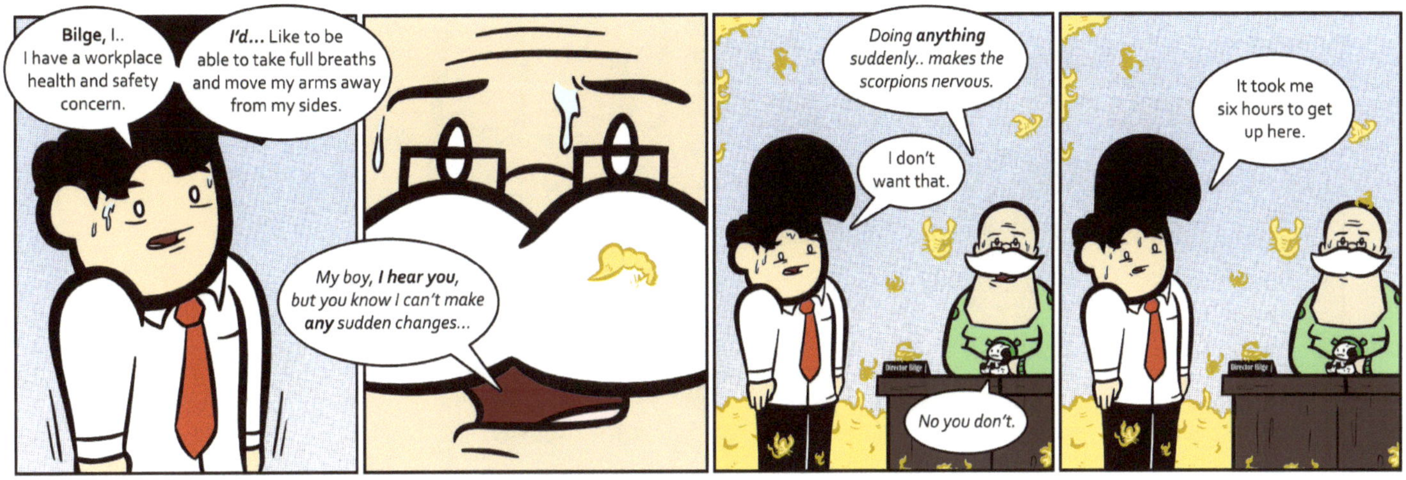

Bilge, I.. I have a workplace health and safety concern.
I'd... Like to be able to take full breaths and move my arms away from my sides.
*My boy, **I hear you**, but you know I can't make **any** sudden changes...*
*Doing **anything** suddenly.. makes the scorpions nervous.*
I don't want that.
No you don't.
It took me six hours to get up here.

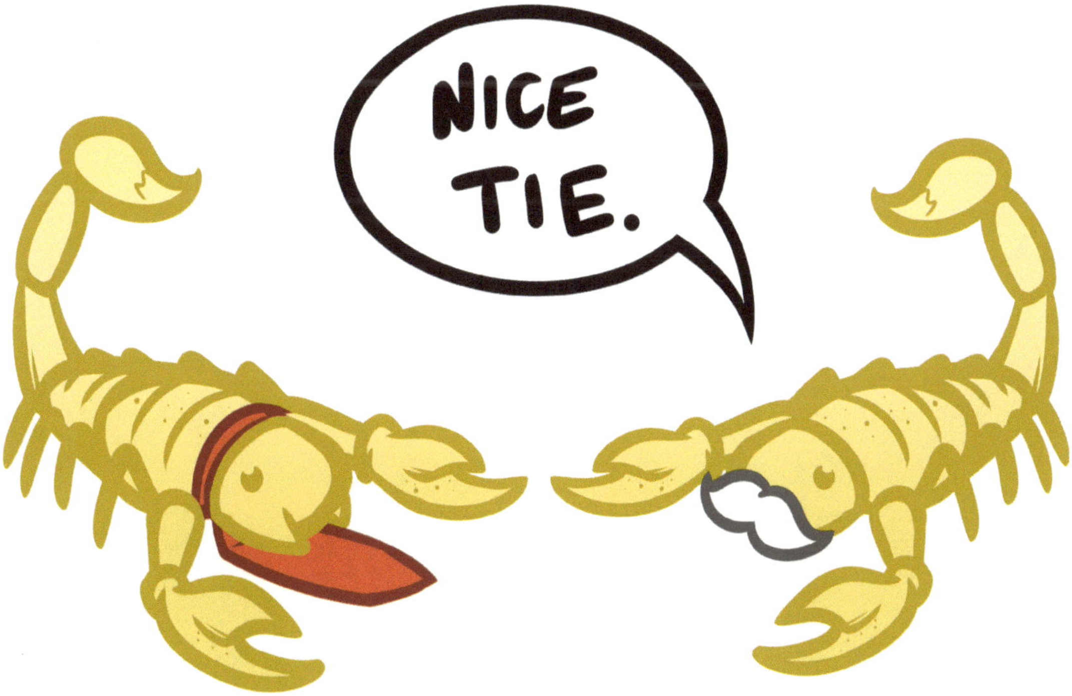

NICE TIE.

"Even Here There Are Rules"

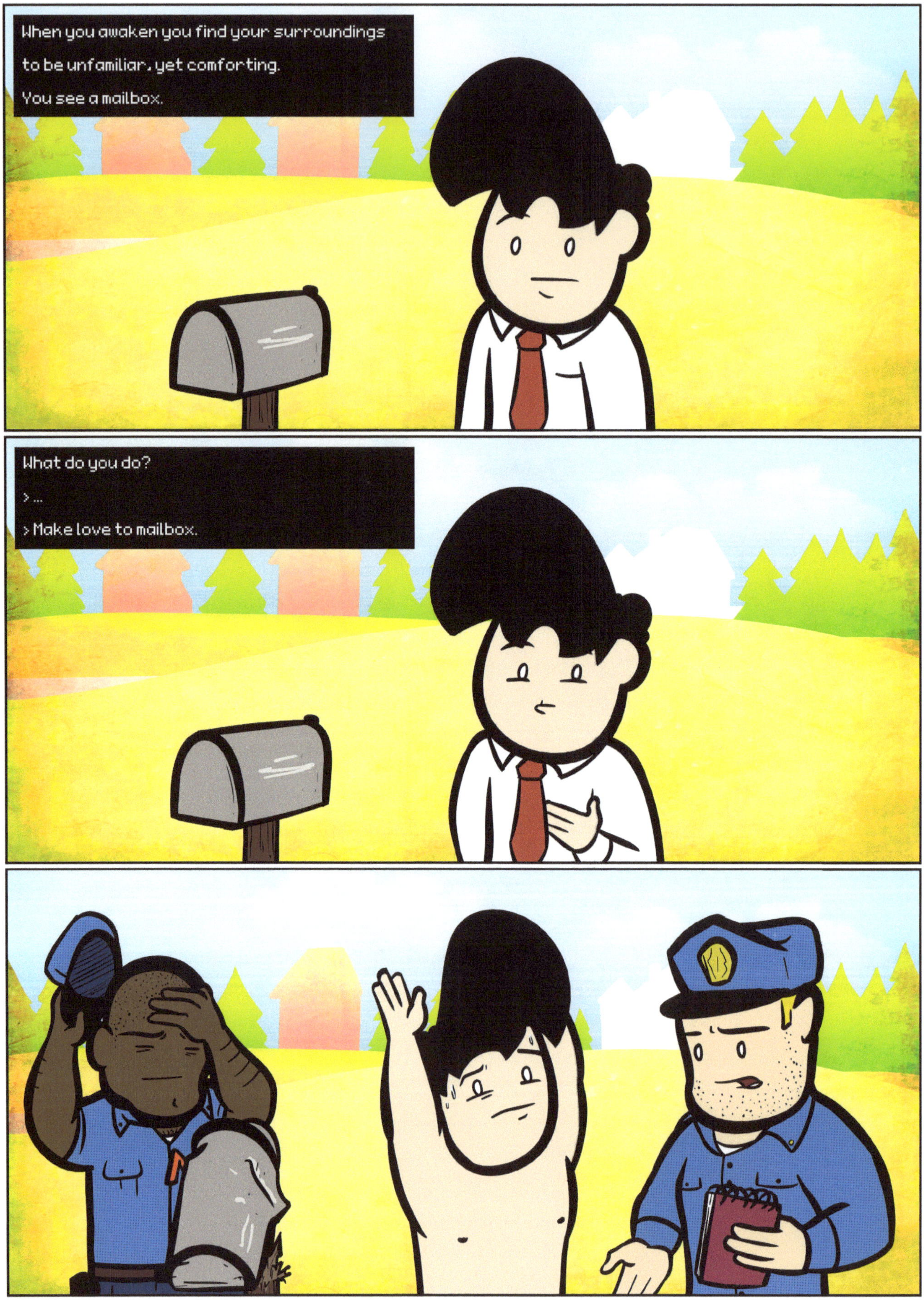
When you awaken you find your surroundings
to be unfamiliar, yet comforting.
You see a mailbox.
What do you do?
> ...
> Make love to mailbox.

"Text Adventure Redux"

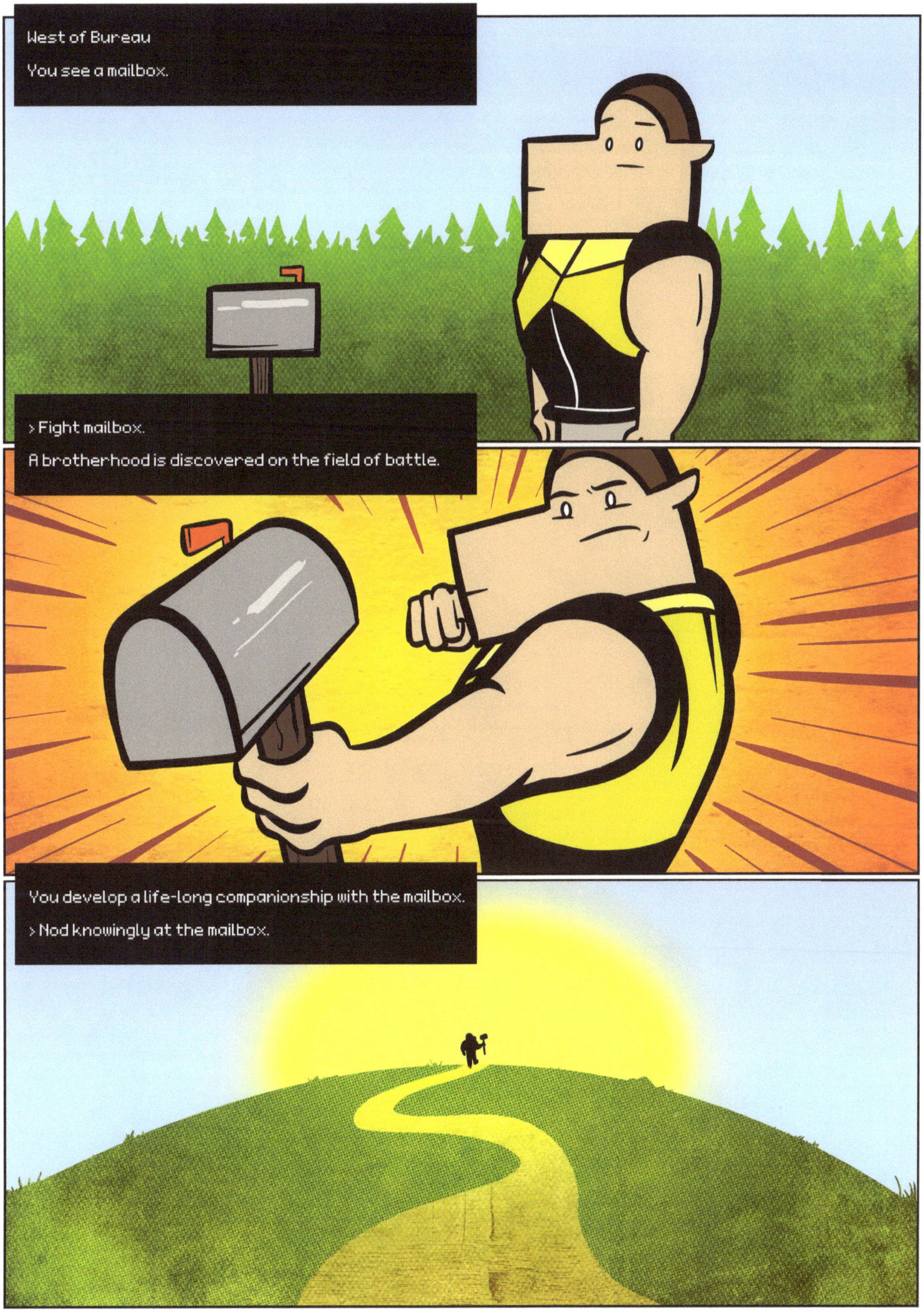
West of Bureau
You see a mailbox.
> Fight mailbox.
A brotherhood is discovered on the field of battle.
You develop a life-long companionship with the mailbox.
> Nod knowingly at the mailbox.

"The Last True Coliseum"

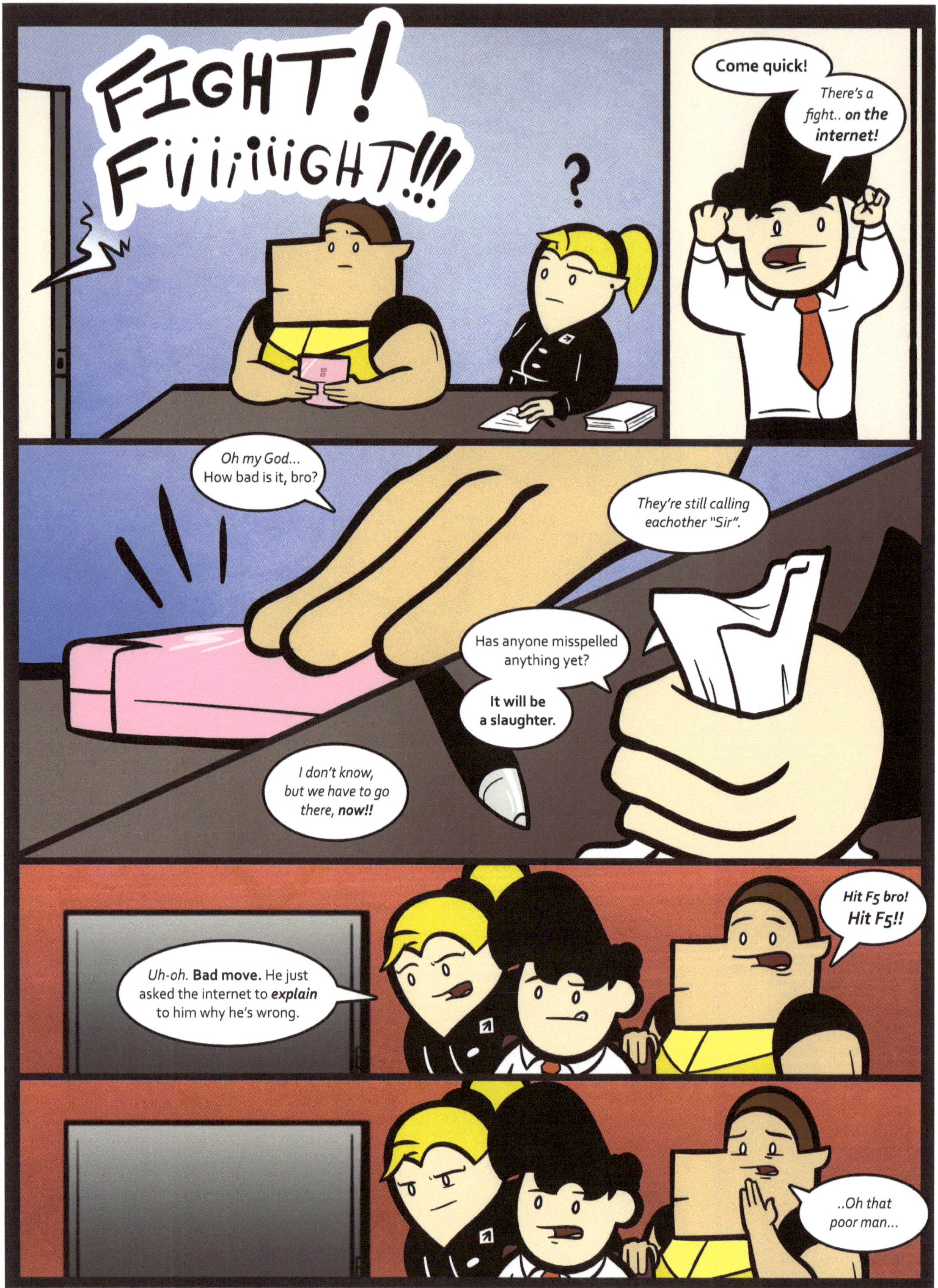
FIGHT! Fiiiiiiight!!!
?
Come quick!
There's a fight.. on the internet!
Oh my God... How bad is it, bro?
They're still calling eachother "Sir".
Has anyone misspelled anything yet?
It will be a slaughter.
I don't know, but we have to go there, now!!
Hit F5 bro! Hit F5!!
Uh-oh. Bad move. He just asked the internet to explain to him why he's wrong.
..Oh that poor man...

"Spotless Sunshine Of The Eternal Mind"

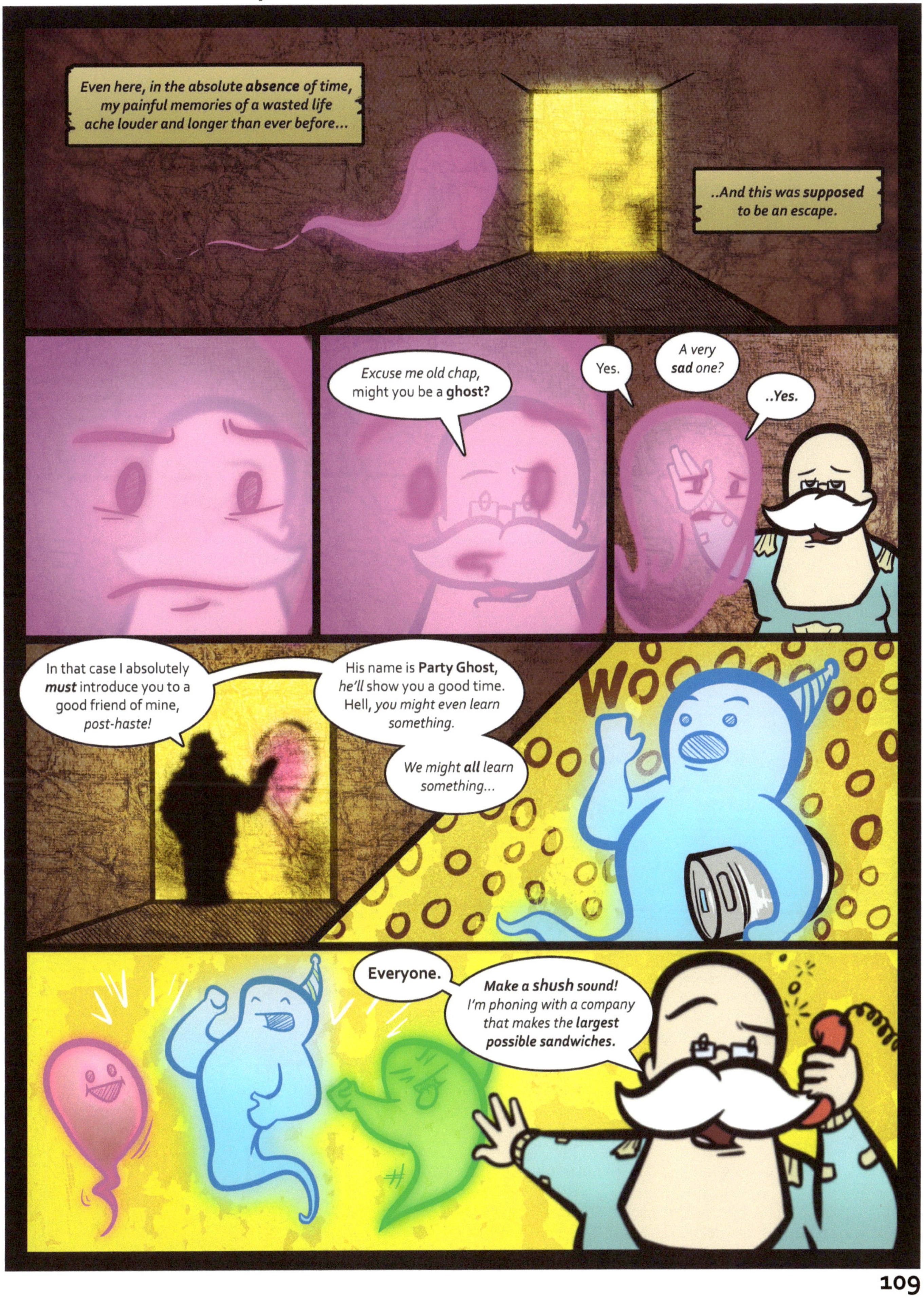

Even here, in the absolute **absence** of time, my painful memories of a wasted life ache louder and longer than ever before...
..And this was **supposed** to be an escape.
Excuse me old chap, might you be a **ghost?**
Yes.
A very **sad** one?
..Yes.
In that case I absolutely **must** introduce you to a good friend of mine, *post-haste!*
His name is **Party Ghost,** *he'll* show you a good time. Hell, *you might even learn something.*
*We might **all** learn something...*
WOO
Everyone.
*Make a **shush** sound! I'm phoning with a company that makes the **largest possible sandwiches.***

"Just A Coincidence"

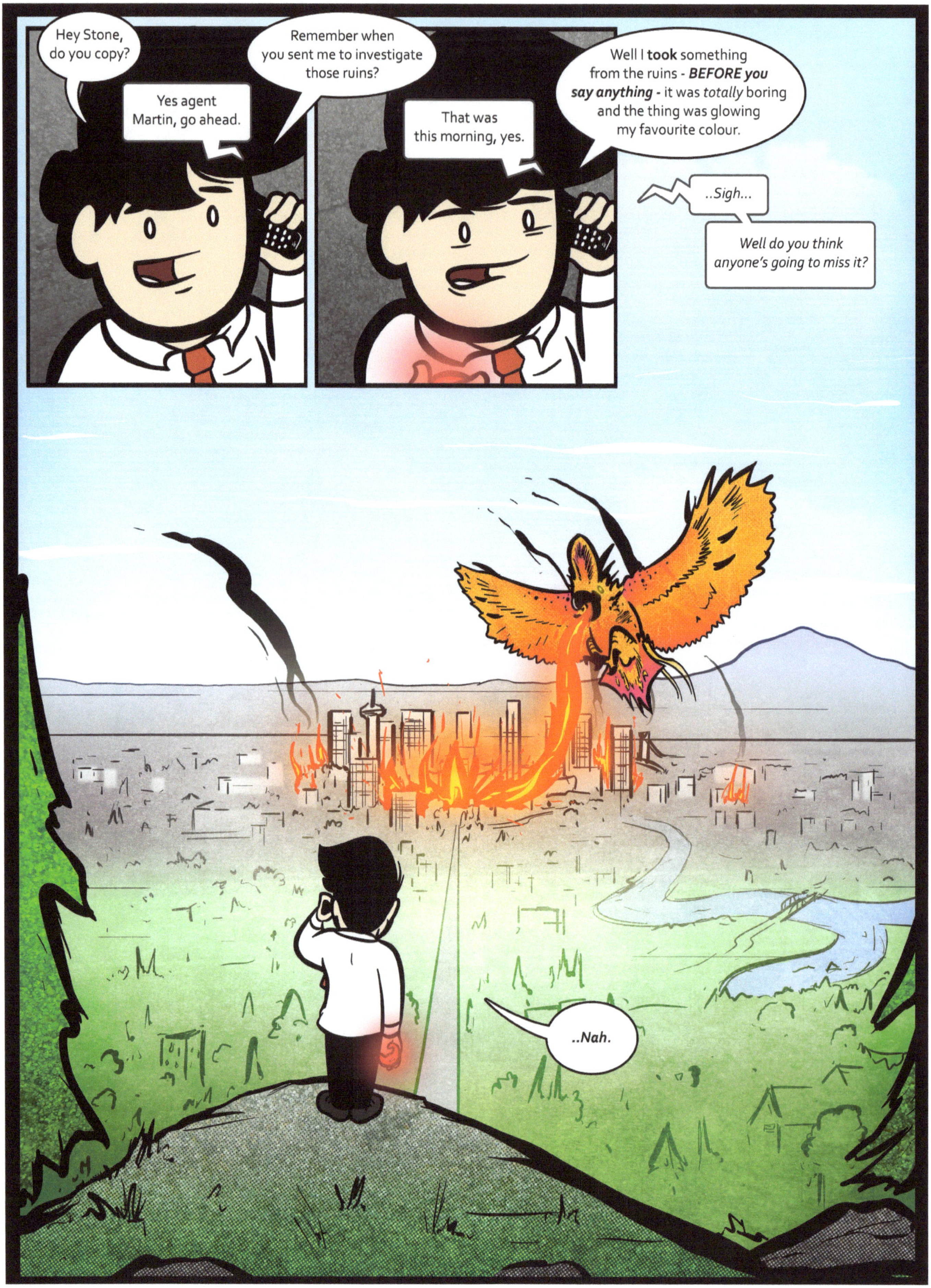
Hey Stone, do you copy?
Yes agent Martin, go ahead.
Remember when you sent me to investigate those ruins?
That was this morning, yes.
Well I **took** something from the ruins - ***BEFORE you say anything*** - it was *totally* boring and the thing was glowing my favourite colour.
..Sigh...
Well do you think anyone's going to miss it?
..Nah.

"You Got The Touch"

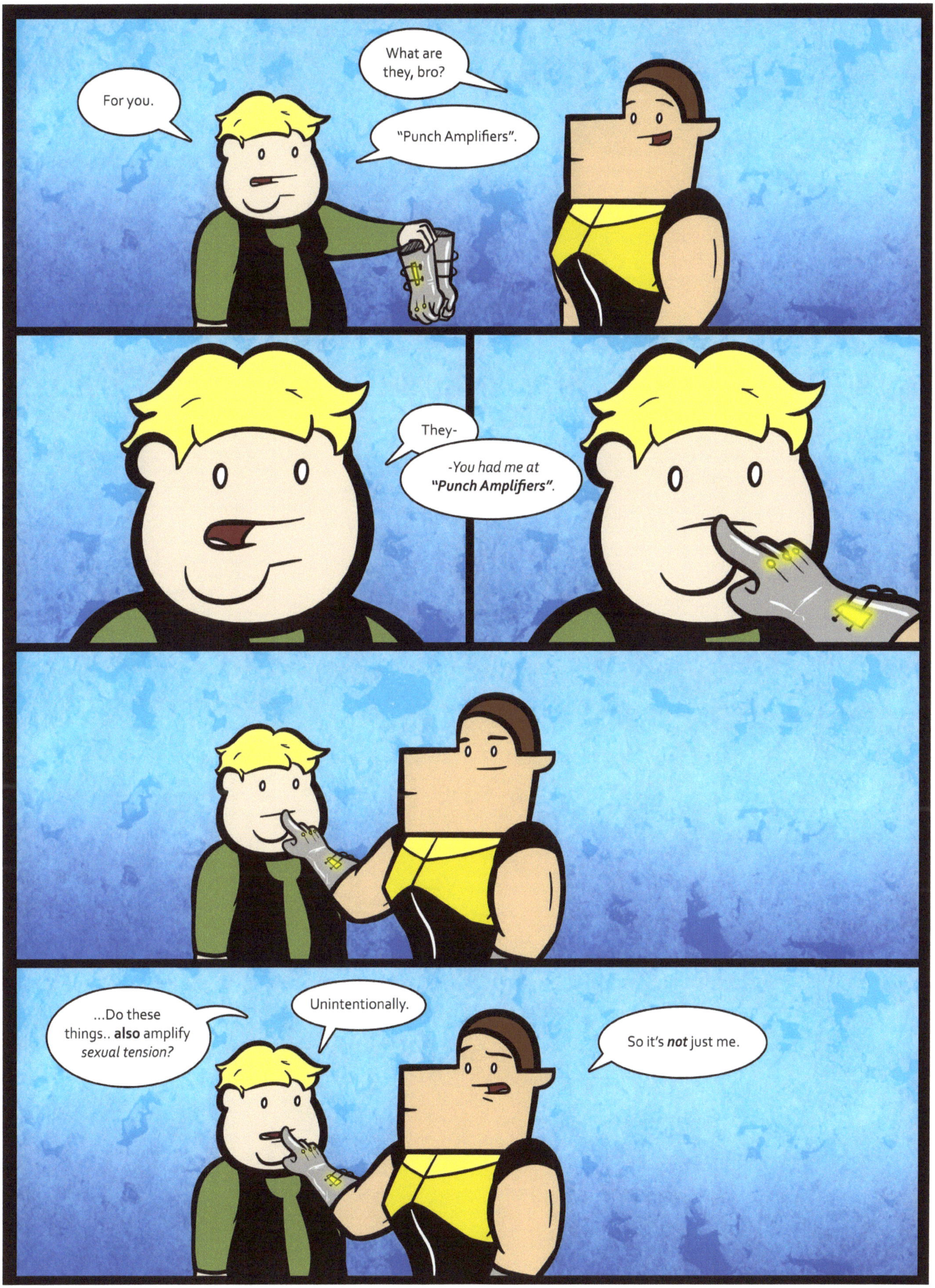

For you.
What are they, bro?
"Punch Amplifiers".
They-
-*You had me at* ***"Punch Amplifiers"***.
...Do these things.. **also** amplify *sexual tension?*
Unintentionally.
So it's ***not*** just me.

"All Rights Reserved"

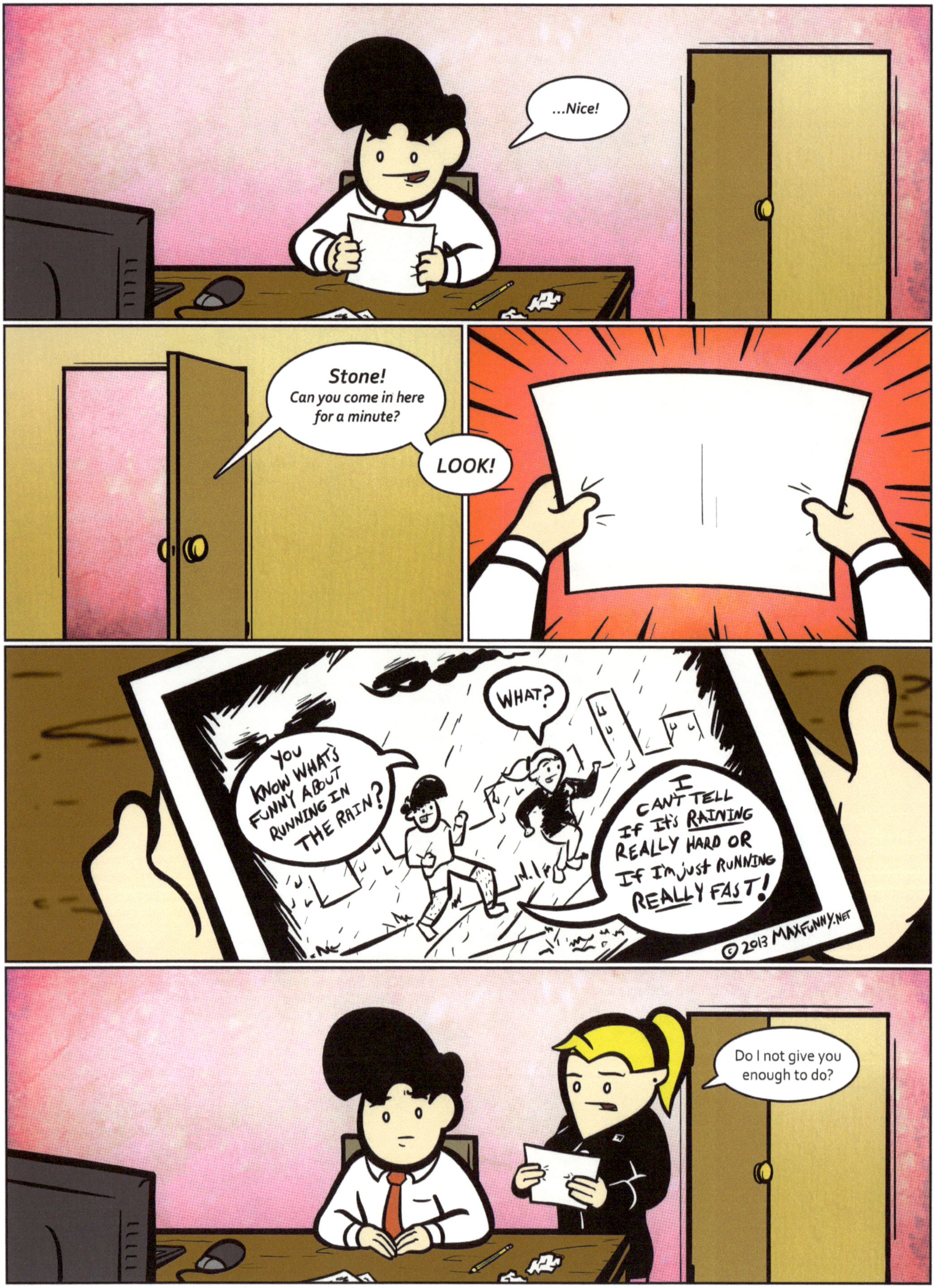

...Nice!
Stone!
Can you come in here for a minute?
LOOK!
YOU KNOW WHAT'S FUNNY ABOUT RUNNING IN THE RAIN?
WHAT?
I CAN'T TELL IF IT'S RAINING REALLY HARD OR IF I'M JUST RUNNING REALLY FAST!
© 2013 MAXFUNNY.NET
Do I not give you enough to do?

"Everyday Situations"

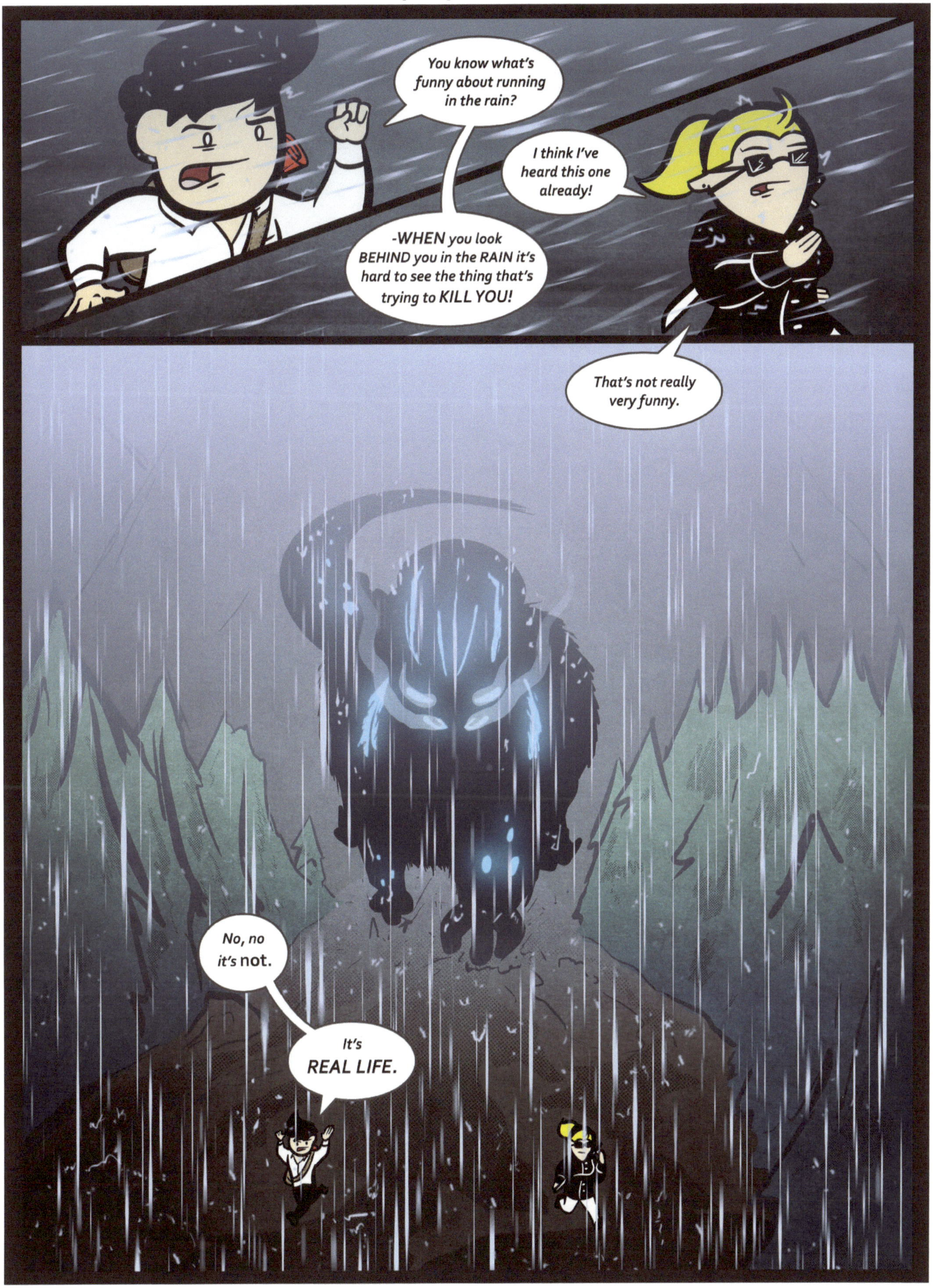

You know what's funny about running in the rain?
I think I've heard this one already!
-WHEN you look BEHIND you in the RAIN it's hard to see the thing that's trying to KILL YOU!
That's not really very funny.
No, no it's not.
It's REAL LIFE.

"A Whole Blog's Worth Of Lady Facts"

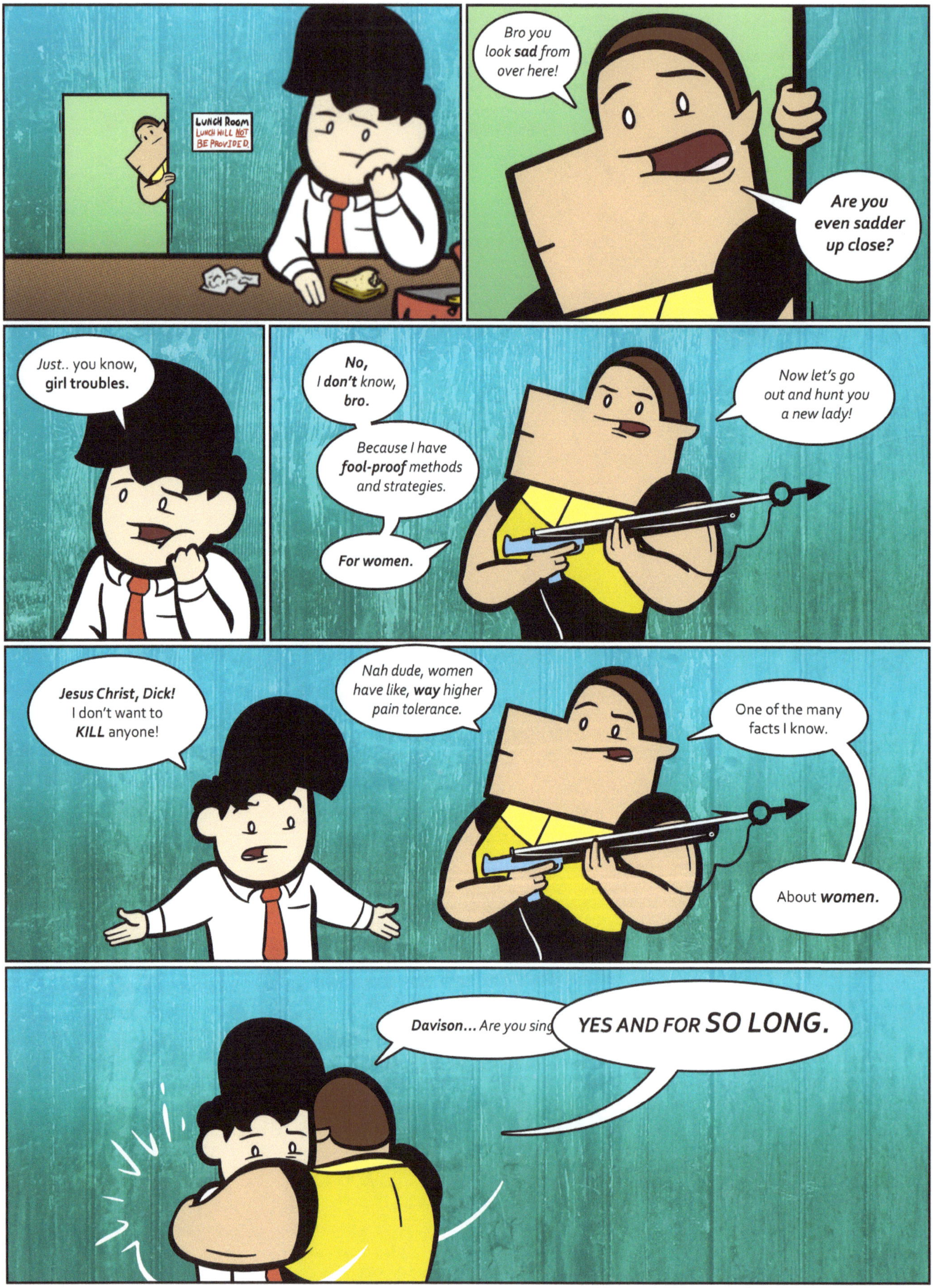
LUNCH ROOM
LUNCH WILL NOT BE PROVIDED.
Bro you look **sad** from over here!
Are you even sadder up close?
Just.. you know, **girl troubles.**
No, I **don't** know, **bro.**
Because I have **fool-proof** methods and strategies.
For women.
Now let's go out and hunt you a new lady!
Jesus Christ, Dick! I don't want to **KILL** anyone!
Nah dude, women have like, **way** higher pain tolerance.
One of the many facts I know.
About **women.**
Davison... Are you sing
YES AND FOR **SO LONG.**

"Kill Steal"

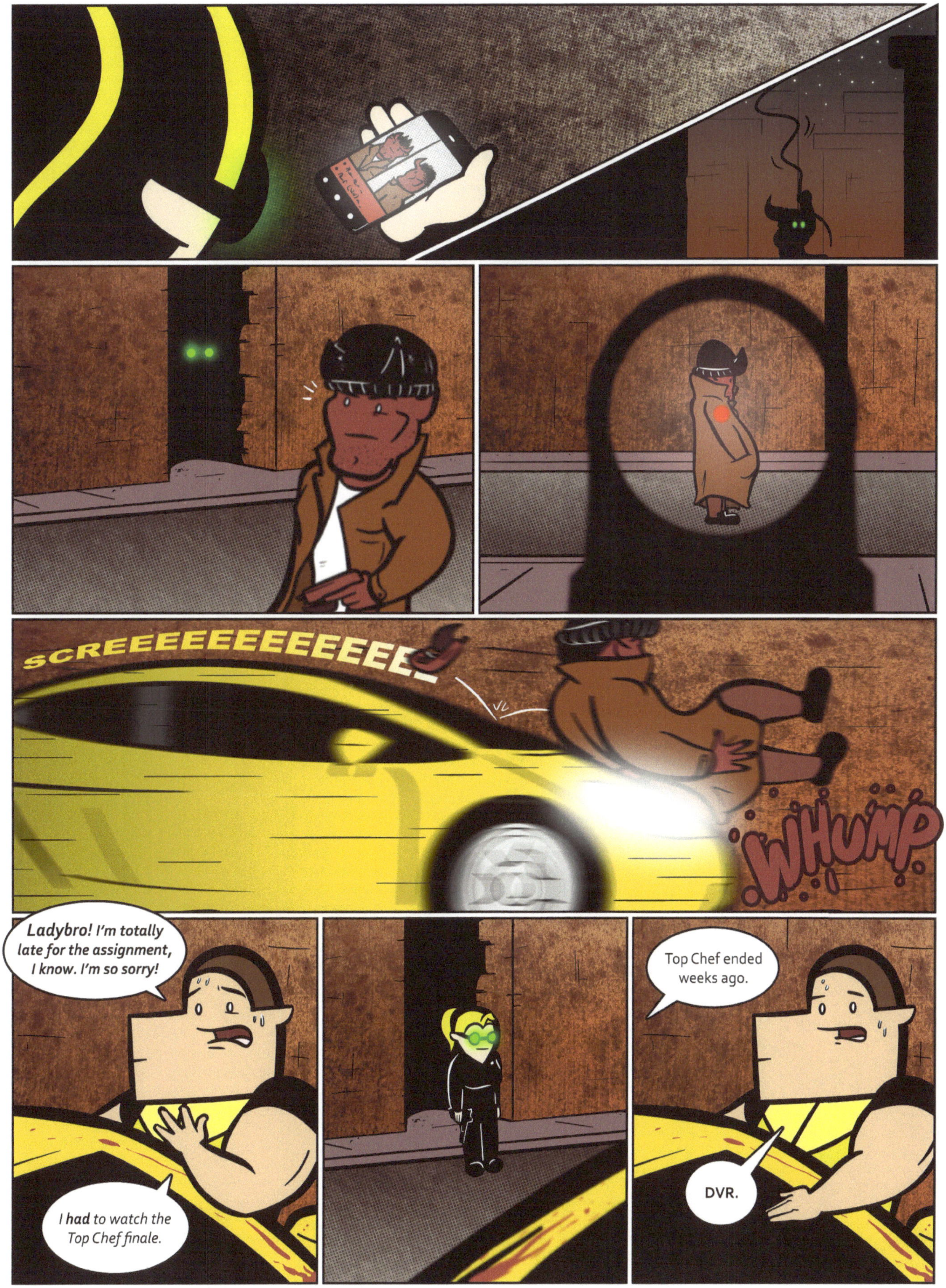
SCREEEEEEEEEEEEE
WHUMP
Ladybro! I'm totally late for the assignment, I know. I'm so sorry!
I **had** to watch the Top Chef finale.
Top Chef ended weeks ago.
DVR.

"Ashamed To Call You Bro"

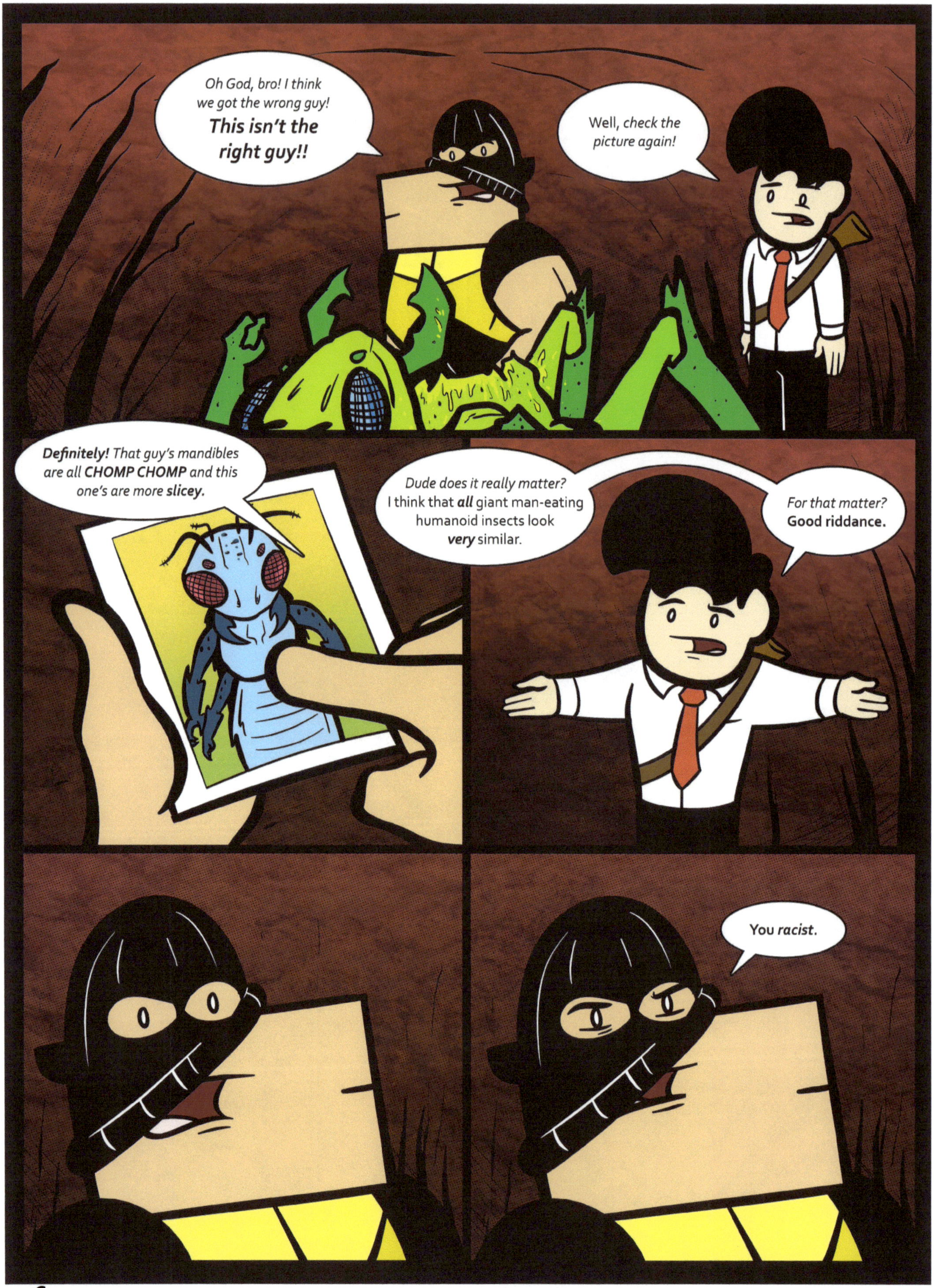
Oh God, bro! I think we got the wrong guy! **This isn't the right guy!!**
Well, *check the picture again!*
Definitely! That guy's mandibles are all **CHOMP CHOMP** and this one's are more **slicey.**
Dude does it really matter? I think that **all** giant man-eating humanoid insects look **very** similar.
For that matter? **Good riddance.**
You *racist.*

"And That's All We Will Say About That"

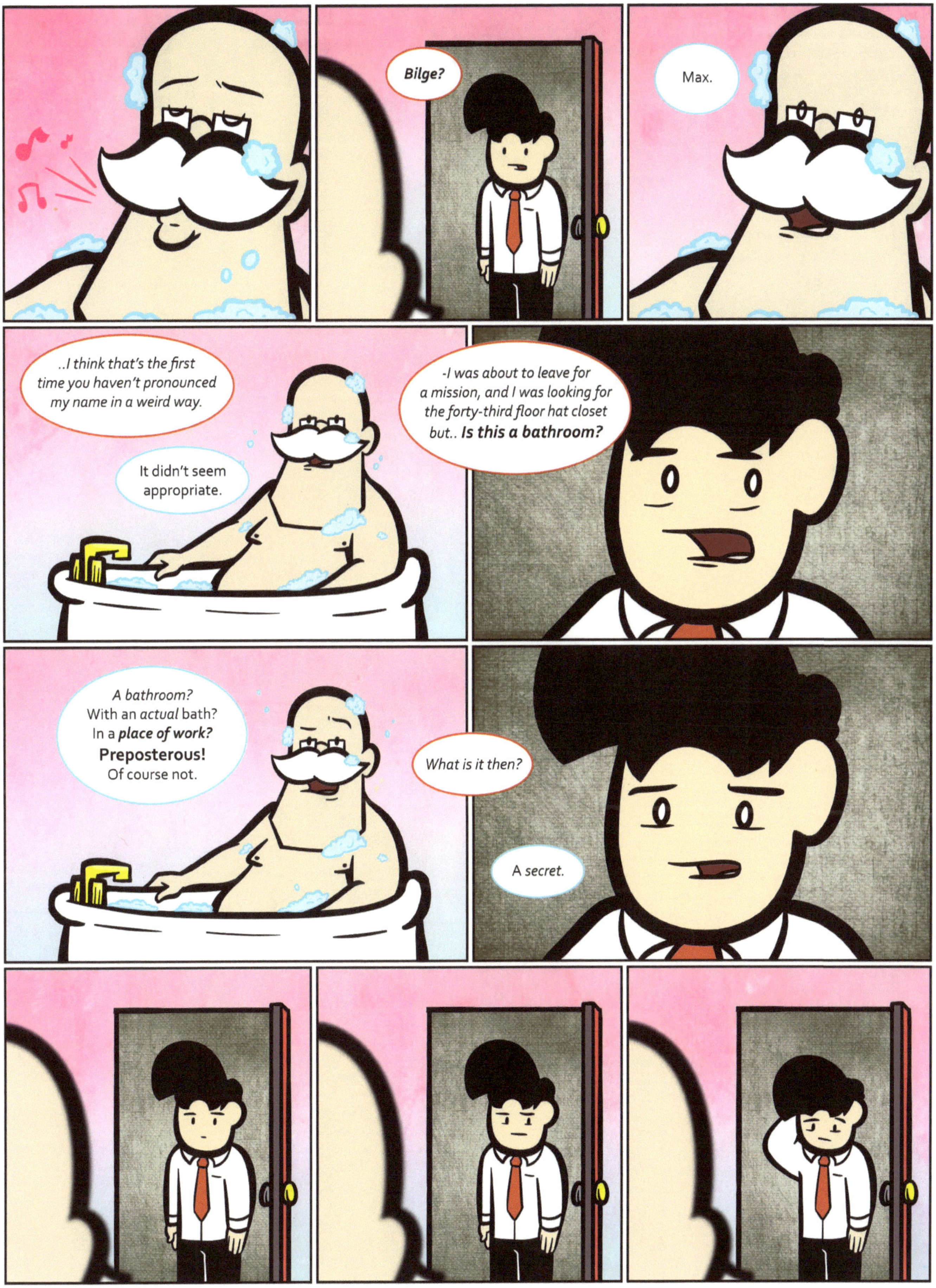
Bilge?
Max.
..I think that's the first time you haven't pronounced my name in a weird way.
It didn't seem appropriate.
-I was about to leave for a mission, and I was looking for the forty-third floor hat closet but.. **Is this a bathroom?**
A bathroom? With an *actual* bath? In a ***place of work?*** **Preposterous!** Of course not.
What is it then?
A secret.

"Controlled Escape"

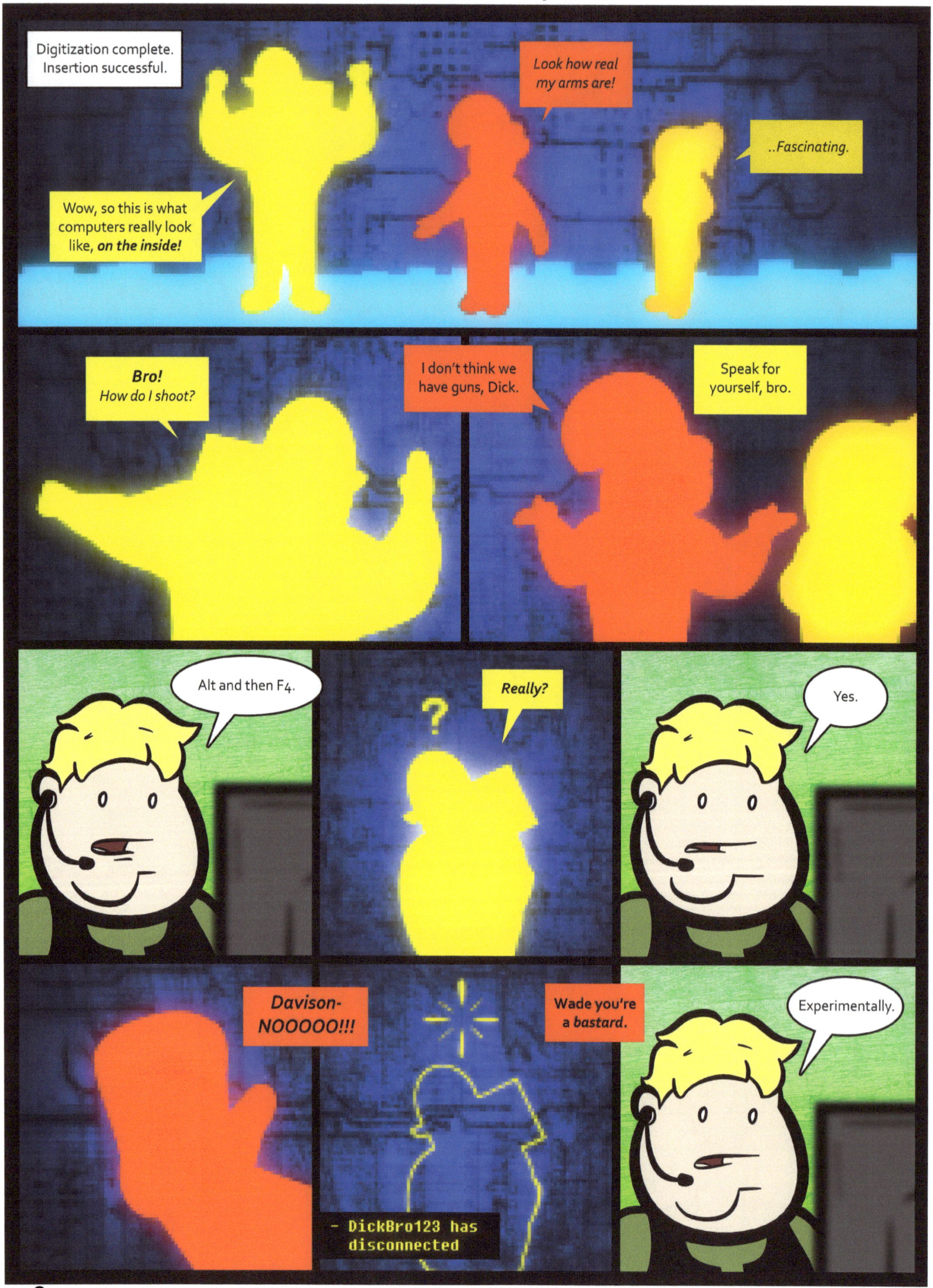

Digitization complete. Insertion successful.
Look how real my arms are!
..Fascinating.
Wow, so this is what computers really look like, ***on the inside!***
Bro! *How do I shoot?*
I don't think we have guns, Dick.
Speak for yourself, bro.
Alt and then F4.
Really?
?
Yes.
Davison-
NOOOOO!!!
Wade you're a ***bastard***.
- DickBro123 has disconnected
Experimentally.

"Latency With Malicious Intent"

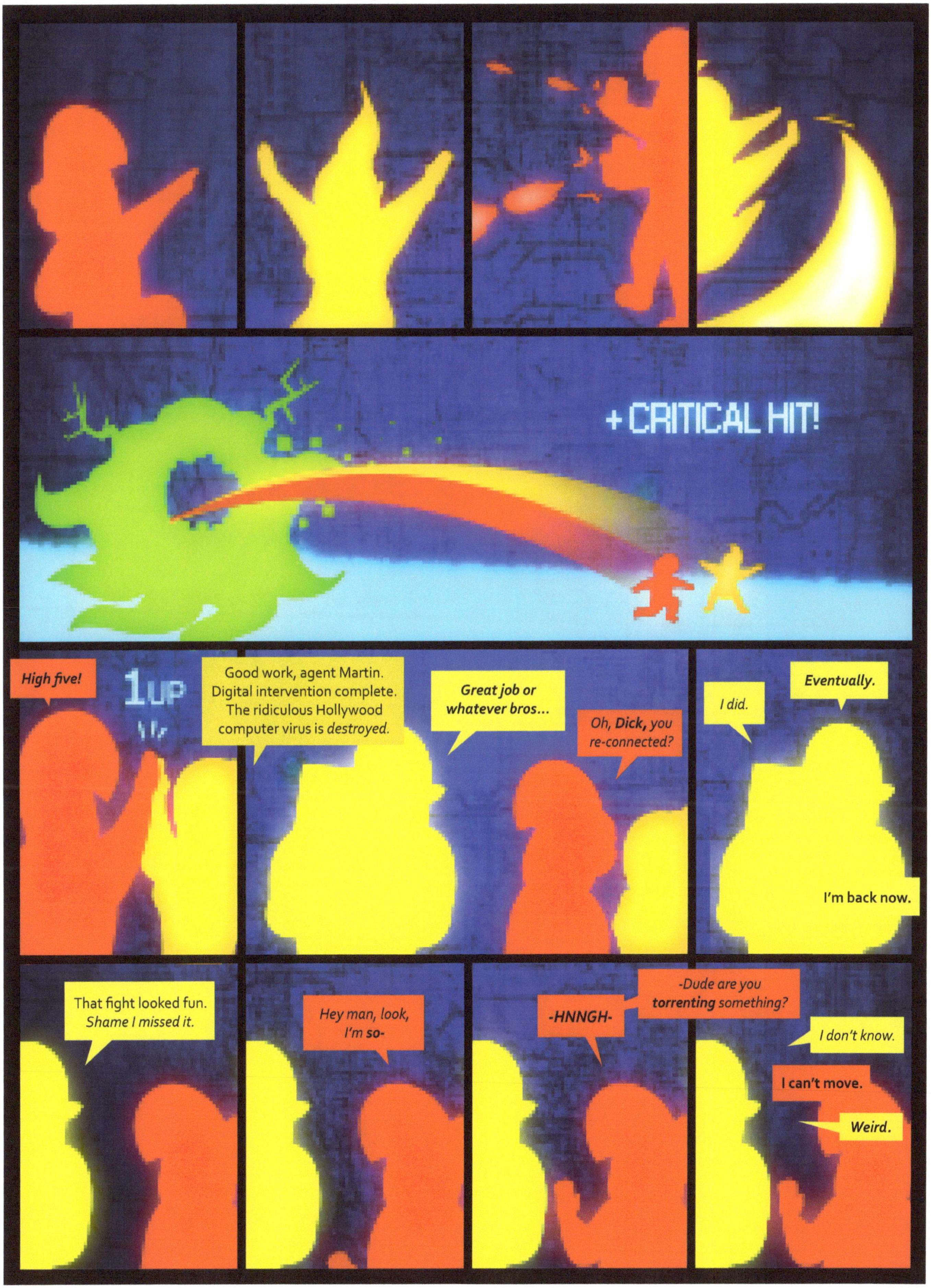

+CRITICAL HIT!
High five!
1UP
Good work, agent Martin. Digital intervention complete. The ridiculous Hollywood computer virus is *destroyed*.
Great job or whatever bros...
Oh, **Dick**, you re-connected?
I did.
Eventually.
I'm back now.
That fight looked fun. *Shame I missed it.*
Hey man, look, I'm so-
-HNNGH-
-Dude are you **torrenting** something?
I don't know.
I can't move.
Weird.

"Reflecting Pool"

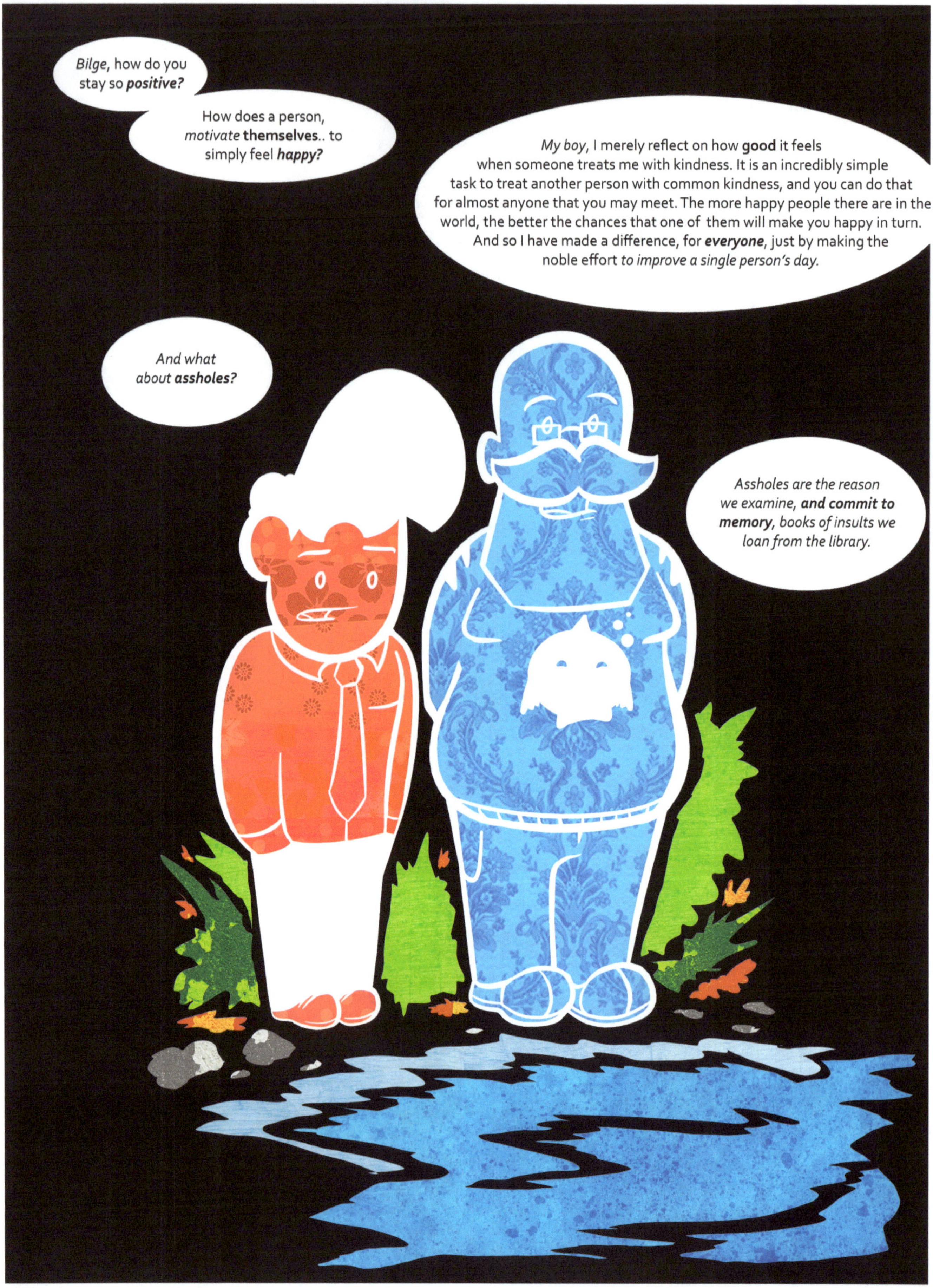
Bilge, how do you stay so ***positive?***
How does a person, *motivate* **themselves**.. to simply feel ***happy?***
My boy, I merely reflect on how **good** it feels when someone treats me with kindness. It is an incredibly simple task to treat another person with common kindness, and you can do that for almost anyone that you may meet. The more happy people there are in the world, the better the chances that one of them will make you happy in turn. And so I have made a difference, for ***everyone***, just by making the noble effort *to improve a single person's day.*
And what about ***assholes?***
Assholes are the reason we examine, ***and commit to memory****, books of insults we loan from the library.*

"Just Like On The Television"

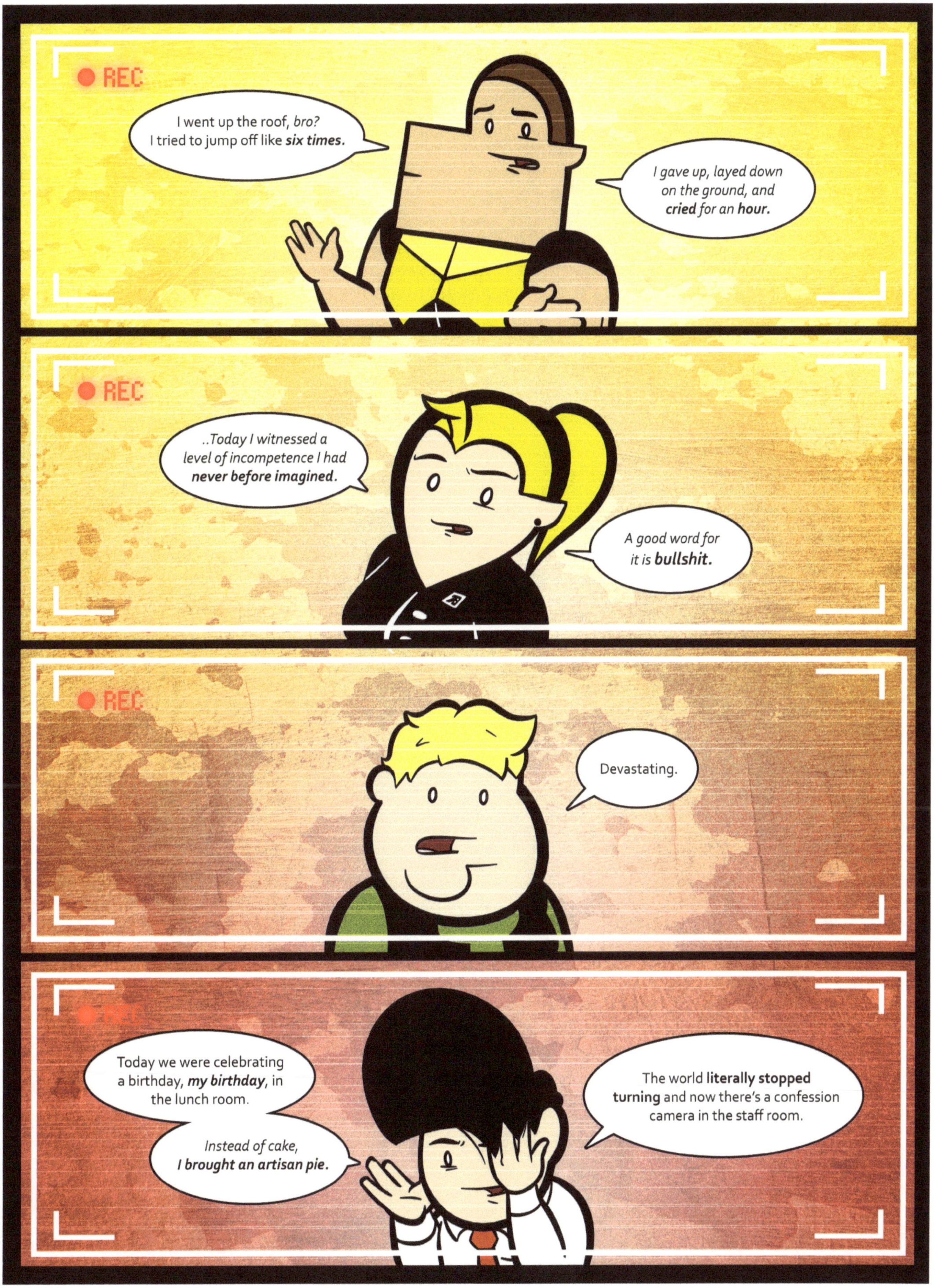

REC
I went up the roof, *bro?*
I tried to jump off like ***six times.***
I gave up, layed down on the ground, and ***cried*** *for an* ***hour.***
REC
..Today I witnessed a level of incompetence I had ***never before imagined.***
A good word for it is ***bullshit.***
REC
Devastating.
Today we were celebrating a birthday, ***my birthday***, in the lunch room.
Instead of cake, ***I brought an artisan pie.***
The world **literally stopped turning** and now there's a confession camera in the staff room.

"Nothing Really Matters"

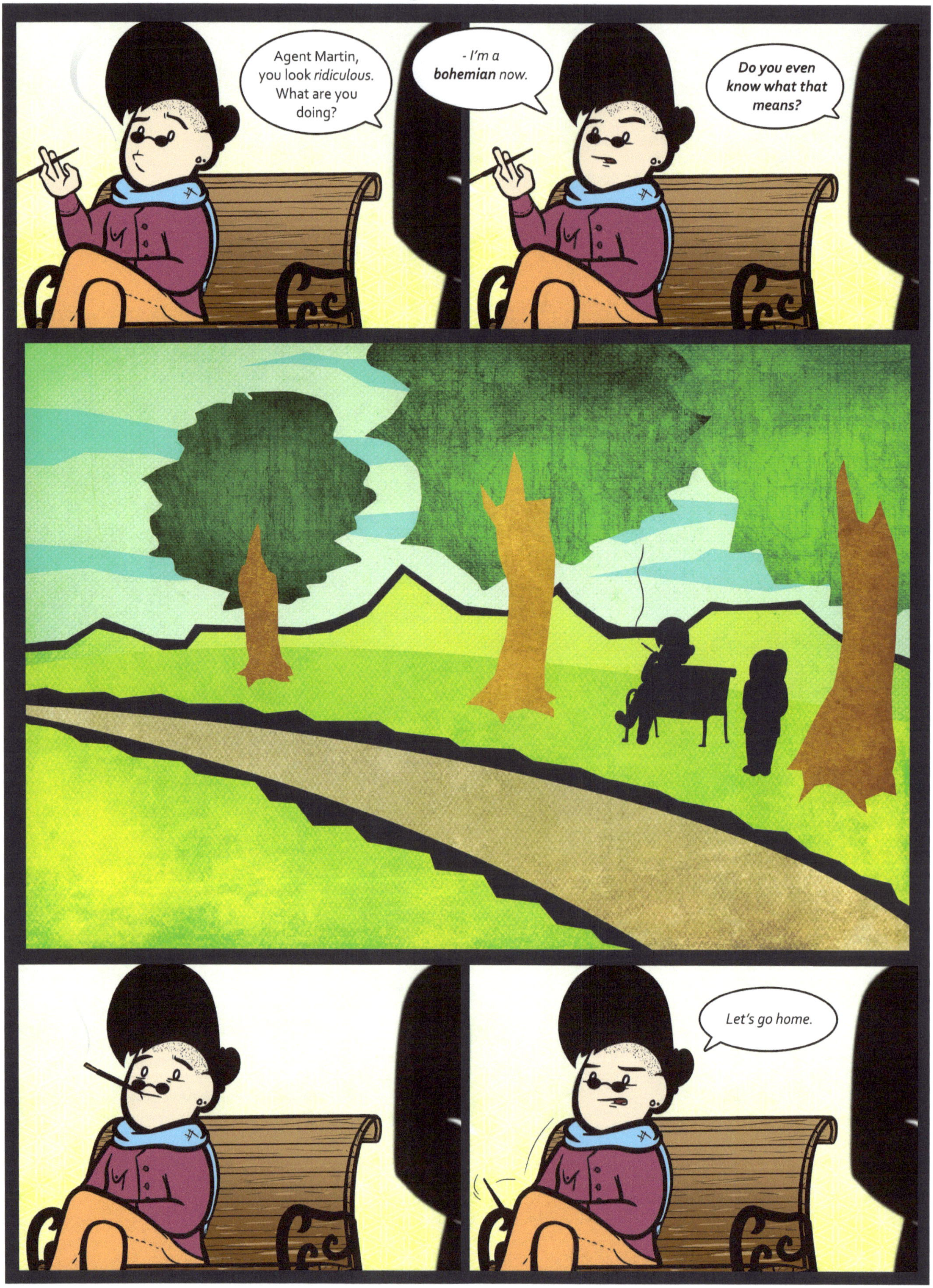

Agent Martin, you look *ridiculous*. What are you doing?
- *I'm a* ***bohemian*** *now.*
Do you even know what that means?
Let's go home.

"A Lesson In Disguise"

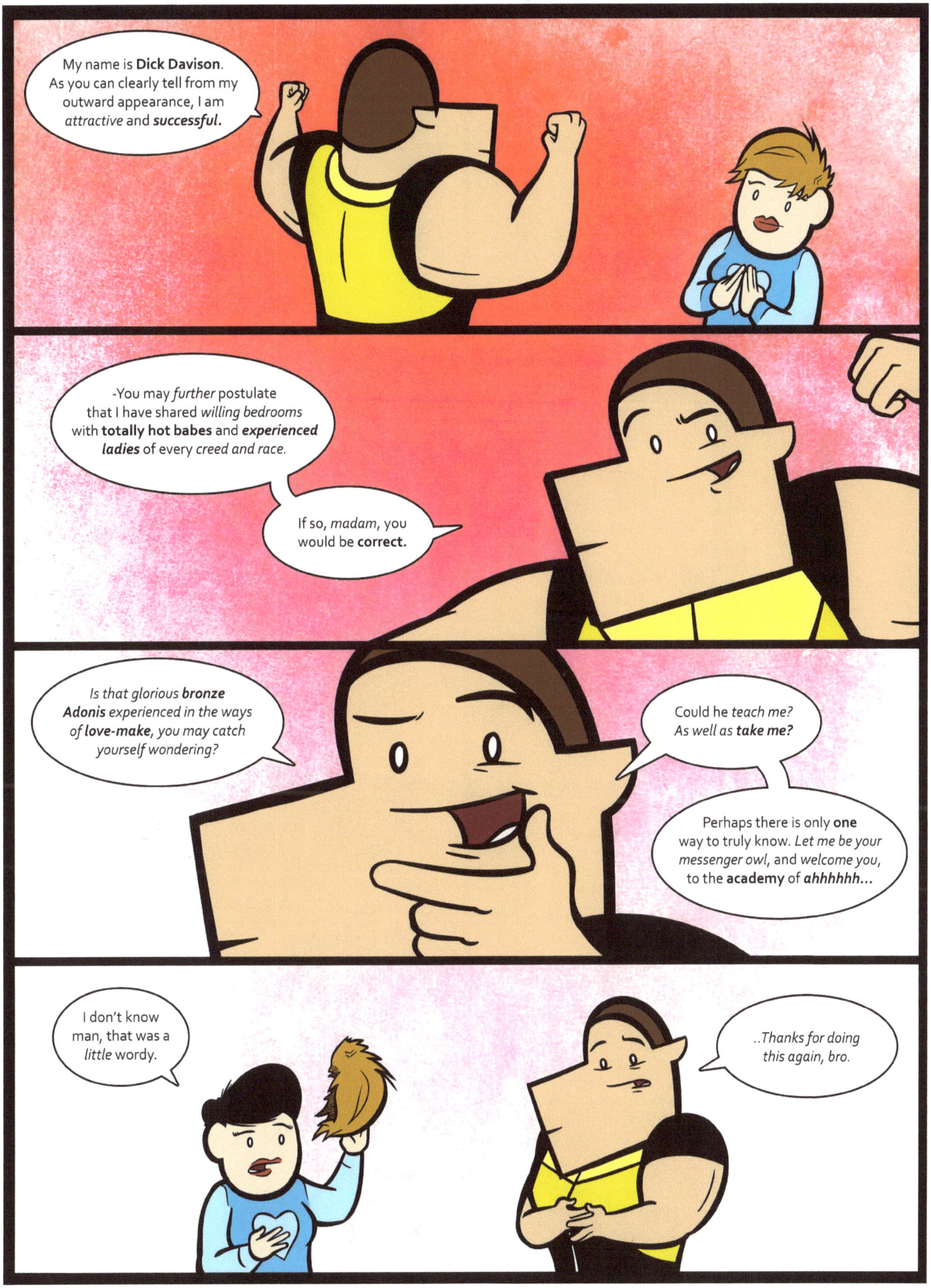

My name is **Dick Davison**. As you can clearly tell from my outward appearance, I am *attractive* and ***successful.***
-You may *further* postulate that I have shared *willing bedrooms* with **totally hot babes** and ***experienced ladies*** of every *creed and race.*
If so, *madam*, you would be **correct.**
Is that glorious ***bronze Adonis*** *experienced in the ways of* ***love-make****, you may catch yourself wondering?*
Could he *teach me?* *As well as* ***take me?***
Perhaps there is only **one** way to truly know. *Let me be your messenger owl*, and *welcome you*, to the **academy** of ***ahhhhhh...***
I don't know man, that was a *little* wordy.
..Thanks for doing this again, bro.

"Paranoia"

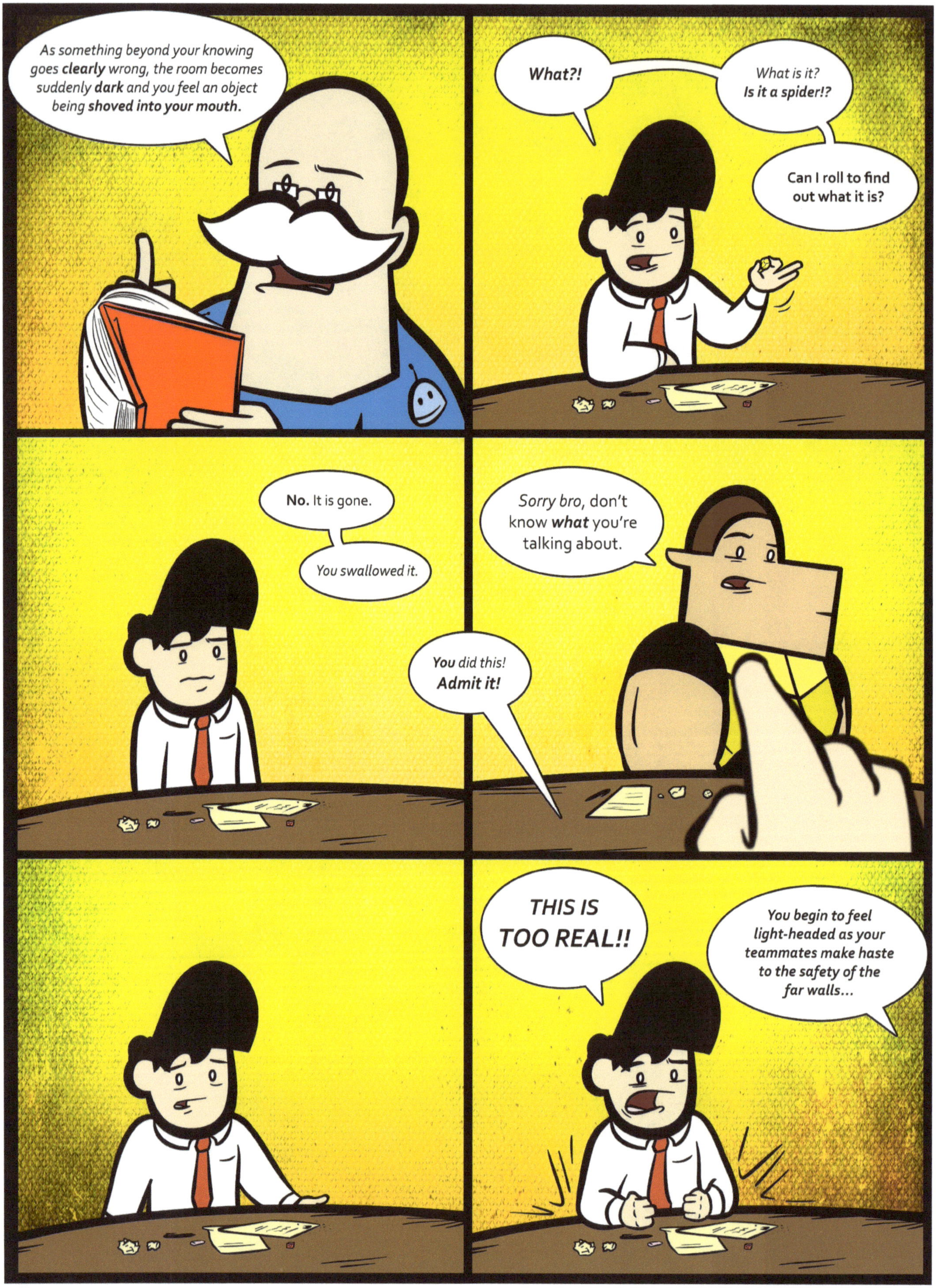

As something beyond your knowing goes **clearly** wrong, the room becomes suddenly **dark** and you feel an object being **shoved into your mouth.**
What?!
What is it? Is it a spider!?
Can I roll to find out what it is?
No. It is gone.
You swallowed it.
Sorry bro, don't know **what** you're talking about.
You did this! **Admit it!**
THIS IS TOO REAL!!
You begin to feel light-headed as your teammates make haste to the safety of the far walls...

"Further Paranoia"

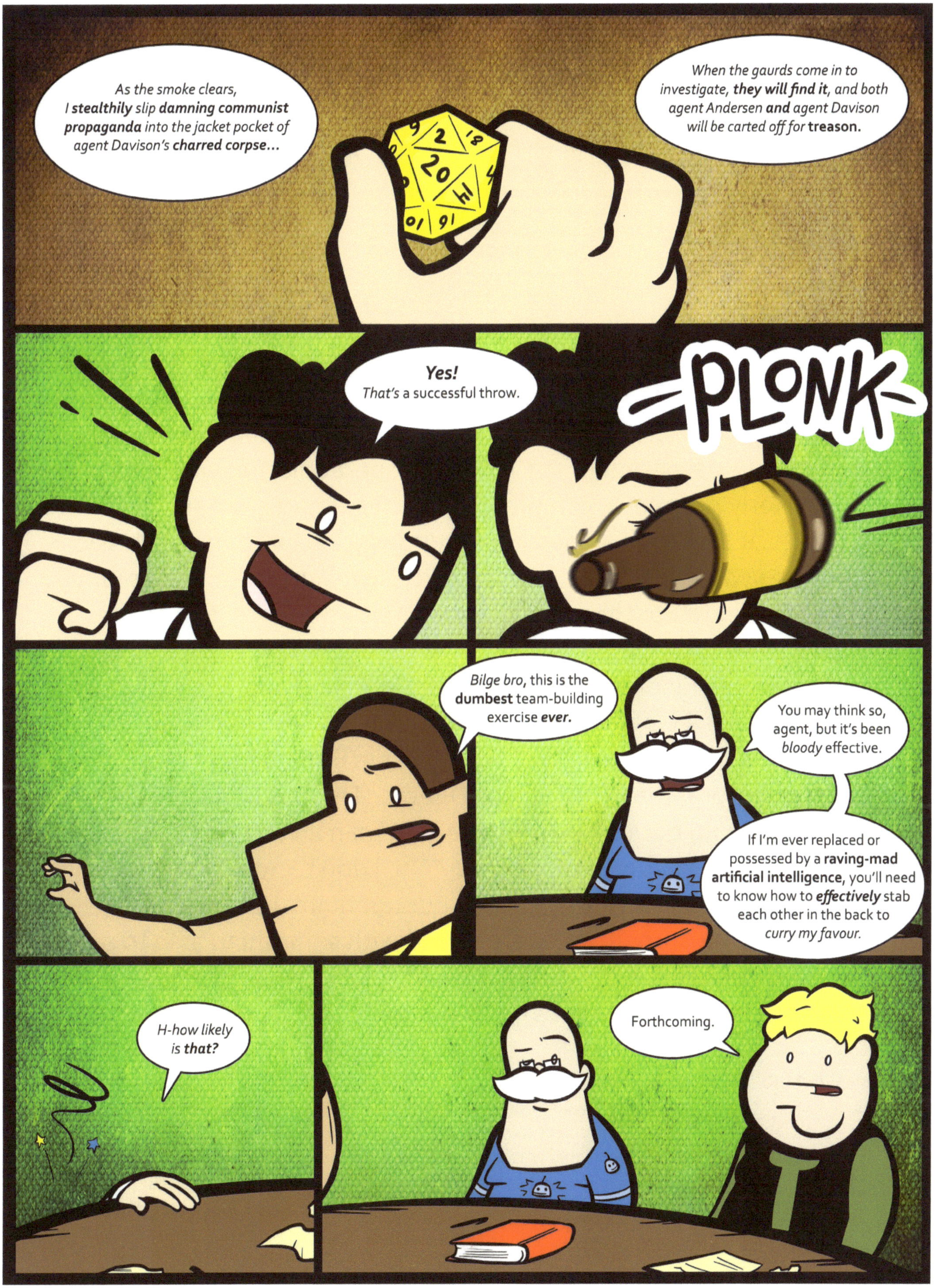

As the smoke clears, I ***stealthily*** *slip* ***damning communist propaganda*** *into the jacket pocket of agent Davison's* ***charred corpse...***
When the gaurds come in to investigate, ***they will find it****, and both agent Andersen* ***and*** *agent Davison will be carted off for* **treason.**
Yes! *That's* a successful throw.
PLONK
Bilge bro, this is the **dumbest** team-building exercise ***ever.***
You may think so, agent, but it's been *bloody* effective.
If I'm ever replaced or possessed by a **raving-mad artificial intelligence**, you'll need to know how to ***effectively*** stab each other in the back to *curry my favour.*
H-how likely is ***that?***
Forthcoming.

THE LOST SUNDAY STRIP

So I found this thing.

The thing that I found, was a sketch. This sketch was the plan for a Sunday strip that never was made. I found it while looking through all the old Aversion Bureau notes trying to come up with ideas for extra content to put in this book. Clearly, this was one of those ideas that was created in a state of *true* desperation. The kind of desperation that would have me draw an utterly ridiculous, completely pointless image rather than have no update at all. That's a good kind I suppose, better than the classic "*Sorry, no update today :(!*" message. But *so much* worse, than *so many* other things. For this is the dumbest comic in the entire series.

Now if you could ignore the page to your right, and imagine with me for a moment, a frog. *A big frog.* Give that frog some suave-ass facial hair. Give him a saddle. Put Max Martin of the Aversion Bureau in that saddle and give him a Sombrero . Then place Director Thomas Bilge (also of the Aversion Bureau) beside him and give that man an arcane walking stick. *Don't ask why.* What is Bilge wearing? Oh, I don't know, just a poncho I guess. Now you're pretty much there, but not quite. Put them against the backdrop of a mushroom kingdom mixed with something akin to a small house that might inhabit a fish tank. That's good, whatever you've got is probably better than what's on that other page. *Don't believe me..?*

<u>**The least fun fun-fact in the world:**</u> There is actually one other "Lost Sunday Strip", I found it at the same time. In that strip, Max is a talking head walking around town, thinking about suicide, using the words that were always in my head on the subject. With great positive creative energy, comes great moments of hopelessness. It was a dark time when I wrote that stupid thing, and I came very close to tainting this world with it. Making that strip would have been a bad idea second only to putting it in this book as the extra strip for this section. Which almost happened. That strip, my friends, is **super** lost. *Good riddance.*

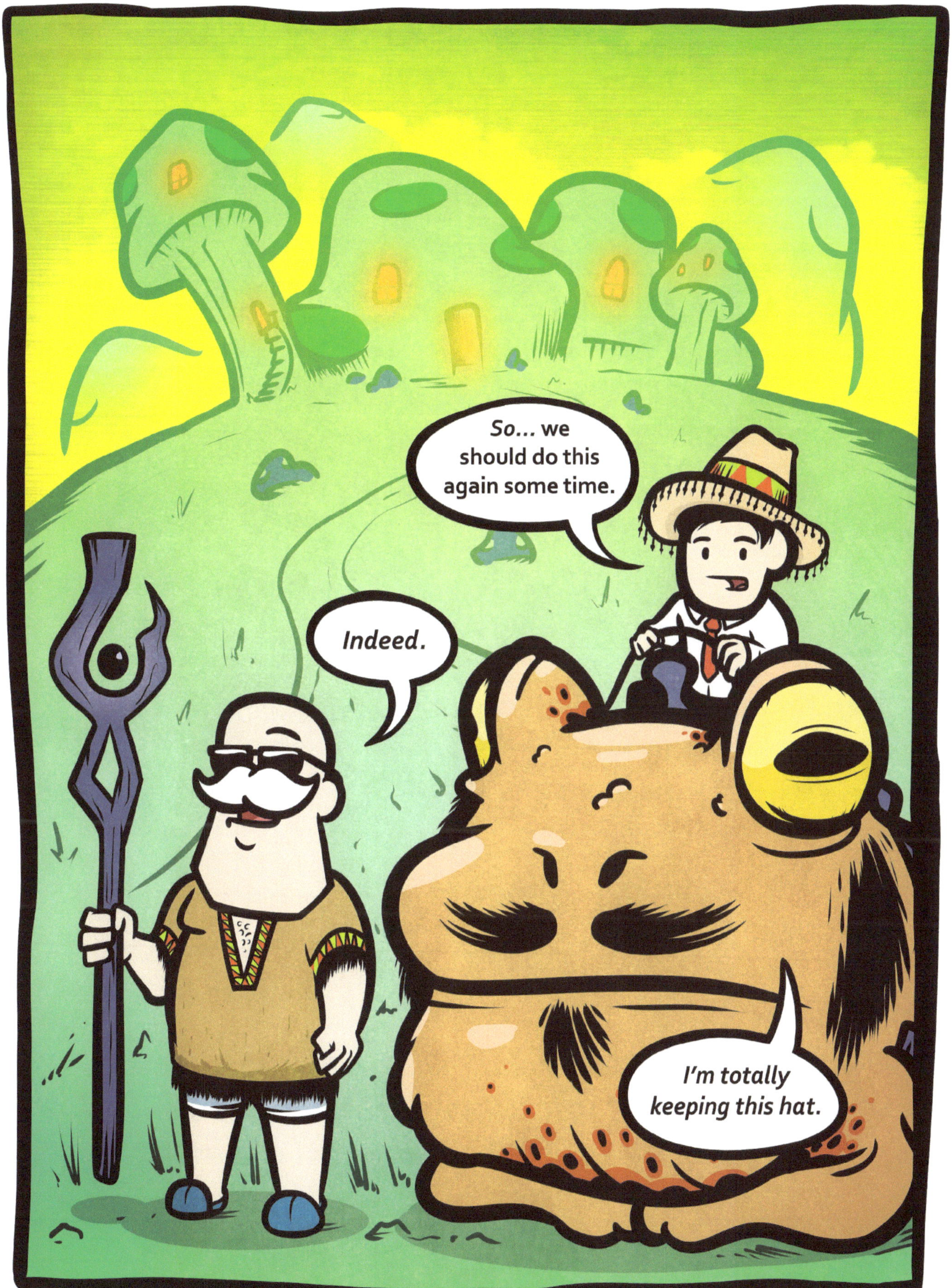
So... we should do this again some time.
Indeed.
I'm totally keeping this hat.

aversionbureau.com

RUNNING THE BUREAU IS <u>HARD, YOU KNOW</u>

For a man who captains a sinking ship,
my knees are **especially** dry!

One finger can fix *plenty* of leaks,
just by keeping a watchful eye...

And though this ship I am sailing breeds *foiling* and *failing*
in the plots of the *evilest* of guys, the problem with agents
who battle with ancients is they tend to just up, and *die.*

So wages, vacations, mental e-valuations, so much business
kept taught as a whip – munitions and direst anti-venom
and virus with big jars for making a tip.

The *aquatic, necrotic* and *Cthulish-exotic*, foes faced in
a regular week, leave those unprepared quite paddle-impaired
leagues deep up the brownest of creeks.

~

Then equip them, *I must!* **Turn baddies to dust!**
With *missiles* and *crystals* and *rays*...

Grab *katana* and *phaser*, *mace* and/or *laser* –
arakhs and *M-sixteens* too... Offer *bolter* and *blaster*,
but *beamswords* are faster, to pwn evil in myriad ways.

In the face of this all, my agents stand tall,
ne'er do-wells forestalled, t'was their oaths as cabal.

And the ones who live long enough become friends of mine still,
those who strode *up* and *downed* the red pill.

Like family now, death bonds us in spates,
as we pro-tect the world, from its various fates.

OUTTROFAREWELLADUCTION®

Another mind-blowing compound word from the *clustermind* of the corporate think-tank that brought you last collection's *"AbOUTroduction (the author)"*. They really have outdone themselves this year, and I believe that their bonuses will be appropriately grotesque.

Now, to the business of closing this papery monster out.

This book's very existence is a testament to my love of the comic that I dedicated so much of my life to, in such a small amount of time. At time of writing, *The Aversion Bureau* comic strip hasn't updated in almost a year, so truly, this book never needed to be made. The majority of it was in fact created many months ago, however when I realized how expensive colour printing would be and how few people were left to read it, I laid it to rest.

Things are different now, and so wonderfully better! Due to a recent revelation in the world of myself printing books, *Ancient Magicks And Feelings And Stuff* can finally exist. Even though it doesn't have to. But every time I re-read these strips, any amount of them, from any point in the run, I am reminded why TAB might remain my favourite thing I've ever made until the day I die. So, true to those feelings, this book needed to happen no matter if *anyone* read it, and I am exceedingly glad that it did.

I speak so deathly of the series though, when all is in fact *not* lost. The year that this collection was put together I also happened to try my hand at something new. I authored a (longish) short story based on the world of TAB but not written so that has to mean anything to anyone. The response was awesome and it reinforced a notion inside of me that writing had been the stronger of my two creative loves all long. *Regicide On The 51st Floor* became the first, albeit brief, novel in the newly existing series of Aversion Bureau novels. A very new thing even now, as I write this Outtrofarewelladuction®. I may have burnt myself out on the absurd art workload this comic used to be for me, but I never stopped loving the characters, and I never stopped thinking about the world. I now have a new way to explore adventures with these guys again, without having to spend days in front of the tablet, and it's all very exciting.

(Aside, that is, from the mythic day when the strip eventually returns.) (**Wink**.)

Now, finally, I tried to think of something to put here other than yet another picture of myself and thanking you for reading but hell, it's classic. It's just what you do.

Thank you and good night!

aversionbureau.com

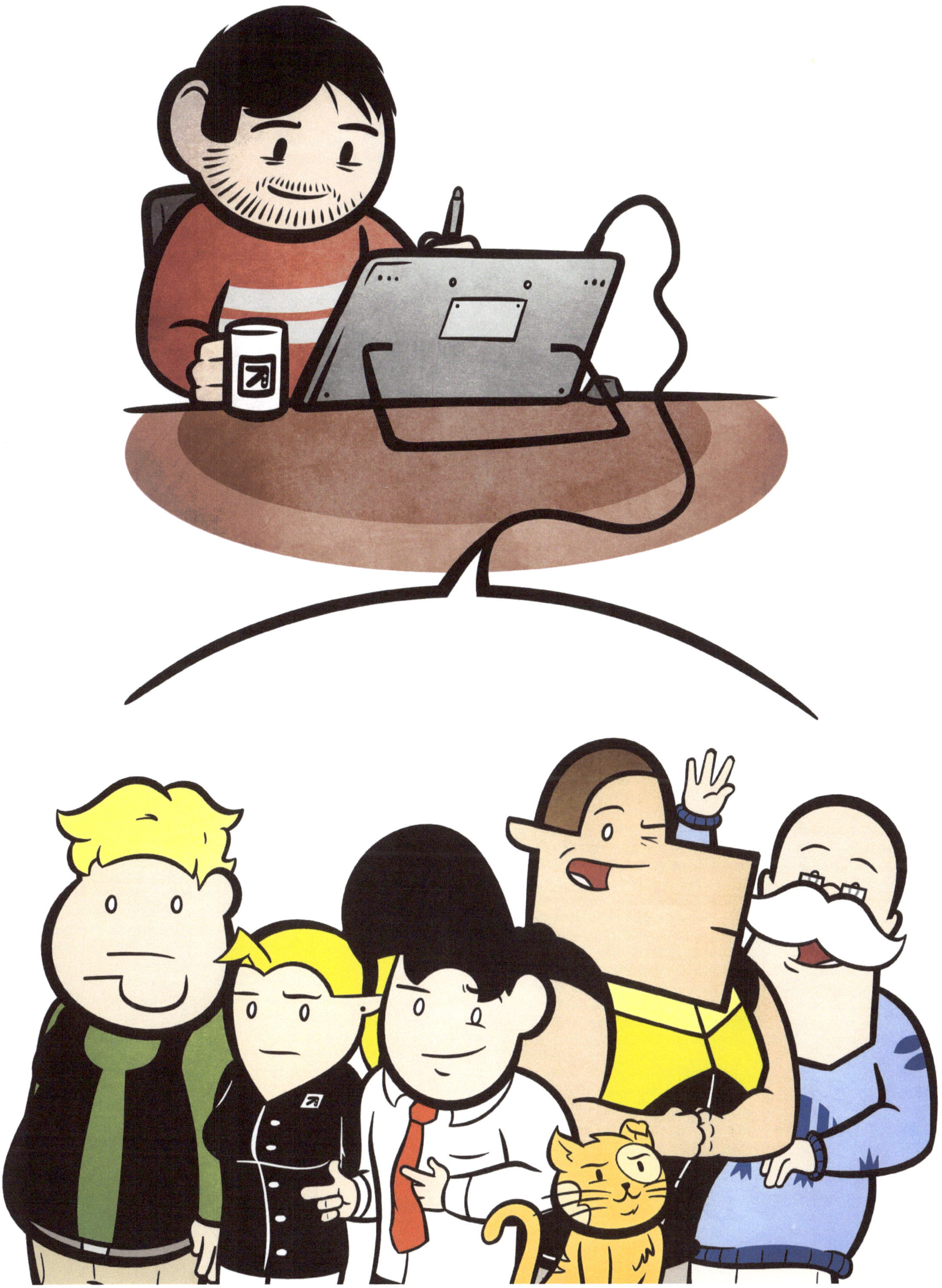

Woooooo!!

THE END

(OF THE BOOK)

HEY THIS IS THE LAST BOOK, RIGHT?
CAN I GET MY CHEQUE NOW?

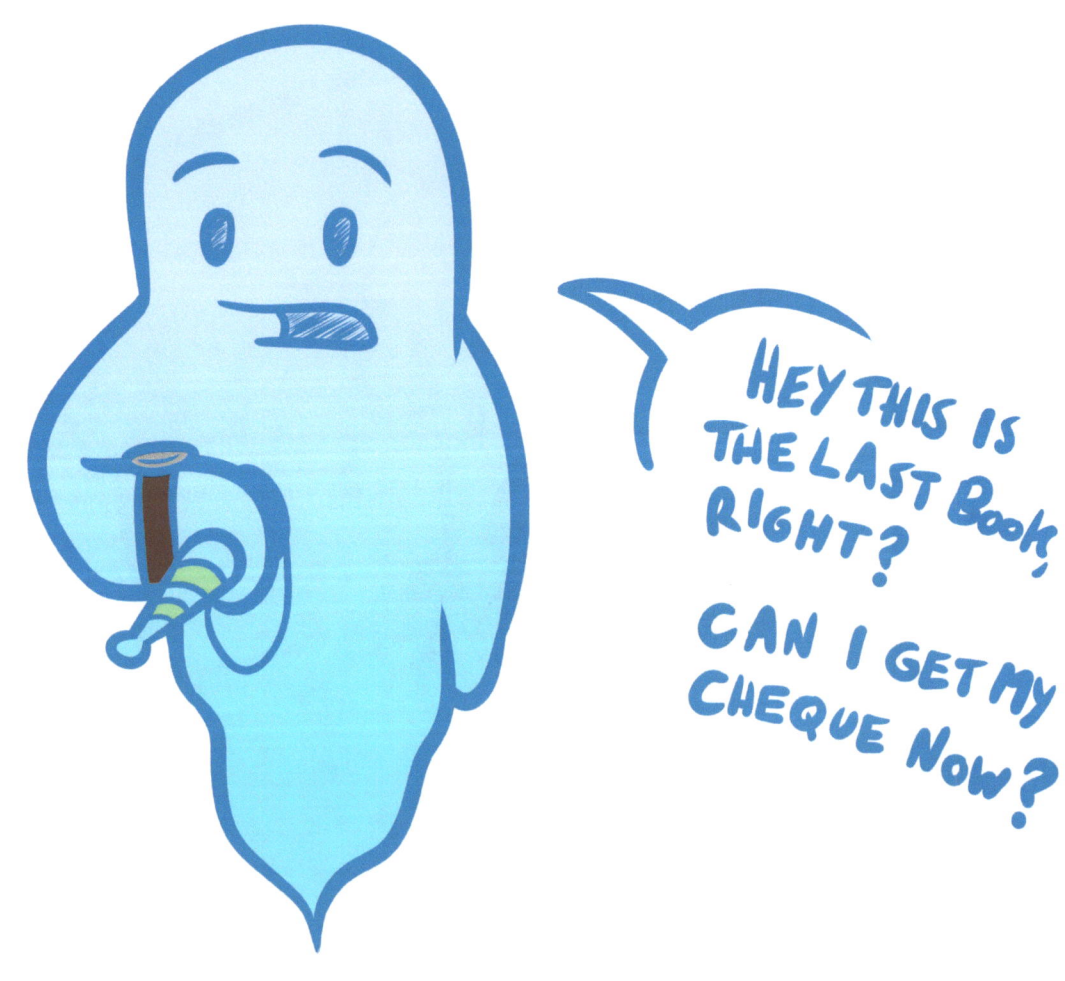

www.ingramcontent.com/pod-product-compliance
Lightning Source LLC
Chambersburg PA
CBHW042020150426
43197CB00003B/88